Theaters of War

Theaters of War

America's Perceptions of World War II

Vincent Casaregola

THEATERS OF WAR

First published in 2009 by
PALGRAVE MACMILLAN®
in the United States—a division of St. Martin's Press LLC,
175 Fifth Avenue, New York, NY 10010.

Where this book is distributed in the UK, Europe and the rest of the world,
this is by Palgrave Macmillan, a division of Macmillan Publishers Limited,
registered in England, company number 785998, of Houndmills,
Basingstoke, Hampshire RG21 6XS.

Palgrave Macmillan is the global academic imprint of the above companies
and has companies and representatives throughout the world.

Palgrave® and Macmillan® are registered trademarks in the United States,
the United Kingdom, Europe and other countries.

ISBN: 978–1–4039–6486–1

Library of Congress Cataloging-in-Publication Data

Casaregola, Vincent.
    Theaters of war : America's perceptions of World War II / Vincent
Casaregola..
       p. cm.
    ISBN 978–1–4039–6486–1 (alk. paper)
       1. World War, 1939–1945—Literature and the war. 2. World War,
    1939–1945--Motion pictures and the war. 3. American literature—20th
    century—History and criticism. 4. Veterans—United States—Biography—
    History and criticism. 5. World War, 1939–1945—Veterans—United
    States—Biography. 6. War in literature. I. Title.

PS228.W37C37 2009
810.9'358—dc22   2008055915

A catalogue record of the book is available from the British Library.

Design by Newgen Imaging Systems (P) Ltd., Chennai, India.

First edition: October 2009

10 9 8 7 6 5 4 3 2 1

Printed in the United States of America.

For my father, Joseph Casaregola, T/5, U.S. Army, 1943–1945,
and for my mother, Concetta Isabella Casaregola,
and for all of their generation—the ones who went,
the ones who waited.
May we never forget their struggles
or their stories.

CONTENTS

PREFACE

I started my research for *Theaters of War* over seven years ago, before the date September 11, 2001, held any special significance. While beginning to write about our cultural history of World War II, however, I have witnessed that same history become a source for narratives, imagery, and metaphors in our War on Terror, as well as in our specific campaigns in Afghanistan and Iraq. It is no surprise that, when Americans want to frame a war as necessary and just, they use World War II as an analogy. After all, it was the "Good War," and in winning it, we defeated unquestionably oppressive forces, particularly those of Nazi Germany. To achieve that victory, millions of Americans left home to fight, and even more millions devoted themselves to the war effort at home. Never had war so unified our nation and brought such massive government spending and subsequent prosperity. Our standard narrative of World War II therefore suggests that wars make sense and, if pursued properly, they bring closure to international conflicts and potential economic benefits at home. As a careful study of our nation's history suggests, these can be dangerous and self-defeating assumptions.

Theaters of War has grown from my ongoing study of how Americans have come to understand and represent the history of their wars, particularly those in the twentieth century. Because World War II is so central to that history, I have chosen to focus solely on it, and specifically on how we have represented combat in that war. Even within this narrower focus, my original plan proved too ambitious, and I have had to cut much material because there was neither space nor time. Also, some very recent films, such as Spike Lee's *The Miracle of St. Anna* (2008), have appeared too late for me to study. Ken Burns' comprehensive television documentary, *The War* (2007), certainly deserves mention as a major effort to provide a balanced exploration of America's World War II experience; unfortunately, it still came well after my manuscript was in the editing stages. I can, however, acknowledge its high quality and lasting significance—it will do much to help a new generation of Americans understand their history. Despite such limitations, I have tried to examine representative works of literature and film about the war from every decade since the 1940s. Of course, my study still continues because new publications, films, or other representations emerge every month.

This book explores how World War II became part of America's basic cultural mythology, and how our representations of that war have fundamentally shaped our vision of ourselves and our nation. At the heart of this book lie several analyses of our cultural history. First, I consider how America shifted from the antiwar, isolationist attitudes of the 1920s and 1930s to vigorous support for our fighting in World War II. I try to explain how political and cultural forces arrayed themselves during the transition period from 1939 to 1941 and what rhetorical strategies they used to shape the public national consciousness. I also examine how the propaganda efforts during the war created a consensus narrative that has continued to provide our basic historical understanding of the conflict: the "Good-War" narrative. Subsequently, as the Cold War emerged during the late 1940s, and America shifted from fighting fascism to opposing communism, the narrative and rhetorical strategies of the postwar period continued to follow the "Good-War" pattern. By the 1950s, our mainstream narrative of World War II had become a vehicle for supporting our Cold War policies. Of course, when those policies led America into the disastrous war in Vietnam, many Americans began to question both that narrative and the policies it helped to support. During the next phase, we paid less attention to World War II, focusing instead on the aftermath of Vietnam, a war that we watched on television. During the 1970s, Vietnam veterans, having experienced a traumatic war and a painful homecoming, began to publish graphic accounts of their combat experience. I believe that these memoirs and oral histories also awakened the consciousness of World War II veterans, who had remained silent for decades about the trauma they had suffered. By the late 1970s, however, this older generation finally began to express itself, and since then, a steady flow of personal memoirs about World War II have been published. This new literature by veterans has provided Americans the opportunity to achieve a deeper, more complex understanding of World War II—not that all of us have made use of that opportunity. During the past decade, as we observed the sixtieth anniversaries of events in World War II, Hollywood has once more returned to the World War II genre, with some films reviving the traditional "Good-War" narrative and others critiquing it energetically. I try to anticipate how our evolving understanding of World War II will continue to shape attitudes toward war and to influence our actions on the world stage. I believe that, if we can come to terms with these questions, we might understand better how to act responsibly in a world so fraught with conflict and so ready to make war.

A Note on Methodology

The basic method of this book is a combination of applied rhetorical and cultural analysis of works of fiction, film, journalism, and memoir. I describe the broad patterns of cultural narrative (found principally in literature and film) that have shaped our understanding of World War II and the American identity. I also provide detailed analyses of specific rhetorical techniques and strategies in particular works, along with the ideological perspectives either expressed or embedded in those works. I follow a largely chronological pattern, examining how work from each period embodies and alters what has come before, shaping an evolving national consciousness about World War II and American identity.

In pursuing this project, I have drawn on my reading of various rhetorical and literary theories. As a scholar of literature and film, I am an eclectic pragmatist, without any strong allegiance to one particular theoretical school but with a particular concern for the rhetorical power of narrative art. Still, I do try to draw what seems useful from the array of theories available, virtually all of which have something to offer the careful reader. I make few specific theoretical references in the text of the book, but rhetorical theory serves as a background influence that informs both my description of broad cultural patterns and more detailed examinations of specific novels, films, memoirs, and other materials. I do, however, provide some connection with theoretical concerns in the notes.

I also claim some specific influences in developing and deploying my approach. My reading of Kenneth Burke informs my sense of how a broad range of cultural discourses can be examined as dramatic constructs that initiate, replicate, preserve, and adapt a particular cultural vision. Burke's concept of identification is also important as a fundamental aspect of persuasive discourse. I have been influenced by Mikhail Bakhtin's work as well, particularly his concept of "heteroglossia," which I find can explain the ways in which complex patterns of cultural understanding, often with conflicting or contradictory elements, can be revealed in the imagery, characters, and stories of large narratives. The materials of our culture thus flow into the construction of such works, regardless of the artist's full awareness or acknowledgment. Likewise, interpreting such works must be an ongoing, open-ended, and "unfinalizable" project, as Bakhtin also notes. The richness and diversity of Burke and Bakhtin serve as a foundational structure that underpins my approaches to interpretation. At the same time, I employ a great deal of specific rhetorical analysis, at both technical and thematic levels, drawing on methods developed by critics such as Wayne Booth and modified by what might be labeled as either "neo-Boothians" or "Booth revisionists" (I think particularly of the excellent work by Professor James Phelan in this regard). Still, it is fair to say that this tradition of rhetorical analysis of cultural expression goes as far back as Aristotle. I am also influenced, somewhat more by example than by adaptation, by the current work in what is generally labeled "cultural studies." Insofar as I examine a broad range of cultural discourses and productions, viewing them as part of extensive patterns through which America constructs its sense of both history and identity, I am engaging in rhetorical analysis informed by cultural studies. At the same time, I am also drawing on approaches that one might label as structuralist, in that I am concerned with broad patterns of genre and form, along with how specific works exemplify those patterns. Yet, since the basic questions I am seeking to answer are rooted in particular cultural processes and historical moments in American history, the cultural basis for my work is equally strong. I am interested in the specific issues of what constitutes propaganda, though I do not necessarily subscribe to one definition. I do employ elements of Jacques Ellul's well-developed concepts of integration and agitation propaganda; though they have been around for some forty years, they are still quite useful. I should note as well that media studies has also influenced my approach, especially the work of Walter J. Ong and his emphasis on how new forms of media can reshape cultural consciousness. Certainly the development of film and broadcasting as means for representing modern war, particularly World War II, has profoundly affected how we understand that conflict. As noted originally, I am an eclectic pragmatist, but one who focuses on what I might label the cultural rhetoric modern America. My methods, influenced by these and other theorists, ultimately lead to a pattern of reading, analysis, and interpretation that examines the ways in which fiction, film, journalism, and memoir help to shape our national consciousness about a major set of historical events. Insofar as I am looking at very particular cultural processes and historical moments, my approach is cultural; insofar as I am examining pervasive patterns, it is structural; and insofar as I am analyzing persuasive strategies and techniques, it is rhetorical. I suppose I could call this "culturalist rhetorical analysis," which is itself not a theory but, indeed, a methodology derived from an eclectic blend of theories.

ACKNOWLEDGMENTS

I owe thanks to a number of people whose help and support have made it possible for me to pursue this project. I came to it with a fundamental influence from my father, Joseph Casaregola, and my grandfather, Luigi Casaregola, each a veteran of a World War. From my childhood, they encouraged me to study the history of these events so that I might understand my future role as a citizen. Thus, I grew up reading about World War II and watching countless films and television shows representing it. All this served as a foundation for my current study and for my views on the subject matter.

Having determined to pursue this project, I studied the work of a number of scholars and critics who have explored the material before me. Although I have developed my own analyses and conclusions, I have found several of these scholars to have been invaluable resources for my study. Although I may not always agree with their opinions, I have the greatest respect for them and their work. Among these are Jeanine Basinger, Philip Beidler, Bernard Dick, Thomas Doherty, John Dower, Jay Hyams, and Lawrence Suid. Of course, the foundational historical study *Hollywood Goes to War*, by Gregory D. Black and Clayton R. Koppes, has been indispensable. Naturally, Paul Fussell's rigorous interrogation of the "Good-War" narrative has shaped much of my understanding and approach. In a different way, the work of Stephen Ambrose has provided excellent connections with the experience of World War II veterans. The veterans themselves must be acknowledged, for their service but also for their willingness to reconstruct their wartime experiences so that we might better understand the war. Finally, I should note that I have relied on film credits for information about filmmakers and cast, but I have frequently depended on the *Internet Movie Database* (imdb.com) to check my memory or my notes.

A number of people have helped directly with the development of this project, especially graduate students who have assisted me during the last seven years. In particular, Robert Blaskiewicz, William J. Rable, Laurie Britt-Smith, and Joseph Webb have worked with me for extended periods, helping with both research and editing, as well as with computer issues. Without their assistance, I would have been lost on many occasions. Rachel Reynard and John Walter also served for briefer periods in this role. Other graduate students have helped with tasks outside the book project, thus freeing up some of my time, and these include Janet Garrard-Willis, Kathleen Lancia, Gina Merys, Deborah Scaggs, and Paul J. Stabile. Of course, the conversations and discussions with all of my students, graduate and undergraduate, have provided a constant stimulus for new ideas.

I wish to thank my department chair, Dr. Sara van den Berg, for her ongoing support and encouragement, and all of my fellow faculty members in the English Department at Saint Louis University. I also appreciate the support of our College of Arts and Sciences and our Graduate School, along with that of Dean Donald G. Brennan. The reference staff at the Saint Louis University Library has also been extremely helpful and kind, including English Department liaison Jamie Schmid.

My early research was facilitated by the librarians and staff of the Military History Institute at the U.S. Army War College, especially Dr. Crane Conrad and Dr. Richard Sommers. Colonel George Reed, who was then on the faculty of that college was also of great help. I owe them all a debt of thanks.

I wish to thank, as well, the editorial staff at Palgrave/Macmillan, especially editors Farideh Koohi-Kamali and Brigitte Shull for their patience and support of my slow process. I also thank all the editorial assistants who have been so kind and considerate during the book project, particularly the current editorial assistant, Lee Norton, and production assistant, Matt Robison. I also wish to thank the copy editor Maran Elancheran for his patient and careful work during the production phase.

My agent, Giles Anderson, was essential in developing the original book proposal and helping to secure a publisher.

I want to offer special thanks to my long-time friend Patrick Mannix, with whom I have shared countless conversations about film. His insight, wit, and support have been invaluable throughout all my academic work, and his own book, *The Rhetoric of Anti-Nuclear Fiction* (1992), was an inspiration.

I want to thank my brother, Louis, for our many conversations about military history and technology, as well as for his encouragement to complete the project.

Finally, I thank my wife, Victoria, and my daughters, Maya and Marina. They have been kind, patient, loving, and endlessly supportive. They make my work possible and worthwhile.

Vincent Casaregola
Saint Louis, Missouri
December 24, 2008

INTRODUCTION

Faces of the War

In my garage lies the artifact of an old war, a poster-sized Coca-Cola advertisement. It represents but a single fragmentary picture of that war—the painted image of a young woman, fresh and vibrant, and of a young man in uniform. They share a tandem bicycle, she in front and he behind. The wind lifts her curly, auburn hair but leaves untouched his close-cropped military cut, held firm by his neatly pressed overseas cap. A basket attached to the bicycle's handles holds a six-pack of Coca-Cola bottles, and the ad's cutline states "For the Party." With bright eyes and an enthusiastic smile, she dominates the picture. She wears a classic 1940s-era skirt, sweater, and bobby socks. Images like hers probably rode through World War II in the wallets and imaginations of millions of servicemen. The man also smiles with confidence and pleasure though his image is rendered more superficially.

The poster is torn, its edges chipped and frayed. A dark, brownish-red stain, like oil or varnish, mars its center, seeming to spill over the woman's skirt. Perhaps someone used this poster to cover the floor when refinishing a piece of furniture. Yet in certain lights, the stain takes on the quality of dried blood, as if the poster cannot conceal the wartime violence beneath its smiling image. The stain speaks to me of the war no poster would attempt to reveal. The man wears the unmistakable shoulder patch of the U.S. Third Army, Patton's Army. Campaign ribbons decorate his chest, suggesting that he has been in combat. These facts place the poster sometime after mid-1944, when the Third Army became operational in Europe. Does this represent the celebratory homecoming at the war's end? Is this man, so surreal with his two-dimensional clipart face, the returning veteran? In 1945 an actual combat veteran would probably have been so distant from the poster's advertising enthusiasm that he would have said nothing. The superficiality of the image is so obvious, in some ways so callous, and yet so much a part of the commonplace world of representations, that it lacks any surprises. If he has survived to this day, that same veteran would find the poster merely a reminder of another time, long ago, and its far simpler approach to advertising if not to life itself.

Whenever I think of Americans in World War II, and of all the great panoply of images and icons—from the deformed and smoking superstructure of the dying battleship USS *Arizona*, to a triad of faceless dead Americans on a beach in New Guinea, to Robert Capa's blurred figures on Omaha Beach, or the determined team of flag raisers on Iwo Jima—this Coca-Cola poster also comes to mind. Perhaps it reflects the hope of a "Good War," a war where combat veterans return physically and mentally unscarred, and where the honor of American identity, as viewed naively in advertising imagery, is maintained. If so, the poster's own superficiality betrays the limits of such sanitized views of war. Of course, this poster is merely an artifact of an era, yet in its current state of decay, it speaks to me of the images constructed to represent that era, and of how those images begin to change and speak in voices other than those they originally intended.

★   ★   ★

I recall that poster as I begin trying to put a face to the experience of World War II. What I and so many others of postwar generations know of that war is a series of images, a pattern of words and stories—merely representations. Yet these representations have fundamentally shaped American experience and identity through all ensuing decades. So this seemingly empty advertising icon is not at all empty; it is a tattered veil that opens to reveal a host of faces that I can neither fully understand nor forget. Sometimes, they are even faces of people I have known, but only in recent years have I thought of them in relation to this poster and the history of the war. They are faces with real names and histories, often painful histories that I learned in fragmentary narratives.

Call one of these faces "Eddie"—a World War II combat veteran who lived in the old neighborhood where I grew up. People said that Eddie was "shell-shocked," meaning he probably suffered from what we now call Post-Traumatic Stress Disorder (PTSD), and he was permanently disabled by this affliction. From dawn to dusk, he silently wandered the streets of our neighborhood, oblivious to all around him, his mind seemingly thousands of miles away. He never actually spoke, making only incomprehensible, mumbling sounds. He chain-smoked relentlessly. His face was brown and weathered from constant exposure, and his eyes never lost their "2,000-yard stare." If his aging mother had not brought him in every night, he would have forgotten to go home. Years later, after his mother had died, Eddie did wander off one winter evening. He was discovered the next day, curled up in a doorway of an abandoned store. There he had fallen asleep and died from the cold. When I heard of this, I could not help but wonder if he had been one of those who had survived the Battle of the Bulge and the horrifically cold European winter of 1944–45. In his last moments, did he mentally return to his lost comrades from so long ago? Or perhaps, with the irony of fate, his 2,000-yard stare had been acquired in some stifling Pacific jungle. Maybe some long-ago wish for a cold winter wind, a wish made deep in the steaming rainforest, had come back to haunt him on that final night. Perhaps, he just lost consciousness and found his long-sought peace.

Call another face "Randy," who worked at a neighborhood grocery. Unreliable and prone to heavy drinking, Randy was mocked by coworkers as "Randy the Red-Nosed Reindeer." He had fought in Europe, returning with an insatiable thirst and a German war bride. Their marriage had dissolved quickly, and when his drinking increased, his gnarled face grew ever redder and more wrinkled. Ultimately fired from his job, he began to wander through the cheap bars and rooming houses on the fringes of the neighborhood. Years later, I heard that he had succumbed, like Eddie, to hypothermia. Intoxicated, he apparently froze into the sleep that may have eluded him for many years. Perhaps Randy was one of the many survivors of those combats depicted in the histories I had read as a child. Not listed as a casualty, he had marched on and eventually home. There he had lived in his own particular envelope of memories and pain, marching down the street to work, marching through the illusory relief of an alcoholic daze, looking for a sense of home that neither mind nor body could any longer recover. Drink, fitful sleep, and ultimately, a very cold death offered his only release.

★　★　★

Eddie and Randy are merely two individuals among the millions of Americans who served in combat in World War II, so many of whom suffered wounds—physical, psychological, or both. By chance, I was a naïve witness to the traumatic consequences of war in those two lives.

I had not seen the war, only its imprint on the faces of these men, but it would be years before I could connect their painful expressions with the World War II stories and films that shaped my simple knowledge of the war. It is a sad but telling irony that, even as I watched the gradual disintegration of these men, I was growing up in an environment increasingly shaped by the much better-known, more influential faces of the war—faces from films and television that represented the war principally as a triumph of the American way.

In America's mainstream story of World War II, the face of war is a celebrity face in an ordinary Joe's uniform. Though streaked with dirt and sweat, the face is still identifiable. The uniform is G.I. fatigues, topped by the classic World War II helmet, tilted back slightly to allow a better view of the actor's face. The face could belong to Randolph Scott, or Dana Andrews, or Van Johnson, but more likely, it is the face of John Wayne in *Sands of Iwo Jima*. The Duke's rugged features are forever embedded in our cultural iconography of World War II. He wears the uniform of a U.S. Marine and a camouflaged helmet. His expression is tired but tough and confident, and from beneath the surface comes a slight hint of affection. He is Sergeant John Stryker, the "tough-love" squad leader who will do whatever necessary to complete the mission yet keep his men alive. More than any other actor, Wayne symbolizes the qualities that Americans associate with their mainstream narrative of World War II. His characters are forceful but not boastful, strong but not bullying, and tough but, though rarely acknowledging it, deeply emotional. In short, he is the romantic hero, the apotheosis of the G.I. Already well known as a star in Westerns, especially those of John Ford, Wayne used *Sands of Iwo Jima* to establish himself as the quintessential American soldier.

It is indeed ironic that, in the American consciousness, the faces of John Wayne and other celebrity actors stand for the G.I. in World War II because anonymity was the essence of being a G.I., whether a "dogface" or a "raggedy-ass Marine." Like an American coin, the G.I. literally was "E pluribus unum." This universal anonymity was celebrated and critiqued at the same time in the very label "G.I."—a title that soldiers both endured and embraced as a badge of identity. Seen in so many newsreels and still photographs, the real G.I. image was the ordinary American face in its multiple realizations. In the photographic record, we find it to be both young and middle-aged, black as well as white, and displaying the full range of human emotions. It was a particular face with a real name, and yet it was also an unknown face with no celebrity content—thus, the citizen soldier. It was all the more ironic, therefore, that this citizen soldier came to be represented not so much by his own image but by Hollywood's most dramatic and romantic male figures. The war came to be known to the next generation much more through the famous faces of actors playing soldiers than from the everyday faces of fathers and uncles who had actually fought in the war.

Despite the lasting influence of iconic images like John Wayne's, reactions to the Vietnam War significantly changed many Americans' perspectives on war. During the two decades after the fall of Saigon, Hollywood released few World War II films. Only after the nation had commemorated the fiftieth anniversaries of the war did Hollywood return to World War II subject matter in a major way. The 1998 film *Saving Private Ryan*, staring Tom Hanks and directed by Steven Spielberg, inaugurated this new generation of World War II films, many of which represent the war in more complex and challenging ways. But the face of Tom Hanks is still the face of a Hollywood celebrity. A more authentic face of the G.I. is represented in the Hanks-Spielberg collaboration *Band of Brothers* (2001), an HBO miniseries based on Stephen Ambrose's 1992 book about one company from the 101st Airborne Division. The ten hours allowed by this venue freed the producers to develop a rich, nuanced dramatization of Ambrose's interview-based history. Hanks and Spielberg collected unusually effective writer-director teams for each episode, selecting the cast largely from then lesser-known actors, whose faces more easily suggested the ordinary G.I. Moreover, each episode opens with brief comments from surviving Easy Company veterans reflecting, with both pride and sorrow, on their wartime experience. Neither pro- nor antiwar, *Band of Brothers* achieves a remarkable sense of authenticity for a dramatization of combat experience.

Yet even docudrama is merely a representation, and so I speak here about the potential of any representation to achieve some degree of authenticity. My concern is to find those books, films, and other works that give space for and voice to the often-silenced experiences and perspectives of combat veterans themselves. Such works come closest to conveying, with some honesty and accuracy, the experience of World War II combat. For this reason, Ken Burns' *The War* is a welcome addition to documentary record because its whole structure grows directly from the veterans. The stories are told by those who experienced them, either through old letters and diaries or through contemporary interviews with survivors. Combining such testimony with significant archival film and photography (some never used before), *The War* offers one of the most authentic representations of World War II to date, one in which the voices of combat veterans are the essence of the war's history. Indeed, it is the war as the G.I.s themselves tell it.[1]

Authenticity, however, is not always valued by those who interpret history, and many historical commentators have tried to refocus the war's narrative for ideological purposes. Yet to the dismay of critics and scholars from both the left and the right, the experiences of combat veterans rarely conform to ideological prescriptions. Many feature films and books tend to move to one or another end of the political spectrum (though films more often reflect conservative views). Recollections of actual combat veterans, however, tend to be more balanced and more ambiguous. For them, telling the story of the war is often a painful struggle to recover *meaning* from the memory of horrific events. Even when expressing both pride and patriotism, the veterans also acknowledge the profound cost of war. They neither forget the lives lost nor the memories of all they experienced.

After the fact, representations of war can be seized upon to offer evidence for whatever agenda someone wishes to put forward. Those who wish to see America's history as glorious and the experience of World War II as a justification of American policies—past, present, or future—selectively focus on American achievements. While acknowledging the trauma of combat, these interpreters emphasize the pride that veterans express for having served. Others, who wish to see all American wars as examples of disreputable imperialism and of a violent national identity, select representations that demonstrate the hypocrisy and insensitivity of the American military, as well as the suffering endured and inflicted by the ordinary soldier.

World War II veterans do not generally abstract from their experiences with the same level of political absolutism. Their expressions of pride are often tempered with loss and grief, and their expressions of patriotism are laced with acknowledgments of America's failures. Although individual accounts vary, in the aggregate, veterans' combat narratives tend to focus on a number of points:

- They express pride at having served in the military and having endured the hardships of training and combat.
- The enlisted veterans often criticize both the military structure and the officer corps.
- Soldiers who were older and/or more educated at the time of the war chafed at the limits of military life and were more critical of military hierarchy.

- As Oliver Wendell Holmes said, the experience of combat is "incommunicable," but the expressions of energy, excitement, horror, pain, loss, and grief that come from veterans provide some consistent sense of its psychological intensity.
- Combat in World War II was always horrific just as all modern combat is horrific.
- Films in particular, and books as well, cannot or will not portray the full range of veterans' experiences (some exceptions come from the veterans' own combat memoirs).
- Many combat veterans frankly acknowledge that they witnessed and/or participated in actions that now seem unusually cruel and brutal, but they also see many such actions either as necessary or inevitable, given the stresses of the modern battlefield.
- Most veterans do not think of any war as "good" though they can see some wars as "necessary"—having known war's cost, they believe it should be avoided if at all possible, but they also believe that America's fighting in World War II was necessary and unavoidable.

The stories of World War II veterans, found in their memoirs and oral histories, testify that the experience of combat in modern warfare is deeply traumatic and leaves lifelong scars. Still, many veterans also celebrate the intimate friendships formed during their time in combat, and they speak with pride and satisfaction of what they endured, individually and collectively. Thus, their experiences cannot be easily reduced to any political position, but their testimony does serve as a baseline against which to measure any film or fiction that attempts to represent the war. In addition, the voices of combat veterans remind us of the tangible consequences of life and death in battle. They call us to recognize that war, however successful, is inevitably costly, and that no war, however necessary, should be entered into lightly or with naïve enthusiasm. They advocate no particular policy; rather, they urge the wisdom and restraint born only, as the Greek playwright Aeschylus once claimed, through the experience of pain.

★   ★   ★

I have been speaking of the faces of war—faces recorded in photojournalism, in drawings by combat artists, in the writing of historians, and in the still vivid memories of the veterans themselves. With every face comes a story, a small narrative thread of the complex experience of

Americans in World War II. I seek the meaning in these faces, and in the stories that grow from them. Whether offered by veterans themselves or reconstructed through powerful forces of media, these stories have shaped the American character and culture of the past sixty years. Even in this new century, our sense of ourselves as Americans is shaped by the experience of World War II.

This book attempts to explore and explain our culture's struggle to construct and interpret the American story of World War II. In part, the book examines how, when the war ended, most combat veterans did not or could not tell of their experiences, and how those few who tried found their stories submerged in a powerful, mainstream narrative of World War II, one constructed largely to carry a Cold War message. This grand narrative represented the war as a triumph of the American Way. While early counterstatements were sometimes powerful (such as Norman Mailer's 1948 novel *The Naked and the Dead*), perceptions of the broader public were shaped by the mainstream version of events, especially as constructed by Hollywood.

The vast majority of Americans, who had never learned the hard lessons of war, uncritically accepted this "Good War" narrative. Having remained at home during World War II, they experienced personal sacrifice and loss but were spared the direct evidence of warfare—no bombed-out cities, no streets filled with the unburied dead. For most Americans, combat and all its horrors had been at a great distance, so they could afford the luxury of viewing the war as uplifting and "good." In addition, war had proved the road to economic achievement unimaginable during the depth of the Great Depression only a decade earlier. As a nation, we grew disturbingly comfortable with our story of World War II.

The military encouraged and promoted these popular views, using them as leverage to maintain appropriations in the face of feared postwar cutbacks. Although the interwar experience certainly justified some fear of military cutbacks, the postwar organizational culture of our armed services also suffered from unhealthy obsessions, including increased interservice rivalries. All such excesses were justified by perceived Cold War threats that, while substantial, were often exaggerated. When the Vietnam War dramatically illustrated many of these problems, many Americans began to criticize the military rather aggressively. But our military does not exist in a vacuum—our nation as a whole creates it, and we all share responsibility for its actions. Collectively, our nation built the "military-industrial complex" to such a size that, by 1961, it troubled even the departing President Dwight

D. Eisenhower, himself one of its early architects. But our narratives of World War II had established the foundation for the edifice. Only after Vietnam infiltrated the living rooms and psyche of America with graphic combat footage did our nation begin to question how we told our stories of war and to consider any war's true cost.

As a result, Vietnam combat veterans returned not to victory parades but to an undeserved atmosphere of quiet embarrassment and sometimes overt hostility. Immediately after Vietnam, neither government nor Hollywood offered any triumphal narrative for none could be offered. Few wanted to discuss the conflict except veterans themselves, and they began to tell their stories of the excitement, terror, and trauma of combat in modern war. From these many individual narratives grew a national understanding of the Vietnam War as both a personal and collective loss. Our nation began to recognize not only our failure to achieve military and political goals but also the deep personal cost of combat itself.

As these stories emerged in print and, a bit later, on screen, our veterans of World War II combat heard a familiar tale, one they knew all too well and which decades of patience could not erase from their memories. They also realized that Americans might finally be willing to listen to the complex stories of World War II veterans. As we began to reach the thirty-year anniversary of the World War II years, and as the participants reached their fifties, their desire to tell the untold story grew more powerful. One by one, memoirs and oral histories appeared, two of the earliest and best being William Manchester's historical memoir *Goodbye, Darkness* (1979) and Studs Terkel's oral history "*The Good War*" (1984). Many others followed. Some earlier memoirs, written immediately after the war but remaining unpublished for decades, finally emerged, such as Raymond Gantter's *Roll Me Over: An Infantryman's World War II*, published in 1997. The Vietnam generation brought fewer victory pennants home from overseas than had their fathers' generation; instead, they returned mostly with their scars, their grief, their pride, and the stories that, if told honestly, might reveal their courage and begin their healing. Doing so, they revealed to the World War II generation the opportunity and the need for all veterans to speak openly of their experiences in order to heal their old wounds. Perhaps one of the bravest acts of each of these generations of veterans has been their willingness to acknowledge their own psychic trauma so they might help others to heal.

This book examines the history of how we have retold the story of combat in World War II, and how that storytelling has shaped our national identity. I neither praise nor blame the military, nor do I compare the relative value of generations; rather, I am exploring how the genres of contemporary memoir and oral history, compared to more culturally hegemonic forms of traditional fiction and film, have allowed combat veterans a more effective venue from which to tell their stories. These stories provide a chorus of voices, resonating with an authenticity that commands readers' attention. It is also vitally important that Americans understand the consequences of combat in modern war so that they might enter into it only when it is absolutely necessary and just.

This book is not encyclopedic in its presentation of material—no single volume could be. Many books, films, and other materials and sources will be mentioned, but only selected works can be assessed in detail; indeed, earlier drafts had proved unwieldy by trying to cover too much. My organizing principle, based on years of studying such materials, is that a dialectic exists between those who wish to represent World War II as a personal and cultural trauma and those who wish to represent it as a national triumph. These are not contradictory narratives; rather, they are stories told from different perspectives and concerning distinct varieties of experience. Our national mythology—how we understand our cultural values as represented in powerful stories—has benefited from balancing both narratives, but that balance is difficult to maintain. Our national policies have suffered when that balance is lost, when our sense of history is narrowed to a single perspective. The facts suggest that the more celebratory narrative, because of its institutional authority, has often dominated and, as such, has thrown off the necessary balance. Although some might argue that the post-Vietnam critique of American institutions achieved similar domination in its own right, the weight of evidence suggests otherwise. Many Americans have continued to accept uncritically the mainstream story of America's World War II triumph while largely ignoring the true costs of that triumph.

Because of a brave effort of veterans, and of historians who have given veterans a vehicle for telling their particular stories, a new sense of balance has recently returned to the telling of World War II. It is not a perfect balance, but no representation of history is ever perfect. However, the face of war is no longer mediated exclusively through celebrity images from film and television; rather, it is the face of each soldier that comes to mind, rising from so many letters, diaries, and memoirs of a youth challenged by war. It also comes from the aging veterans themselves, in both oral histories and interviews. Voices once obscure or silent have now spoken and had their words recorded for posterity, profoundly enhancing Americans' sense of their history and national identity. The effort and sacrifice that veterans put into telling such stories mirrors the courage they once displayed when facing the dangers of war itself. Only they can tell which effort carried the greater personal sacrifice for them—to experience the horror or to reconstruct it so that others might learn from it.

In an 1884 Memorial Day speech, Oliver Wendell Holmes said of his fellow Civil War veterans that "in our youths, our hearts were touched with fire."[2] This poetic language suggests and conceals the horror of combat, a horror that Holmes and so many other veterans have called "incommunicable." Combat veterans of World War II, dying off every day now, often spend their last days leaving something for the record, despite the profound difficulty of conveying their experiences. They once more face the fire, letting it touch their hearts again, if only in memory. Having passed through that ordeal, they offer stories that are unusually direct and honest. When taken together, these simple stories provide the means for knowing not only the war but also how our culture has grown from that war to this day. We inherit these stories, and we are charged with keeping them alive, exploring their meaning, and revealing their lessons. We make this effort for ourselves, and we also do it for those who follow. Out of the past fires, we must discover and preserve the light.

CHAPTER ONE

A War Warning

It Can Happen Here: Strange Prelude

It *could* happen here. It *had* happened here. Fear of a second global conflict had been building throughout the decade, especially as Europe had militarized, and as peace in Asia had fallen victim to Japan's attacks on China. But all those dangers were far from our shores, across the vast oceans whose very extensiveness had always seemed our best defense. No more. Attacked. Attacked without warning.

The Japanese at Pearl Harbor in 1941? No, nothing so tangible. It is the "Martian" attack in New Jersey and New York in 1938. Mere fiction had captured our suppressed fear and anger although news reports and commentary about actual wars had failed to shake us from our isolation. The fiction had come originally from the imagination of H. G. Wells, adapted for radio by the mercurial leader of the Mercury Theater on the Air, Orson Welles. Afterward, it seemed only a nightmarish pre-Halloween prank, except that unexpected panic had ensued. A few people, fearing the arrival of an enemy even more alien than the Axis, had actually chosen suicide over capture by the Martians.

Even today, this event continues to baffle us, despite the strange obsessions of our own postmillennial culture. It now seems absurd that people could so easily accept, at face value, the fiction of a Martian invasion. Yet in another sense, it seems so typically American to grant absolute authority to a new medium of communication as radio was in 1938. Like the voice of the "great Oz" in the film that would be released the following year, the disembodied voice of radio was like the voice of a god. Certainly, national and international leaders had already grasped the power and influence of the medium. Adolf Hitler, Winston

Churchill, and Franklin D. Roosevelt, each in his own way, would make radio into one of the principal propaganda weapons of World War II.

Despite its absurdist qualities, the *War of the Worlds* incident does seem prophetic of the war to come and emblematic of the power of fiction to capture the subtle but persistent undercurrents of the public unconscious. Just as scenes from H. G. Wells' original novel (1898) seem predictive of World War I, with poison gas and mechanical fighting machines, so the 1938 radio version anticipates the panic that would sweep across Europe in the next seven years as people fled from earthly invaders even crueler and more relentless than the fictional Martians. Scenes of invasion, panic, and terror had already occurred in Asia, a place for many Americans as strange as Mars. In July 1937, Japanese armies assaulted China, which was in no position to resist the well-trained and well-equipped Japanese forces.[1] Many of China's most populous cities fell quickly, with civilians paying the greatest cost. Those who could not flee often paid a high price, especially in places such as Nanking, where Japanese troops tortured and murdered an estimated 300,000 Chinese, mostly civilians, in a period of three months.[2]

These horrific events shocked Americans, making them more sympathetic to the Chinese and more willing to provide aid, but few seriously considered going to war on China's behalf. The "Rape of Nanking," as it came to be called, along with all the other events of the Sino-Japanese War, became for Americans just more terrible manifestations of the distant and "inscrutable Orient." Still, knowledge of events in China and elsewhere could not but affect America's cultural subconscious—the nightmare world of sociopolitical and military fears that already sought gratification in various popular culture venues. It was this apocalyptic nightmare world that Orson Welles and his players inadvertently exposed on that October evening in 1938.

More Than a *Rumor* of War

On September 1, 1939, the Wehrmacht rolled across the Polish border, and two days later England and France, honoring treaties with Poland, declared war on Germany. Yet after Germany (and the Soviets) had dismembered Poland, this new war settled into a low-level routine, suggesting that neither side wanted to prolong the fighting. Although some Americans viewed these events with alarm, most still wanted no part of another European conflict. Americans also felt relatively well protected, falsely assuming their military to be strong and the danger to

America to be low. Moreover, despite their general repugnance for the
aggressiveness of Nazi Germany and its führer, many Americans also
doubted the motives of England and France, especially because these
Allied powers had misrepresented Germany during the early years of
World War I. Now, England and France wanted our support again, but
they seemed hypocritical for having failed to confront Germany's aggressiveness years before.
    Even in this isolationist atmosphere, alternative perspectives had
some influence. President Franklin D. Roosevelt's administration
clearly favored England and her Allies, but it expressed this position
in ways that would not alienate the uncertain political mainstream. In
addition, the American film industry, traditionally dominated by conservative politics, had provided a haven for European émigré writers,
directors, producers, and actors who had fled the growing power of
Hitler. While still a minority, these artists had witnessed far too much
to remain silent. Increasingly, they struggled, against considerable resistance, to produce films openly critical of Nazi Germany.[3]
    By mid-1940, after Nazi Germany had conquered most of Western
Europe, the American public began showing increased support for
England, the last Allied nation capable of opposing Hitler. Recognizing
the obvious threats to our own security, FDR's administration insti-
tuted the "Short of War" policy, allowing direct aid to England
while America mobilized its forces.[4] Meanwhile, the American media
reported on how the English were defending themselves against
the largest air assault in history. As coverage of the Battle of Britain
touched America's deep sense of sympathy for England, Roosevelt
carefully analyzed evolving public opinion about the war, initiating
further programs to aid the Allied cause. An increasingly supportive
Congress passed new appropriations bills, both to aid England and to
rearm America. They authorized a massive, though belated, expansion
of the Navy, and they allowed the Army to call up reservists, to fed-
eralize National guard units, and to institute an unprecedented peacetime draft. Outdated but still serviceable U.S. warships were offered to
England in exchange for American use of English bases in the Western
Hemisphere, and later, the Lend-Lease Act provided aid to England
without creating a drain on the already exhausted English treasury.
    Between 1939 and 1941, America thus moved from isolation to in-
volvement. Writers, photographers, broadcast journalists, and filmmakers, working in harmony with an increasingly active Roosevelt
administration, helped make this political evolution possible in so short
a time. Yet the processes of political change seemed far slower and

more uncertain in those years than they appear now in hindsight. The conventional wisdom of two decades of American foreign policy had been definitively isolationist, and even as late as 1941, many Americans still believed that the United States should not enter the new World War as a combatant. FDR and those who favored U.S. involvement had to be determined and patient in order to overcome this isolationist tradition.

For the most part, Hollywood had encouraged isolationism throughout the 1930s. Filmmakers who wanted to confront the Nazi menace often ran afoul of both the Hays Office and congressional conservatives.[5] In addition, the growing America First movement, working with conservative senators such as Gerald P. Nye, pushed for American neutrality. Nye and like-minded politicians raged against what they termed "warmongering" by filmmakers, and Senate hearings about the political content of films spread considerable fear in Hollywood. Indeed, hearings proceeded right up to the brink of the Pearl Harbor attack. "Hollywood," however, was merely a collection of businesses whose principal ideology was making money. Studios sold much of their product abroad, often in countries influenced by or sympathetic to Germany, and feared losing these profitable markets. Well into 1940, industry-imposed censorship and conservative politics combined with existing financial motives to limit the number and scope of films critical of Nazi Germany.[6]

In contrast, the news media, especially in its newest forms, had been energetically reporting on international crises since the Spanish Civil War. During the late 1930s, CBS began developing its network to cover international broadcast news, while print journalists, especially photographers, had already made media history with their innovative coverage of foreign affairs. Both broadcasting and this new brand of photojournalism emerged at a time when international events were providing just the kind of material that fledgling media needed to establish their power and authority. Representing the drama of international conflict and the intensity of modern combat called for the immediacy of broadcasting and the focal concentration of photography. Historic events were now broadcast live into our homes, and many Americans' first knowledge of such events came through radio. Likewise, many of the period's iconic images first appeared as classic black-and-white photography in publications such as *Life* magazine.

Newsreel films also contributed to the rising war consciousness of the American public. Perhaps most prominent among these was *The March of Time,* produced by Henry Luce's media conglomerate Time, Inc.

Begun in 1935, this cinematic news series provided powerful support for a more internationalist American foreign policy even prior to 1939.[7] Once war broke out, *The March of Time* focused additional coverage on the growing global conflict, becoming more openly antifascist. From the mid-1930s to the Japanese attack on Pearl Harbor, *The March of Time* and its brethren print publications, *Time* and *Life*, confronted the mainstream American public with relatively graphic images of war. Thus, whether Americans sought escape and diversion through magazines, radio, or movies, each week millions came face to face with the growing menace of Axis power. From 1939 onward, newsreel viewers saw the anguish of people in countries that had once sought to avoid war by appeasing Hitler. Such representations made it increasingly clear that there was no fantasy world so powerful—in print, on air, or on screen—that it could not be ruptured by the major news events of the day. Audiences finally began to realize that no nation could isolate itself from these events.

Despite these media influences, American opinion would not have coalesced so powerfully in favor of the Allies had not events developed with such ferocity during the spring and summer of 1940. Suddenly, England alone opposed a Nazi Germany that actually surpassed the worst images of the rapacious "Huns" in World War I propaganda films. Moreover, imperial in scope but small in actual size, England now appeared a courageous underdog. What emerged was a classic narrative pattern that characterized England as the besieged but unbowed island "democracy," standing in stoic opposition to an authoritarian continental power. This pattern recalled previously popular representations of the Spanish Armada and the Napoleonic Wars. Of course the Nazi menace was genuine, and England's opposition to the Nazis was absolutely necessary. Yet the imagery of a noble and dogged English resistance also ignored a history of imperialism and oppression whose effects were still being felt worldwide. Many colonized people, from Ireland to India, had difficulty conceiving of their colonial oppressors as the "underdog defenders of democracy and freedom." Had the Nazis not been so obviously evil and so relentless in pursuit of world dominance, England could never have been successfully represented in such glowing terms.[8]

By late summer 1940, the American media increasingly showcased the brighter side of English history and culture, reflecting the virtues being demonstrated in the fight against the Nazis. With their outnumbered Royal Air Force (RAF) in a desperate battle against Nazi bombers over London, the English appeared as sympathetic victims and as tough citizens of the last democracy able to oppose Hitler. Hollywood also found greater reason to intervene even if the American government was still unable to do so. In August 1940, shortly after the Battle of Britain began, the Nazis banned all American films from areas under their control.⁹ In doing so, they effectively eliminated the major financial worry that had kept Hollywood from confronting fascism: with no pro-German market to lose, producers and directors were able to make explicitly anti-Nazi films. Despite the Hays Office's intransigence and the vocal political pressures of America First, conservative Hollywood finally shifted to open support for the Allied cause.

★   ★   ★

Despite all the newspaper coverage and motion picture footage, World War II was also radio's war. Only network radio had the ability to bring the sounds of war into America's living rooms, often in real time. Since the international radio hookups necessary for such broadcasts had been developed only shortly before the outbreak of hostilities, this was the first real broadcast war, setting the standard for future wartime broadcast journalism. Broadcasting also helped shape how Americans would come to think of World War II. Never before had those on the home front felt themselves so immediately connected with the events of a war on foreign soil. The secure emotional environment of the home could now be suddenly shattered by breaking news from far away. First came the voice of the network announcer: "We interrupt our regularly scheduled program to bring you a special broadcast. We now take you to. . . ." Then came the correspondent from some distant site: "I am speaking to you from Berlin," or Rome, or Prague, or Paris. Even during the years just prior to the war, Americans grew familiar with such interruptions and frightened by their implications. It was this new "radio consciousness" that Orson Welles had exploited with his fictional *War of the Worlds* broadcast. As war began for real, many Americans at home would experience it most intimately through the magically disembodied voice of radio.

Early in the war, one foreign city became particularly emblematic for America's radio audiences, and one voice seemed to speak for all those who covered the war. "This is London," said the voice, and Americans immediately recognized the rich, somber tones of Edward R. Murrow. Moments later, they might hear sirens, guns, and bombs as well. Throughout the Battle of Britain and the Blitz, Murrow kept broadcasting from the embattled English capital. His style compelled attention, and his obvious respect for the English people and his opposition to the Axis shaped the political tone of the broadcasts. Having covered Europe for several years, and having previously helped émigré intellectuals and artists escape from Germany, Murrow had personally witnessed Nazi terror.[10] While not explicitly politicizing his broadcasts, he could easily draw attention to the suffering caused by Nazi aggression.[11] He gave voice to the facts, and he gave weight to the issues that would lead people to consider those facts seriously. His own judgment, but not overt bias, shaped his reporting. Essentially, he told the radio audience that this is what I have seen and heard, and this is what it means in my view—now you decide what to believe. Fellow journalists, such as Eric Severeid, claimed that Murrow's influence grew from his willingness to speak frankly but not to proselytize directly. Of all American correspondents, he set the standard for coverage.

Broadcasting from London, Murrow focused America's attention on daily air battles and nightly bombings. In a clear, understated manner, he presented not only the intensity of the battle but also the simple human-interest stories that so effectively connected the average American with the ordinary Londoner. Avoiding exaggeration, Murrow created a calm media persona that made the new war familiar to Americans, while characterizing the English people as America's besieged brethren. He could convey the war's powerful drama and terrible cost while also maintaining a sense of irony that brought occasional lightness to the otherwise dismal experience of the Blitz. Many broadcasts were given after the fact, but his "rooftop broadcasts," conducted at great risk during the actual bombings, brought listeners into the thick of battle. In the background, sirens wailed, bombers droned, antiaircraft guns barked their defiance, and bombs screeched earthward to thunderous explosions. All the while, Murrow's cool demeanor kept listeners' attention and sustained their spirits, as he demonstrated the same courage manifested by the tough London population. A September 22 broadcast gives one example of Murrow addressing listeners during an ongoing air raid:

> I'm standing again tonight on a rooftop looking out over London....there's been considerable action up there, but at the moment there's an ominous silence....a silence that has a great deal of dignity.[12]

In contrast, he could also see the war from a broader perspective. During an August 25 broadcast, Murrow spoke ironically of the young

German aircrew responsible for the bombing. His words provide an accurate sense of the unreality of this new kind of war:

> ...three or four high-school boys with some special training had been flying around over London in about $100,000 worth of machinery. One of them had pressed a button—the fire and a number of casualties was the result.[13]

Here, Murrow captures a feeling of distance between agent and effect in the acts of modern war, and how otherwise harmless "high-school boys" cause horrific destruction. The images are telling, and the insights prescient. When he describes an unseen agent behind the very graphic destruction from night bombing, Murrow speaks for civilians throughout the war, in places as distant from one another as London and Tokyo.

In many broadcasts, Murrow also speaks of the lives, sacrifices, and simple courage of ordinary Londoners. On August 18, he describes the aftermath of one raid, offering an almost cinematic vision of the destruction. Then he focuses on details of a bathroom, cut open by the bombing, where a "red sponge was still in the soap dish...."[14] The same broadcast summarizes qualities of the English people that Americans have come to associate with the Blitz:

> After watching and talking with those people this afternoon I am more than ever convinced that they are made of stern stuff. They can take what is coming.[15]

As Murrow expressed his growing respect for these people, his on-air persona acquired some of the same cachet that he discovered in the English—he sounded cool, calm, slightly ironic, but unperturbed in the face of danger. For Americans, his broadcasts represented the *ethos* of the English, a character of quiet courage, and he enacted that character on the air. In a sense, he was calling Americans to witness courage, and in doing so, to emulate that courage in their own responses to the threats of Nazi tyranny. He did not have to proselytize; he needed only to describe the demeanor of the English under fire while representing similar qualities in his own reporting. Murrow, who started his career in education-related work, became America's great educator on the developing conflict, didactic and persuasive without seeming to try.

After more than a decade of radio dramas, the American audience could already appreciate radio's power to bring even fictional events to life. Murrow and his correspondents had pioneered live-event coverage even before the war.[16] When war came, they built on their experience and honed their skills, becoming one of the most influential news teams in history. Although distinctive in individual style, they all strove to maintain Murrow's high standards of quality and integrity. Yet it is Murrow's voice that lingers in our ears even today; his words "This is London" carry an authority that was his alone. He brought the American people not only the news but also a human perspective and an underlying political context that gave meaning to the news. Murrow, as much as anyone, led Americans to see the Nazis for the evil they were and, consequently, to see the English people as the defenders of freedom.

The Yanks Start Coming

From 1939 to 1941, American films began to insert into stories of England's struggle the additional narrative of brash young Americans who come to England's aid, though often with initially selfish motives. The questionable American protagonists soon learn the meaning of English stoicism and, ultimately, combine it effectively with vigorous Yankee courage and ingenuity. It is a narrative pattern that has many precedents, including some aspects of Henry James' fiction and specific works, such as Mark Twain's *A Connecticut Yankee in King Arthur's Court* (1889). In the commonplace characterization of these World War II narratives, Americans bring energetic bravery and native cleverness to the fight, whereas the English, a bit stuffy at times, bring quiet courage and steady discipline. This narrative of the Anglo-American Alliance promises the best of both worlds in fighting culturally distinct continental enemies.

The structure of this new narrative appealed to an uncertain American public by reversing an older characterization of England as the more powerful and senior partner in a historical tradition of parallel, if sometimes rival, democracies. This older pattern grew largely from mid-nineteenth-century assumptions concerning the relative status of the two nations. Perennially on the frontier, America had been seen as wilder and more violent, while England had been depicted as the old bastion of civilization and the new center of industrial and commercial power. The mother country had thus been in a better position to advise and support the "advancing forces of civilization" in frontier America. Though England had maintained its own colonial frontiers, America had been seen typically as *all* frontier. By 1900, however, America had "closed" its frontiers and largely caught up with or surpassed England in most industrial development. Thus in 1940 and 1941, it would be England in the front lines and America, with its vast resources, providing the financial and technical support, a reversal of the nineteenth-century pattern. The new images appealed to Americans' sense of industrial and economic supremacy while still reinforcing the cultural links with England.

On a policy level, the relationship came to life with Roosevelt's concept of America as the "Arsenal of Democracy," the site from which the resources for war might be sent to England.[17] Supporting this pattern were a broad range of cultural narratives representing English heroism, Nazi evil, and American support of the righteous. As one American poster from the 1939–1941 period proclaimed, "America's Answer! Production."[18] We worked on the production lines while the English soldiers fought on the front lines. Many Americans viewed this as a reasonably good deal, especially as more high-wage industrial jobs opened up. At the same time, we expressed our compassion by collecting and sending such aid as "Bundles for Britain" to provide resources for an English population made needy by the U-boat war in the Atlantic.[19] The "bundles" were literally relief packages for beleaguered English civilians, but in another sense, the entirety of our lend-lease aid to England consisted of "bundles" for the besieged nation. In this latter case, the bundles included artillery, tanks, planes, and supplies of every kind.

American armed forces also played a role in the conflict before any official declaration of war. Throughout 1941, American escort vessels were increasingly responsible for guarding conveys in the western half of the Atlantic. What is more, American troops were sent to Iceland, relieving the English garrison for combat elsewhere. Roosevelt and Churchill met to plan joint war-fighting goals and strategies months before the Pearl Harbor attack. Many believed that when war broke out officially between America and Germany, it would come as a result of the already active combat in the Atlantic shipping lanes. On the other side of the globe, the increasing aggressiveness of Japan also led to more American aid to China. In the case of the well-known "Flying Tigers" (the AVG, American Volunteer Group), U.S. Air Force pilots worked clandestinely and independently in China to oppose Japanese attacks.[20]

Back in the European theater, a few Americans began fighting the Nazis before America was officially a combatant. These were mostly pilots who volunteered to fly and fight with the RAF in England during the Battle of Britain. Some flew in "Eagle Squadrons," volunteer units under RAF command, while others joined up individually and flew in otherwise English squadrons. Stories of these volunteer pilots provided great opportunities for dramatic interpretation, and it was natural that the film industry would quickly move such stories to the screen. During 1940 and 1941, several films featured the adventures of these young Americans, with the plot lines consistently following the pattern of the brash American whose personality at first offends, but whose humor, courage, and ingenuity ultimately win the day. In the process, he usually learns to respect the English and their culture even as he fights to preserve it.

The most important film of this type was *A Yank in the RAF* (1941), coupling the star power of Tyrone Power with the sex appeal of soon-to-be favorite pinup girl Betty Grable. The film focuses on Tim Baker (Power) as the talented but rebellious pilot who, ferrying bombers to England for a fee of $1,000 per trip, discovers his old flame Carol Brown (Grable), a volunteer medical worker by day and London nightclub singer by night. He tries to revive the romance, joining the RAF so that he can stay in England and appear heroic. The film includes many seriocomic romantic scenes, with the persistent Tim still possessed of a wandering eye whenever Carol is not within easy reach. But the film cuts from the romance episodes to scenes of training and combat that involve increased danger and intensity. Tim's group commander, John Morley (John Sutton) becomes a staid but persuasive rival for Carol's affections. Just as Germany assaults the Low Countries and France, Tim seems to be losing the romantic struggle. Finally, he proves himself in the climactic air battle over Dunkirk but fails to return from the mission. Morley comforts Carol, who demonstrates her obvious love for Tim now that he is lost. When all hope seems gone, a telephone call announces the arrival of a ship with the last survivors. Tim, bandaged but undaunted, slowly walks down the gangplank to the waiting arms of Carol and the proud handshake of his erstwhile rival.

As clichéd as any film can be, *A Yank in the RAF* captures both the spirit of the time and fundamental aspects of our characterization of American heroes. Its prowar, pro-English stance was welcomed by those who called for greater American opposition to the Nazis. As critic Howard Barnes put it in a *New York Herald Tribune* review:

> ...It is neither imaginative nor conventionally captivating. What makes *A Yank in the RAF* a rather stunning entertainment is the

fact that it keys right into memorable events which constitute the pattern of this present chapter in history.[21]

For all its weak humor and sexism, the film typifies the story of a brash Yankee in, if not King Arthur's Court, at least in His Majesty's service. The film is especially noteworthy because its high-profile male lead makes it a major production. Likewise, with Darryl F. Zanuck as producer, it shows greater Hollywood muscle behind a prowar film. *A Yank in the RAF* is also important in relationship to later films. The producer-director team of Zanuck and Henry King, along with cinematographer Leon Shamroy, subsequently collaborated on a much more effective World War II aviation drama, *Twelve O'Clock High* (1949). Even a simple comparison of the two films reveals how much the team had learned during the war, as well as how actual gun-camera combat footage would influence, and be incorporated into, postwar aviation films. The flying sequences in *A Yank in the RAF* seem awkward and stagy, with plenty of room for pilots to make ironic comments in the face of danger. These scenes in no way suggest the speed and savagery of World War II air warfare. World War II combat photography reveals slashing fighter attacks—a speeding plane, a few seconds of heavy machine gun bursts, and a disintegrating opposing aircraft. There is little time to think or reflect, much less to give a gallant speech, however brief. But only the war itself, still in its early stages in 1941, could provide the knowledge and the combat footage to allow the Zanuck-King-Shamroy team to evolve beyond the crude representations used in *A Yank in the RAF*.

A Yank in the RAF also influenced subsequent films made during the first half of the war, setting up a title form that focuses on an individualistic American in search of wartime adventure. *A Yank on the Burma Road* (1942) and *A Yank in Libya* (1942) repeat a similar pattern. Embedded in all these stories is the spirit of Yankee ingenuity and independence. These films show American heroes as free spirits who fight on their own terms and do not easily conform to a group. In contrast, later war films like *The Story of G.I. Joe* (1945) will emphasize the military unit almost as a character in itself, subordinating individual personalities to the mission and character of the group. An additional contrast comes in the training-film genre of roughly the same period. This type of film shows how the selfish young male character learns to suppress his ego and sacrifice some of his independence so he might become a valued member of a fighting group, as in the popular film about aviation training *I Wanted Wings* (1941). After the war, serious

American war novels and films would draw much of their psychological complexity and narrative power from these contradictory qualities in the American national character. But prior to America's official entry into the war, as well as during the months immediately following Pearl Harbor, Americans who went to war represented a kind of independence that became the central feature of characters in the "A Yank in..." films.

Almost a quarter of a century later, the satirical film *The Americanization of Emily* (1964), starring James Garner and Julie Andrews, would offer a satiric treatment of the brash American in conflict with a stodgy English culture. Interestingly, a number of scenes between Garner and Andrews suggest subtle connections with those in *A Yank in the RAF*, particularly the return of the wounded protagonist from across the channel. Allusions also can be found in a scene in which American naval officer Garner fakes a limp, claiming to have been injured "flying with the RAF in 1940." In 1964, such satire would be possible, but back in 1941, for all its limitations, each film like *A Yank in the RAF* proved one more demonstration of Hollywood's solidarity with the embattled English people, one more call to arms against the Nazis. Such films both revealed and predicted that, as in World War I, the "Yanks are coming," again.[22]

CHAPTER TWO

"Why We Fight"

War as Narrative

Strategic and operational planning in war, while dependent on many different aspects of military thought, is also a narrative art form. War plans present a hypothetical future, constructing a fiction that shapes one side's actions while also anticipating those of the enemy. War games test these fictions, but combat remains the real test, subjecting narratives to actual circumstances that, along with the counternarratives of an enemy, force violent "revisions." Through this rough narrative process, military planners practice their art. In contrast, actual combatants experience the very real chaos and violence that rarely resembles those elegant plans. With the battle over, planners use after-action reports to craft new narratives from these recorded fragments of experience. This process demands interpretation as well as reconstruction, adapting narratives in light of actual events to develop a deeper understanding of their significance—a kind of military hermeneutics. Both sides take away from battle a different set of interpretations, and so the process continues. In the end, imaginative or interpretive failure can lead to military failure. If one cannot imagine more comprehensively than an enemy, one risks being subjected to the enemy's narrative of events. Many factors make for victory, but at one level, wars are won by the most honest, imaginative, and resilient storytellers.

Joan Didion once wrote that "we tell ourselves stories in order to live," and we might add the corollary that we also tell stories in order to fight, to kill, and even to die.[1] Beyond the range of specific military planning, wars also grow from the cultural narratives of one nation, or group of nations, coming into conflict with those of other nations. Fighting a war depends on governments and armies, but these must be supported by whole populations and cultures. Even totalitarian regimes must motivate their peoples to support a war actively. Narrative art, especially in its most mythic forms, provides a sense of order and purpose that makes human actions meaningful. Declaring war is a decision of government policy, and fighting a war is a matter of military action, but wars often succeed or fail based on the rhetorical effectiveness of the narratives used to persuade a nation's people to give their support. Without a sense of common purpose, no nation can sustain the human and material costs of war, particularly a modern war. Certainly no level of conviction can overcome completely the uneven odds between mismatched opponents, but the impact of such conviction can never be discounted. Recent history provides numerous examples of a militarily strong nation that loses in conflict with a weaker one, either because the stronger nation's belief in a common narrative for war has failed or because the people are failed by a government that poorly or dishonestly constructs the narrative of war—examples include the United States in Vietnam and the Soviet Union in Afghanistan. People will suffer the costs of war only if they are convinced that those costs are justified, and common narratives, more than abstract analyses, provide the deep justification required by a national psyche faced with the potential horror and trauma of modern combat.

Of course, for those who will actually fight the war, such large-scale narratives provide only a beginning—perhaps enough motivation to enlist. As numerous personal narratives of combat testify, soldiers fight largely for their own survival and for that of fellow soldiers in their unit. The organized chaos and overwhelming violence of combat become specific in the idiosyncratic experience of each individual and small group. Most combat veterans agree that no representation conveys the emotional intensity of combat. Yet many still find it necessary to tell their stories, for the sake of the psychological release that may come from the act of telling or from the opportunity to leave some record, however limited, of their experience. Even given the futility of conveying the combat experience, many veterans try to manifest it through words and images.

Thus, from the most abstract levels of national policy and military staff planning, to the most concrete level of recollecting combat, constructing narratives is a basic aspect of fighting a war. To paraphrase Carl von Clausewitz, war is *narrative* by other means.

★　★　★

When the Japanese Combined Fleet staff planned the attack on Pearl Harbor, they did so as an act of military strategy and operations, but they also believed the attack plan to be a *very good story*. Like most good stories, the plan showed some respect for history and conventions. It paid homage to the courage and boldness of the Samurai tradition while also adding something new. Moreover, it depended on the latest military technologies and the most innovative tactics. In contrast, the U.S. military planners had been slow to craft new stories, slow to explore the multiplicity of possible narratives that could shape their experience. They did have a master narrative for a possible war with Japan, originally called the Orange Plan, which assumed a Japanese attack in the Western Pacific, perhaps in the Philippines, requiring a determined defense by the available forces.[2] Relief would come from the U.S. Navy's slow progress across the Pacific, capturing strongholds where necessary, and ultimately engaging the Japanese forces somewhere near the site of the original attack where, it was hoped, the defending U.S. forces would still be holding out.

During the interwar decades, the vaguely defined Orange Plan had undergone many revisions, but by the second half of 1941, its original assumptions prevailed by default. By the eve of war, however, many American military planners realized that no such trans-Pacific campaign could be carried out in the early stages of a war. The United States lacked the tactical forces and the logistical support to do so. The military could not, however, acknowledge that our forces in Far East Asia had become "expendable," or that our leadership had consciously accepted the inevitable loss of those forces. We persisted in a state of denial, by pretending that the untenable Orange Plan defined our strategic objectives and operational guidelines, and by stationing our fleet at the advanced base of Pearl Harbor in 1940. Ironically, the Japanese themselves "read" this plan in the very fact that we had moved the fleet. Accepting our own flawed narrative of a possible war, the Japanese felt obligated to counter it. Despite the weakness of the Orange Plan, Japanese war planners assumed that we might still achieve our unrealistic objectives. Their preemptive countermeasure of attacking our fleet at Pearl Harbor grew from this assumption. So our own outdated plan for fighting in the distant waters of the Far East called forth the tactically excellent Japanese plan to circumvent our strategy by attacking us at Pearl Harbor. In the event, December 7 revealed not only the failure of U.S. strategic intelligence analysis; not only the failure of operational planning, tactical training, and local reconnaissance; but also the underlying failure of narrative and imagination, much as we saw with the 9/11 terrorist attacks in 2001.

Although the Pearl Harbor attack became a tactical and operational victory for the Japanese, it was turned quickly into a broader political victory for the United States. Victorious as they were, the Japanese soon became captive to their own narrative of success. Attached to their story's power, they were not prepared for any counterinterpretation. For them, the event's meaning was clear—a vindication of cultural superiority made manifest by their military. This superiority was not a matter of numbers and technology but of mind and spirit. A warrior people, represented by a select warrior caste, could certainly defeat a larger but undisciplined rabble with no such martial values. The Japanese pilots and aircrew who wrought the devastation at Pearl Harbor saw themselves as such a warrior elite, destined to prevail by virtue of superior discipline. The Japanese naval planning staff shared this belief and demonstrated equivalent values in their own practice of the art of war. Their attack plan, their "story," was of the highest quality. To conceive of such a story, and to craft it into a military operation, was to them an intellectual and artistic achievement of the highest order. To make that story into the concrete reality of a victorious attack had been a great feat of arms, yet all such feats are initially triumphs of the imagination. So both "pencil pushers" and pilots felt a common sense of pride in the stunning victory that confirmed their most optimistic expectations about Japanese military superiority. Having achieved such success at the outset, they naturally began to extend the narrative to the obvious conclusion of a quick and complete victory. The evidence seemed so compelling that it could only justify the Japanese interpretation of these events.

Not so for the United States, where the obvious shame and anger in response to the defeat was interwoven with something more important—the emergent sense of a common cause in crafting new narratives, both militarily and politically. Our overwhelming defeat at Pearl Harbor forced us to make radical revisions in the military thread of our war-planning narrative, but that revision would take time and patience. What could sustain us as we continued on the defensive and struggled to reshape our understanding? Fortunately, the attack provided new elements for our political war narrative, and these gave powerful motivation for Americans to fight a war since there is no better reason to fight than against a treacherous enemy. The attack unified America's determination to fight back, and even if we did not yet know *how* to fight the war, we had quickly decided *why* to fight it. Without the Pearl Harbor attack, such unity of purpose would have been unlikely. In a country divided by its own conflicted narratives of what was happening in Europe and the Far East, little consensus had been achieved about whether we should enter the war. Prior to the attack, any American declaration of war, against any or all Axis powers, would have faced stiff opposition in Congress and among the public. For that reason, Roosevelt's administration had maneuvered cautiously, hoping an enemy action would create the necessary justification for war. The attack on Pearl Harbor did just that—we were now fighting to defend *our* country.[3]

The attack provided additional narrative material and incentive as well. For us, it was not only a surprise but also an act of treachery—defining the Japanese, and by extension all the Axis powers, as the most treacherous of enemies. America and Japan had literally been in peace negotiations as the bombs began to fall. The Japanese had intended to break off negotiations and all diplomatic relations an hour before the attack commenced, legitimizing the action in their minds even though a preemptive strike, prior to an explicit declaration of war, might still be viewed as treacherous.[4] Their embassy staff, however, failed to decode the official statement on time, so the attack began while negotiations were still technically in progress. Ironically, the U.S. government had broken the Japanese diplomatic code and already knew that the unde-livered message meant that war was inevitable.[5] Thus, our government was not surprised that an attack came, but only by where, when, and how it came. In hindsight, Pearl Harbor stands out as a logical target, but until the attack, few military planners seriously believed that an air-craft carrier strike force could deliver so great a blow at such a distance from its home base; therefore, the Japanese preemptive attack on Pearl Harbor took our government and military completely by surprise. Yet it also superseded any prior political narratives in America, providing the necessary justification to declare war.

In addition, the Pearl Harbor attack fit easily into a traditional American narrative about war—acknowledging our own unprepared-ness because we are "not a warlike people" while at the same time justifying our sense of righteous anger in confronting aggressive ene-mies who attack us. But Pearl Harbor as a central narrative is unique in our narrative history, making similar historical events, such as the problematic sinking of the USS *Maine* prior to the Spanish-American War, seem minor by comparison. At Pearl Harbor, American territory had been attacked by a foreign power during a time of titular peace. We had never before and might never again feel so righteous and so unified in pursuing a war as in the aftermath of Pearl Harbor. Perhaps only our response to 9/11 can compare, but since those attackers were loosely structured terrorist groups, not a specific nation-state, our reac-tion was different. So, on December 7, 1941, the Japanese surprised us with a winning military narrative, but the next day, President Franklin

D. Roosevelt counterattacked with an interpretation that snatched that victory back, in political terms if not in military ones. Calling it a "date which will live in infamy," he set the tone for interpretations and the counternarratives, both political and military, that would help bring victory within four years.

Pearl Harbor: Remembering the "Infamy"

For most Americans, the Japanese attack on Pearl Harbor exists in two separate universes: the one a place of historical facts, the other a province of narrative constructs that transform history into national mythology. We must be concerned with both, but our study focuses largely on the mythic elements and their rhetorical power. News of the attack reached Americans relatively quickly as military authorities sent out the message "Air Raid, Pearl Harbor—This is no drill."[6] Planes commenced bombing just prior to eight a.m., Honolulu time, on December 7 (2:00 p.m. on the American East Coast). So throughout the afternoon of December 7, millions of Americans received the news. Though many Americans did not then know even the location of Pearl Harbor, the message was still understood. We had been attacked and defeated in the first battle of a war that had yet to be declared. We were in the war whether we liked it or not, and the time for debate was at an end. Now we were the target, and the call to arms was a call to save our nation.

The combination of shock, fear, and anger that came on December 7 is unfortunately all too clear to contemporary Americans after 9/11. Familiar as well is the intricate way in which the news of distant events can be interwoven into our individual experience and collective cultural psyche through the power of mass media. We can well understand why Americans who lived through that day can never forget it. It was one of a number of significant days that, when mentioned to that generation of Americans, enables them to recall, with crystal clarity, precisely where they were and what they were doing. Other such moments include the death of FDR and the assassination of John F. Kennedy; 9/11 is merely the latest addition to the list.

In such moments of national self-consciousness, we redefine ourselves in the terms and through the imagery offered by our media. We see ourselves not as separate individuals or groups but as a nation made whole by its response to tragic events. We become the "selves" we are shown to be as media represent and reconstruct the national identity in a single process, with our conscious and unconscious cooperation. On a more general level, this process continues every day in a mass-media culture with each news report or advertisement we witness, yet it happens in a special and lasting way on occasion of crisis or catastrophe. In a moment of national tragedy, in the open space of pain, we share common words and images, common narratives, provided through our national media. Furthermore, those reporting the events also draw on the familiar narratives that have, in the past, provided social and cultural solidarity.[7] Using such familiar structures to frame their representations, the media connect present events with the authoritative narratives of a revered past. So from the available images of a sudden crisis come the icons that we will eventually view as sacred images of history.

★ ★ ★

On December 8, President Roosevelt's call for a declaration of war took no one by surprise, and yet his speech would set the tone for America's understanding of this war throughout the next four years. Roosevelt recognized that the nation was both shocked and angered by the Pearl Harbor attack, but he also realized that the disaster could provoke either panic or overly hasty action. In contrast, the long struggle ahead would require patience and firm commitment. Grasping the political importance, mythic significance, and rhetorical demands of this occasion, Roosevelt made his speech the first step in constructing the national "mythos" of Pearl Harbor and a foundation for our whole narrative of the war. As understood in America, this story tells of a peaceful people attacked by treacherous and deceitful enemies, and of a righteous people whose very rectitude confers upon them justice, might, and with God's help, victory.

Roosevelt's address is brief and focused, clearly articulating the events and actions as they had occurred. By pointing out that the Japanese strike forces would have had to set sail weeks earlier, Roosevelt emphasizes that the attack had been planned and executed while peace negotiations had still been underway. Thus, he takes the narrative initiative in framing the attack as treacherous. This theme is articulated even in the first sentence of the speech: "Yesterday, Dec. 7, 1941—a date which will live in infamy—the United States of America was suddenly and deliberately attacked by naval and air forces of the Empire of Japan."[8] The sentence also reveals an important aspect of the rhetorical strategy in the speech: whereas the main sentence structure provides the facts, the theme is carried by a parenthetical expression, standing in apposition to the date. By subtle inversion of normal sentence logic—placing the most important issue in the parenthetical section—Roosevelt thus creates a sense of syntactic surprise. As a result, the phrase "a date which will live in infamy" stands in judgment of the mere facts, making these words particularly memorable. Also arresting is the choice of the word "infamy," stating judgment. Surrounded by otherwise simple language, this more consciously oratorical word exerts even greater force. The first sentence of the speech thus forcefully and directly tells the whole story, indicting and judging in one brief expression.

The body of the speech clearly and succinctly states the charges against Japan. It identifies the attack not only as a "surprise" but also as an act of "premeditated" deceit. The measured pace proceeds through four more short paragraphs, listing additional attacks Japan made following Pearl Harbor. Here, the style changes: the list is not focused into one sentence but extended through six, each one naming a separate attack. Roosevelt begins the series by reusing the word "yesterday," connecting with the first word of the speech, suggesting that he has been building to this climax. The six sentences repeat similar structures, creating a tone of formal ritual in stating the additional charges. Each sentence states that the Japanese were the attackers; however, the list progresses from using "the Japanese government" as the subject in the first sentence, to "Japanese forces" in the next three sentences. In the final two sentences, the subject is truncated to merely the "Japanese." This subtle shifting of reference builds an indictment against the whole nation of Japan, not merely its government and military.

Unlike the usual speeches against Germany, specifically identifying Hitler, here no mention is made of Japan's leadership. Rather, the Japanese government, military forces, and people are identified collectively and in sequence, making them share responsibility for the attacks. Since the list builds in intensity, it also builds to the conclusion, syntactically and rhetorically, that the Japanese people bear ultimate responsibility for the war of aggression in the Pacific. Roosevelt's audience would assume, therefore, that the Japanese people should suffer the consequences of their actions. It is impossible to determine how much Roosevelt consciously intended to indict the whole Japanese people as opposed to just their leaders and military. Perhaps he was merely voicing the fundamental pain, fear, and anger that he and the whole nation were experiencing. Perhaps, as well, he spoke unconsciously for an undercurrent of racism that flows consistently through American culture, while redirecting that racism toward a specific enemy nation.

These qualities, incipient in Roosevelt's speech and likely unconscious in its composition, grew into major influences on how we depicted the Japanese as an enemy during World War II.[9]

In closing, Roosevelt more explicitly speaks for the whole nation: "No matter how long it may take us to overcome this premeditated invasion, the American people in their righteous might will win through to absolute victory." Here he shifts from the first person to the third in the same sentence: "No matter how long it may take *us*," shows unity between speaker and the nation while the phrase "American people" apparently maintains the suggestion that the president speaks for all Americans. But then he shifts to the third person in attributing "righteous might" to the people but not to himself as an individual. *His* will has thus become the *people's* will, and his identity is subsumed into the unified whole of the nation. The individual personality of the president disappears for a moment, and the voice carries on as if at a distance, describing the unity of leader and people. Within the brief space of this speech, Roosevelt progresses from leader of the people, to voice of the people, to will of the people. The speaking voice describes a people so unified that even the president himself disappears into their "wholeness," leaving the voice disembodied and without identity. At the same time, creating such a distant voice suggests transcendent authority and truth, which the speech would not attain if still attached to the individual identity of Roosevelt. Leader and people are one, and the voice becomes almost divine in its comment on their common righteousness. In this godlike, distant voice, Roosevelt's call to war and prediction of ultimate American victory carry almost divine sanction. It is unlikely that Roosevelt consciously engaged in such minute syntactic and semantic analysis of a speech that he prepared in less than twenty-four hours. Yet his gifts and habits, as both a statesman and a rhetorician, helped him compose structures that would ring true to most Americans.

Although perhaps not as eloquent as Lincoln's "Gettysburg Address," Roosevelt's speech seeking a declaration of war is still among the most memorable and important presidential addresses. It can be argued that the occasion would raise any speech to prominence, even one that sounds simple, direct, and deceptively pedestrian. But the general simplicity, as noted above, belies rhetorical sophistication. Indeed, it is a masterful speech in making explicit the case for war and in calling forth a national unity that was, as of yet, only partially realized. At the same time, it begins the process of telling the *American* story of World War II, representing its struggle and combat. In this story, our enemies are "dastardly," having created the date that will "live in infamy," while we are heroic and righteous. This "righteousness," expressed in the speech both implicitly and explicitly as God-given, creates our might, which will manifest itself in victory. Out of infamous defeat, we will become a people called to fight "in our righteous might," not only to avenge that defeat but also to create a world without treachery. From this point on, our national identity began a new and vigorous development. We would see ourselves increasingly as a people whose fundamentally peaceful nature justified its becoming the world's dominant military power. On December 7 and 8, 1941, we were born again as a warrior nation, soon to become the greatest military power in history, all in the name of peace.

First Impressions: Early Images of Our "Good War"

Today, much of our World War II mythologizing grows from more than sixty years of representations in books, films, and other media. Ironically, for many Americans, the most memorable World War II images now come from Hollywood war films. During the war itself, however, it took time to construct such icons. Though Hollywood began producing war-related films just prior to Pearl Harbor, the film industry was largely unprepared for our full entry into the conflict. For the first year, pictures already in the pipeline had to suffice. Thus, films released in 1942 had often been shot largely before Pearl Harbor, emphasizing subjects relevant to the period between 1939 and 1941, including more films about "free-agent" Americans fighting their personal war against the Axis.[10] The most memorable of these was *Casablanca* (1942), in which Humphrey Bogart incarnated the archetypal American protagonist struggling to overcome self-interest and to serve the cause of others. But neither the mythmaking *Casablanca* nor its less memorable imitations represented American soldiers in actual combat; rather, these war films were merely variations of traditional romance, intrigue, or espionage genres.

It was left for journalists, photographers, and combat film crews to shape America's view of the war during its first year. At a time of humiliating defeats and limited victories, they worked to sustain the determination called for in Roosevelt's December 8 speech. In the process, they also began constructing the narrative structures and iconic images foundational for later American representations of World War II combat, whether fact or fiction. In addition, various government agencies

WHY WE FIGHT 37

issued a steady stream of poster art and advertisements that helped create the home-front tapestry of the war, providing a broader context for the public's understanding of the war news. Complementing the government information efforts were extensive advertising campaigns run by big business, major labor organizations, and other private groups.[11] These efforts reflected the themes articulated by FDR on December 8, all of which had grown into government policies. Of course, all media had far more to represent as the war continued, and the government itself eventually allowed greater latitude in revealing the actual costs of war, even in publishing photographs of dead U.S. servicemen. Yet in 1942, when it was necessary to buoy America's fragile morale, most images emphasized a determined, upbeat, at times even glib approach to the war.

★ ★ ★

Much of this material was obviously propaganda, whether coming directly from the government or from the news or entertainment media. After the Pearl Harbor attack, the federal government massively expanded its information campaigns, mobilizing the news and entertainment media in the same fashion as it had all other sectors of American industry. While never establishing a literal "Ministry of Propaganda," the government did consolidate several information services into the Office of War Information (OWI), an agency supervising representations of the war from all sources: government, news, entertainment, and advertising.[12] Like all other belligerents, once the United States officially entered the fighting, it entered the propaganda war as well.

Yet both the American government and our media have perennially engaged in propaganda campaigns, some of them extraordinarily destructive. This was certainly the case with some strains of World War II propaganda, the worst aspects of which were dehumanizing depictions of our enemies. Serving an "agitprop" function, these represented the enemy as everything from a comic caricature to an insidious monster.[13] Rhetorically, such dehumanization serves to legitimize extreme acts of destruction, not only against the enemy's military but also against its civilian infrastructure and its people as a whole. It is much easier to employ the uncompromisingly violent methods of total war when one systematically excludes one's enemies from the human race. This was particularly true in our response to the Japanese because Japanese forces had attacked us and because of the preexisting racism found in various segments of American culture.

As cultural scholar John Dower notes in *War Without Mercy*, the negative propaganda directed against Japan was more contemptuous than that directed against Germany.[14] Dower argues that the character of the Pacific war, on both sides, was heavily influenced by racist assumptions deeply rooted in both American and Japanese cultures, ultimately creating a war of intense racial hatred in which no quarter was given during the fighting. Indeed, some American propaganda went well beyond supporting the war effort to justifying acts of near extermination of the enemy people. Certainly, our willingness to accept the firebombing of Tokyo and the atomic bombing of Hiroshima and Nagasaki was linked, in part, to racist representations of the Japanese. Likewise, the cavalier fashion in which we stripped Japanese Americans of their civil rights—confiscating their property and interning them in camps for the duration of the war—testifies to how propaganda could play upon and reflect the worst threads of racism and xenophobia that were already interwoven throughout our culture. While Dower does overstate his case somewhat, since American propaganda worked consistently to dehumanize all the enemy nations, his overall thesis remains fundamentally accurate: America's war with Japan was intensified, on both sides, by obvious and predictable racist assumptions.

Regardless of this more extreme American propaganda, most of the representations that the government, journalists, and Hollywood produced during World War II were in an entirely different register—positive depictions of America, her Allies, and their war aims. A good deal of such propaganda attempted to portray the heroism, self-sacrifice, humility, and good humor of the "typical" American, whether soldier or civilian. These representations were not merely wartime propaganda; rather, they were the consistent "propagating" of values and virtues of the "American Way" as had already been constituted to support the prevailing cultural power structures. Such constructs drew on a general cultural ideology of America that is most obviously represented in its commercial advertising. In *Advertising the American Dream*, historian Roland Marchand describes American advertising ideology, using Jacques Ellul's concept of "integration propaganda," the broad pattern of cultural discourses that shape our sense of who we are as individuals and as members of a larger society.[15] Advertising is one of the major forces shaping our sense of cultural identity and purpose, and that was particularly true of our advertising in wartime.

Yet despite the claims of advertising, our sense of an "American Way" is not necessarily uniform, and as a result, our wartime propaganda was not monolithic. In fact, because of competing political interests,

America's wartime propaganda could be unusually "polyphonic" when compared to that of nations with more aggressively centralized control.[16] In *Hollywood Goes to War*, Clayton R. Koppes and Gregory D. Black astutely explain how, near the war's beginning, two distinctly different versions of America's dreams and aspirations were voiced respectively by media mogul Henry Luce and by FDR's third-term vice president Henry Wallace.[17] The former stressed how the war called America to take on both global responsibility and hegemony, while the latter represented the war as a way of sharing more fully in an ongoing struggle for universal human rights. The contrast between these two visions illustrates the polyphony of America's World War II propaganda, appealing at the same time to conservative and to liberal political agendas. Like Luce, some Americans understood and represented the war as the struggle for the United States to achieve its destined place as the greatest of great powers—by confronting and overcoming antidemocratic, anti-American nations. Others, following Wallace, constructed a version of the war as a common struggle, shared with all peoples and races throughout the world, to live in freedom and dignity.

Such contradictory narratives grew not merely in response to the complex issues of the war; rather, they were rooted in the American cultural psyche as fundamental but contrary myths, shaping how we understand our national history. During the war and afterward, these preexisting but conflicted cultural myths would shape our understanding of "why we fought." Of course, the multifaceted experience of the war would also restructure the rhetorical and narrative processes through which we fashioned our national identity. Our attempt to mythologize the new war reshaped how America saw itself. As that war became part of our national narrative, that narrative became somehow more warlike. Even before the war's end, the evolving processes of cultural mythologizing had begun to interweave with specific narratives of the war. As World War II itself became part of the American cultural identity, the rhetorical and narrative elements of representing the war became new commonplaces in our national story. In essence, as we began to tell our story of World War II, our whole nation began to take on qualities associated with that story and that war. But implicit in that evolving story was the still-divided national consciousness that perpetuated two contrary American visions: America as a hegemonic great power, remaking the world in its own image, and America as one nation among others, all struggling to achieve greater human freedom and dignity.

Although wartime propaganda presented dehumanizing images of our enemies and more warlike representations of Americans, and while it also perpetuated a conflicted sense of national purpose, its greatest energy went into positive representations of American ideals, acceptable to a wide political spectrum though interpreted differently across that spectrum. These ideals included our commitment to individual rights and freedoms, our support of democratic political structures, and our desire to improve the human condition—fighting global war had now become our means of maintaining and spreading these values. Ironically, throughout our history we had obviously failed to achieve these declared ideals, but we rationalized that we were nonetheless faithful in our struggle to learn from and progress beyond our mistakes. Wartime propaganda therefore focused on our achievements rather than on our failures. It also strove to demonstrate why our cause was just and why our enemies were the aggressors who sought to conquer and oppress millions. Yet in constructing such representations, we were frequently disingenuous about our own history of oppressing various peoples, including the history of slavery and its aftereffects. Our wartime propaganda steered clear of such historical issues while it also largely avoided addressing contemporary problems like the wide-spread racial discrimination that persisted throughout the war. Another example was America's traditional anti-Semitism, which made us less sympathetic and helpful to European Jews both before and during the war, when greater effort might have saved at least some from annihilation. Yet this failure did not stop us, after the war, from using the fact of the Holocaust/Shoah to confirm our own national righteousness in having fought the Nazis.[18]

Despite the hypocrisy evident in our propaganda, the facts of history do unmistakably demonstrate that the Axis powers had engaged in an aggressive war that was comprehensively evil, and that Nazi Germany had pursued an unprecedented policy of genocide. Although our fight against the Axis does not excuse our own social sins, prior or subsequent, that fight was still a just and necessary one that was motivated, to a very large degree, by a desire to save lives and free oppressed peoples. Ultimately, to support that fight, we marshaled our news and entertainment media as vigorously as we marshaled our war industries and our fighting men. In the process, we overproduced not only war material but also war propaganda, a fact that would alter and distort our postwar identity, with many painful consequences. Such is the inevitable cost of propaganda even in an ostensibly just cause.

*   *   *

With our full entry into the war, the government mobilized all the media, Hollywood included, to integrate its traditionally positive representation of American values with the current need to support the war effort. While the OWI served as a nucleus for this activity, the armed services recruited and employed their own filmmakers. Cadres of war correspondents came from the American press corps, accompanying ground troops, aircrew, and sailors to every front. These were almost always civilian reporters and photographers, representing print, broadcast, and movie newsreel media. Visual artists, a number of whom worked for *Life*, were also involved, providing some unforgettable images of the conflict. In addition, the military recruited its own artists, photographers, and writers. Together, these groups created the primary images and narratives that would help shape our later representations of the war.

Thus, the iconography of Americans in World War II began to take shape through the lenses of photographers and cinematographers, on the typewriters of reporters, and in the voices of broadcast journalists. Among the numerous still photos, the countless rolls of movie film, the numberless stories filed from either the rear areas or front lines, some took on unusual significance. The already established journalistic authority and popular appeal of *Life* photographers gave them an automatic advantage. Work by the likes of Robert Capa and Margaret Bourke-White left a lasting impression in the minds of Americans. Endlessly republished after the war in textbooks and numerous *Time/Life* historical volumes, such photographs not only *represent* the events, but for most Americans, they also *become* events in and of themselves. Of course, quite a bit of material was censored during the first year and a half of the war because of fears about home-front morale. This was particularly true of photographs showing American casualties.[19] But painful photographs of American losses did get into print, and we have grown accustomed to images like that of the twisted, charred wreckage of the battleship USS *Arizona* at Pearl Harbor. Such photographs created the initial iconography of America's experience of World War II combat, and they have retained their status through countless reprintings in the decades since the war.

Like their comrades in print journalism, newsreel cameramen, particularly those who worked for the influential *March of Time* series and the Fox *Movietone News,* photographed everything from training to actual combat. Never in history had warfare been so accurately and thoroughly represented in any visual medium, providing not only indelible images for the national psyche but also a treasure-trove of representations for both future filmmakers and historians, whether they wished to confirm or critique the prevailing narrative of the war. In addition to civilian film crews, teams of military combat photographers accompanied men into battle, with every kind of unit and in every theater.[20] Hollywood personnel, both in and out of uniform, and Hollywood facilities often provided much of the professional and technical expertise and specific production technology for such films. Indeed, the U.S. Army and the U.S. Navy became part of a "Military-Movie Complex" for the planning, filming, production, and distribution of vast numbers of training films, documentaries, and features. Men and women in uniform were not only the subjects but often the primary audiences for such films, many of which were eventually shown to civilians as well.

Accompanying these images, reporters' stories touched the hearts of millions of civilians, translating the distant places and events into descriptions and narratives that combined familiar American characterizations with unusual settings and dramatic action. As previously noted, Edward R. Murrow and his incomparable team of reporters led the way for broadcasts from the war fronts. Print reporters, such as Homer Bigart, Richard Tregaskis, Robert Sherrod, Martha Gellhorn, John Hersey, A. J. Liebling, and others, regularly risked their lives to tell stories of Americans fighting across the globe. Most famous of all print war correspondents was Ernie Pyle, known for his ongoing, episodic saga of the ordinary American infantryman.

Of course, in examining coverage of the war, one must naturally consider the relationship between journalists and the government that allowed them a place at the front and provided their credentials. By our standards, these reporters were subject to thorough censorship, but they also felt it their duty to subject themselves to rigorous self-censorship.[21] Many saw their mission not as purely objective war reporting but as a journalistic crusade that paralleled the military one. They usually supported the war effort and wrote their articles to encourage others to support it. In part these practices grew from their sense of national unity and purpose during wartime. For reporters and readers alike, this war called for solidarity in the face of terribly destructive enemies. In addition, some reporters had long been committed to fighting fascism. Having reported from Europe during the Spanish Civil War, they believed that their writing was their contribution to the ongoing worldwide struggle.

Certainly, we cannot fault these journalists for committing themselves to the Allied cause, and we can hardly expect them to have given "equal time" to the Axis. America was at war against powers more comprehensively dangerous than any the world had ever known, and so it seemed natural that the media should support the government in this time of national emergency. Still, whether voluntarily or unwittingly, these journalists helped perpetuate government propaganda, and whenever journalism comes to the service of propaganda, the situation demands scrutiny. Not every report from the field brought good news, nor were all representations of American experience during the war mere sanitized depictions of the American Way—for example, both *The New Republic* and *Fortune* published quite unflattering reports about U.S. internment camps for Japanese Americans.[22] Yet American war correspondents actively supported the war effort, often making pointed attempts to bolster civilian morale by careful selection of content and management of style. This hardly meets accepted standards for news reporting. Such submission to the prerogatives of government during time of war can be understood in the fight against global fascism, but it may have had hidden, long-term costs. The ease with which the American media converted from antifascism to anticommunism during the early Cold War period suggests that following the government line without scrutiny had become a debilitating habit for many journalists. The craze of McCarthyism only reinforced that habit and encouraged greater compliance out of fear. Later on, the credulousness with which the American media accepted government versions of events, such as the Gulf of Tonkin Incident, suggests how seriously our press failed to exercise its own freedom during the postwar period. If truth is the first casualty of war, it is also one of the last to recover from its wounds.

In hindsight, it seems easy to stand in judgment. Faced with the world of 1942, most journalists felt compelled to take sides. Moreover, if one is charged with the task of "pure" journalistic reporting, then any attempt to be persuasive raises questions of professional ethics. One rarely finds "pure" reportage since no narrative of events can be constructed without selecting from among the available facts. Modern American journalistic practices have traditionally attempted to achieve as much neutrality as possible by allowing the weight of factual evidence to shape news reports. The hope is that, in the aggregate, democracy will be served best by such practices. Of course, journalistic practice has never achieved this ideal; even the most thoroughly factual reports can be recontextualized in the overall presentation of the medium, with editorials, advertisements, and other material that can slant how the factual report will be received. Still, journalistic ethics demands that reporters be thoroughly honest, not only in gathering and representing the facts but also in interpreting and contextualizing them. Journalistic features, commentary, and editorials can then be allowed to carry the burden of "advocacy." Indeed, without advocacy journalism, the facts would become a meaningless white noise against which powerful cultural forces might make self-serving claims to even greater effect. If the role of reporter and advocate become blurred, however, then journalists proceed along an inevitably slippery slope. Many correspondents during World War II felt it was necessary to take that risk, especially when they often doubled as both reporters and feature writers at the front. Well intentioned as they may have been, they began to slip. Sliding down the slope of World War II, some would eventually reach the abyss of the Cold War and the McCarthy era, when paranoid fantasy sometimes took on the authority of fact. Thus, the cultural costs of World War II were extensive, and in many respects, we have yet to pay off the full set of debts.

Colonel Capra and Captain Ford

Frank Capra and John Ford powerfully represent the values embedded in the traditional Hollywood vision of America. This is true in the films they directed and in the mythic identities and narratives they crafted for themselves. Ford grew up in a comfortable bourgeois setting that, compared to Capra's impoverished youth, seems almost wealthy. Still, both men represented the American immigrant narrative, expressing the immigrant's essential search for identity and meaning in a new land. As such, these two directors crafted a fundamentally American art. Each left legacies of influential films that, when scrutinized carefully, yield significant insights into the processes of American cultural self-fashioning.

Capra worked mostly with comic forms, integrating them with a kind of moral allegory. Ford, responsible for more than twice as many films, developed an American epic genre set most often in the West; perhaps more than any other director, he captured the Western narrative's essential restlessness. Both men also focused on distinctively different character types. Whereas the classic Capra protagonist is often an outsider, he also is usually naïve and idealistic. This hero may be low on the socioeconomic ladder, or he may possess wealth, but he is usually "poor in spirit"—not driven by a desire for personal material gain. Ford also develops characters who are outsiders, but his is an epic, sometimes tragic vision; and his heroes embody the qualities of the idealized Western figure: taciturn, romantic, powerful, but often haunted. Unlike Capra's comic characters, Ford's protagonists are difficult to domesticate, which suggests how each director worked in a different register of the American myth.

Capra's focal setting was ultimately the home, and he creates a comedy that, through all its tribulations, leads back to the comfort of domestic life. Ford's canvas is far larger, and his drama is one of restless movement—often the desert or the sea. His wounded, romantic loners may be represented best by Ethan Edwards in *The Searchers* (1956), a disturbed man who will never be at peace. The doorway that welcomes Ethan at the film's onset is balanced by the doorway that frames his departure at the film's end. Ultimately, Capra's work leads us back to home and hearth, whereas Ford's sends us chasing an unreachable horizon.

When World War II began, both men were well placed to lend their already established American mythologies to the stories and circumstances brought by war. Each saw the conflict as a call to pursue the art of filmmaking and to serve the country in a time of greatest need. Although the war provided the two directors with new plots, settings, and scripts, the overarching story was still the "American story" that they had been telling on screen for years. They integrated the new war story with their traditional values of individualism, hard work, and achievement, all balanced by a commitment to the greater good of the community. As in the past, their mainstream narrative of American history and culture also obscured internal political conflict by emphasizing how our consensus ultimately triumphs over our division. In the hands of Capra and Ford, therefore, wartime propaganda film came to reflect the traditional commonplaces of Hollywood's American mythology.

Of course, Capra and Ford were far more than directors during the war, and in some respects, far less.[23] As their biographer Joseph McBride has noted, their films were more compiled than shot, stitched together from segments of combat films, newsreels, and other material, making the director's role less important during filming but more so during editing. Since Ford commanded the Field Photographic Branch of the Office of Special Services, he was actually at the war fronts on numerous occasions. Technically in the Army Signal Corps, but actually under the direct authority of General George C. Marshall, Capra worked principally in the United States, and when abroad, he did not personally witness combat. Thus, both Capra and Ford served as military planners and executives, with overall responsibility for producing films most often directed and photographed by others, a far cry from the Capra code of "one man—one film." Moreover, their war films were the product of the military, the "supreme studio" that gave no one a "name above the title." Yet the military also understood command,

and both men were given control over a sizable force of military film-makers, often including some of their most talented Hollywood associates. Each was therefore responsible for overall development of many more films than either could have directed individually.

Each man was also directly responsible for some of the most important works in the history of American documentary film, including Oscar-winning productions—Capra's *Prelude to War* (1943), Ford's *The Battle of Midway* (1942) and the drastically cut version of *December 7th* (1943). In these and other films, they integrated Hollywood's popular history and mythic Americana with their own versions of the American dream—all to convince soldiers and civilians alike of why we were fighting the war. While results at the time were mixed, this effort had long-term effects on how America would represent the World War II experience. During World War II, Capra and Ford helped establish the fundamental nexus that linked the Hollywood "dream machine" to the Pentagon "war machine."

★   ★   ★

Only days after Pearl Harbor, the Army Signal Corps asked Frank Capra to make films for them.[24] By February 1942, he was in uniform and in Washington, beginning what would be a three-and-a-half-year struggle—first to overcome Army bureaucracy, and then to help defeat the Axis by raising the morale of America's soldiers and civilians. In both struggles, he soldiered on stoically though he never fully gained the kind of control he had hoped for; even his best wartime films can be seen as only partial successes. Capra tried in vain for the kind of field photographic command held by John Ford, but the Army saw him as more valuable at home than abroad. He spent his war mostly behind a desk, ensuring that film projects went ahead as planned. He had influence and authority, but like the influence and authority of any Army officer, Capra's was channeled, focused, and controlled by higher command. Yet he did have the respect of General George C. Marshall, no mean achievement, and Marshall allowed Capra to make films his own way. Thus, although the director was making the Army's pictures rather than his own, he still had room to achieve some of his artistic vision.

Despite limitations, Capra supervised numerous productions, some directly, and some at a distance.[25] He is most directly associated with the development of the seven-film *Why We Fight* series, which he supervised and for which he directed several individual films. Contemporary historians and critics debate the success of this series and of Capra's other films for the military; historical evidence about how these films affected military morale is indeed ambiguous. Did men shoulder their rifles and move into action because of films by Frank Capra? Probably not. Why did they fight? Countless interviews, memoirs, and postwar Army surveys suggest that they fought to save their own lives and the lives of those in their immediate units.[26] They fought because they had to, and they kept fighting until they found a way home.

Yet the *Why We Fight* series was appreciated at the time as a clear statement of the circumstances and causes of the war.[27] According to filmographer Charles Wolfe, attendance at *Why We Fight* films totaled over 45 million during the course of the war; some of this series, along with other Army films, were also allowed into commercial release, making their influence even greater.[28] Perhaps their greatest effect was less in motivating troops to go into battle, than in providing them with an overall context for the war. To use Jacques Ellul's terminology, these films were more "integration propaganda" than "agitation propaganda," leading soldier and civilian to understand the war in the relationship to a preexisting national narrative.

Through such films, Capra and the members of his film unit were able to pursue the same cultural project that had occupied them in Hollywood: transforming American history and contemporary life into narratives that confirmed the values of American cultural ideology. By reinforcing a basic vision of America and its values, by differentiating between the war aims of the Allies and of the Axis, the films created a narrative structure through which the war could be understood. The films confirmed who the G.I.s thought themselves to be, establishing for them a relationship to a mythic past and a dramatic present. That process created a psychological framework in which the direct motivations to fight—preservation of self and comrades—could be understood before and after combat. Thus, although the *Why We Fight* series did not directly motivate soldiers to fight, it did help them justify their direct motives and the act of fighting itself. These films also established the fundamental narrative process of historicizing the war in relation to American self-fashioning. As a result, the films became part of the underlying cultural infrastructure on which we have built a long tradition of representing World War II.

Prelude to War (1943), the first of the series, exemplifies the overall pattern of Capra's military projects.[29] This film establishes the war as foreign in origin but still a direct threat to what Americans cherish most: the home and family so celebrated in Capra's prior work. It combines features of the historical documentary and the travelogue, revealing the development of fascism in Italy, Nazism in Germany, and imperial militarism in Japan. Moreover, the film uses extensive footage of the Axis countries' own propaganda, edited and recontextualized into a rhetorical device to undermine the original messages of the enemy films. Although such an approach is not original to Capra, he brings to it particular insights that made the technique successful.

In planning the series, Capra viewed Leni Riefenstahl's technically brilliant *Triumph of the Will* (1935). In Riefenstahl's images of an unconquerable German will to power, Capra and his staff discovered a peculiar weakness that might be used against the Axis. The very arrogance of the Nazi perspective could damn itself, could irritate rather than subjugate the viewers, leading them to resist the domineering images of power. Conceiving of the "two-world" approach—theirs and ours, slave and free—Capra and company could portray the conflict in convenient black-and-white terms, represented literally on the screen as lightened and darkened images of the globe. Entering into the enslaved world of Axis domination, *Prelude to War* portrays the probable experiences of people in settings such as public events and schools, later contrasting these with similar situations in America. The various Axis leaders and their lieutenants are also depicted, usually surrounded by automaton-like soldiers and frenzied crowds of apparently fanatical worshipers. What had originated as Axis propaganda illustrating the people's devotion to their leaders was transformed—through editing, cross-cutting, and commentary—into an illustration of oppressive authoritarianism and mindless fanaticism.

Interestingly, the rhythmic motion so particularly important in Riefenstahl's film can be edited to seem hyperbolic in its regimentation. In contrast, Capra's images of the "free world" reveal a motion that is far less uniform. The visual rhetoric of movement across the cinematic field powerfully reinforces the contrast between the two worlds. While the opening of the film shows U.S. soldiers marching, they seem less regimented than their German counterparts. Capra begins and ends with the motion of U.S. troops, but in the middle, he also contrasts the motion of the two cultures. Viewing these framing images, we recognize that we are now a country and a culture at war. The narrative contained within the frame provides the reasons for war through a contrasting pattern of cultural experience—light/dark, free/enslaved, liberating/oppressive. The film's use of movement contrasts Americans' unfettered motion with Axis regimentation. Of course, although war imposes some regimentation even upon America, the very gait of the American soldiers suggests an inherent sense of freedom not found in the goose-stepping Nazis. This visual rhetoric confirms our cultural assumptions—we fight because we have to, and even in fighting, do not relinquish freedom. They fight because they are part of an aggressive doomsday machine bent on devouring us. Thus, the relaxed freedom of motion, also revealed in homey images of schools, parks, and households, is the essence of who we are. Because that freedom is threatened, we fight.

When scholars critique the series, and *Prelude* in particular, as being ineffective motivation to fight, they miss the level and nature of the motivation—*motivation* as implied through *movement*. Rather than creating the motives for Americans to fight, the film literally reveals the motives as *motions*, as freedoms of *movement*. Our way of life is a free motion, bound only by conscious loyalty and commitment to home and hearth. Capra integrates the stability of home with the freedom of motion, two essential values of American cultural ideology. His film effectively contrasts these values with those implied by the oppressive, repetitive motion of Axis automata. So we march now, to fight for the freedom still evident in our graceful, easy gait that, although less uniform, is more liberating than the step of our foes. The power of the first film, *Prelude to War*, carries a message that will last—throughout the series, throughout the war, and into the postwar world. Ultimately, it was Capra's message as much as the government's.

★   ★   ★

In contrast to Capra, John Ford was a rebel warrior at heart, and he did not wait for Pearl Harbor before becoming involved in the war effort.[30] Brought up in Portland, Maine, Ford was attracted early to the possible adventure of the sea. Since his wife, Mary, was the niece of an influential admiral, Ford made early if informal connections with high-level Navy officers. He joined the Navy Reserve and received a commission in 1934. From the later 1930s up to Pearl Harbor, he used his yacht *Araner* for occasional intelligence missions to observe Japanese shipping off Mexico's Pacific coast. Likewise, he diligently developed techniques for naval reconnaissance photography and for the documentation of combat, ultimately forming his own Naval Reserve unit. In Hollywood, Ford had had his own "Stock Company" of preferred studio actors, writers, and production staff, many of whom would serve with him in the military.

Within days of Pearl Harbor, Ford left home to activate his 200-strong reserve unit of Hollywood film colleagues.[31] Throughout the war,

Lieutenant Commander (later Captain) Ford headed a vast network of production crews who were working across the globe, engaging in photo reconnaissance, and making films that recorded the war for posterity. Although technically a Navy unit, his group was attached directly to William "Wild Bill" Donovan's O.S.S.[32] The Navy did not wish to accept Ford's unorthodox unit for wartime service, but the director used his influence to accomplish an end-run around the Navy and so take his unit to war under Donovan's aegis. Ford saw the war as *his* project, and he brought to it the same restless energy that had driven him to become one of Hollywood's most powerful directors.[33] Yet he could also get himself into the doghouse with the Navy, just as he had with studios. By mid-1943, Ford had alienated powerful Navy officers to such an extent that Donovan moved him out of direct control of the Field Photographic Branch, sending him literally on a slow boat to the China-Burma-India Theater. But even in this often forgotten theater of the war, Ford became involved in O.S.S. operations and continued making important films. He went to England in 1944 to organize filming of the Normandy invasion, and on D-Day, he joined crews filming the landings, on ship and ashore; much of their extensive footage would be used in later documentaries and feature films.

Exemplary among the many films Ford supervised and/or directed are *The Battle of Midway* (1942), much of which he filmed himself, and the flawed *December 7th* (1943). The Midway film is clearly more representative of Ford's style, winning an Oscar for best documentary. *December 7th*, while bearing some of Ford's touches, is a problematic film, even though its drastically edited version won an Oscar for best documentary short subject. While *December 7th*'s subject matter comes first, the Midway film was actually completed and released earlier, and *The Battle of Midway* emphasizes its own authenticity, proclaiming in the opening that it is the actual photographic record. Later in the film, as we see the American flag waving against a smoke-filled sky, the narrator says, "Yes, this really happened."

Although the Battle of Midway was largely fought by carrier fleets hundreds of miles from the island itself, Midway did endure one air attack and also sent its own unsuccessful air attacks against the Japanese fleet. Ford had been sent to Midway to cover what the Navy knew would be a major encounter.[34] He served a dual role during the action, assigned to report on attacking aircraft while also filming the combat. He faithfully kept at both tasks even after being wounded by shrapnel. Also filming on Midway was Navy Photographer's Mate Jack MacKenzie, while Lieutenant Kenneth M. Pier, who flew with the

USS *Hornet*'s air group, provided much of the aerial footage of the attacks on the Japanese task forces.

In composing the finished product, Ford used much of his own excellent footage of the air attack on the island and that of the other photographers. Here the shuddering of the handheld cameras is no affectation but the genuine reaction to explosions. Debris flies into the air while Marine antiaircraft gunners keep at their task, firing at actual planes. The image of a burning Japanese aircraft trailing black smoke is authentic, as are the billowing black clouds and bright orange flames whipping from the wrecked oil storage tanks. Yet it is not the attack footage alone that gives the powerful sense of authenticity to the film; even Ford's shots of the defenders waiting for the attack or cleaning up its aftermath communicate a deep sense of intimacy. We see these men fueling planes, discussing plans, waiting by their guns, and even watching the sunset while one plays the accordion. The tune we hear is "Red River Valley," placing Midway not only in the center of the Pacific war but also in the Old West of Ford's imagination. Though not the focus of the battle's most important actions, the island still becomes the greatest symbol in Ford's film. Early on, the narrator refers to Midway as "our outpost, your front yard." The film intimately connects this distant outpost and the home front, what seems at first a counterintuitive gesture. But we are not only in the register of World War II, we are also in the symbolic register of the Old West, where the frontier fort defends itself against hostile assault. In the Western, the outpost fort is always closely associated with the frontier settlements it must defend. Ford establishes a visual metonymy between the frontier fort and the island outpost through the sunset scene, with the music of "Red River Valley" underscoring the emotional connection. Unsure that audiences could follow such subtlety, Ford makes the connections more explicit by blending fictional voiceovers by Jane Darwell and Henry Fonda into the documentary narration—embedding imaginary, unseen "viewers" into film itself. They talk about the hometown "boys" stationed at Midway, and by extension, more intimately connecting the home audience to our Marines and airmen on that distant island—they are all our sons and brothers.

Burial scenes also provide a typical Ford resolution, first on land and then at sea. Used in many of his Westerns, the burial scene demonstrates group solidarity and the continuity of past and future. It emphasizes renewed commitment to the cause, as well as solemn tribute to those whose new "home" will forever be their grave on the frontier—be that frontier in a fictional West or on a real Midway Island. The burial also represents ties to a home left behind and to the social rituals that shape people's lives. Parallel to Capra, Ford must connect home with the battlefront, but his final movement is always back to the war, to the vastness of the air and sea, and to the danger of the conflict. The closing images of the film (except for the painting out of lists of Japanese ships sunk) return us to the aftermath of the attack on the island. As a Marine looks to the horizon with his binoculars, we see American planes flying over Midway and its still-burning oil storage tanks. This scene visually returns us to the conflict, and as the planes recede into the distance, we recognize the call to press on with the mission at hand.

Though *The Battle of Midway* appears dated today, its visual impact remains powerful. In contrast, *December 7th* confirmed that Gregg Toland could use a camera but not direct a film. The original long version, suppressed for decades after the war, gives half its time to an allegorical dialogue between Uncle Sam (Walter Huston) and Uncle Sam's conscience, "Mr. C" (Harry Davenport). Mr. C repeatedly warns about the danger of Japanese Americans, especially those living in Hawaii, but Uncle Sam dismisses these warnings. The film clearly positions Mr. C as the wise prophet to the Uncle Sam who has literally fallen asleep as the attack on Pearl Harbor begins. The usually likable Davenport sounds like the incarnation of the worst "yellow peril" tract, but the segment remains a useful cultural artifact, giving insight into the deep racism that motivated some Americans throughout the war.

Ford dropped all this material from the shortened version, but even that could not save the film because most of its combat footage was fabricated through transparently bad special effects. The problem was that little of the actual attack had been filmed—a dramatic shot of the USS *Arizona* exploding was one of the few genuine bits of documentary footage. Yet Toland felt a need to show the action of the attack, and so he chose to film with models and staged dramatizations—a grave sin to documentary purists. The studio scenes of ship models have unusually poor production values, and the attack scenes staged on location recall B-movie melodramas. It is not difficult to imagine high-ranking naval officers being insulted by such poor fakery, especially when it also implied that the Navy had been unprepared. Regardless, it is clear that Toland was incapable of documenting the Pearl Harbor attack without resorting to cheap tricks to recreate action. In contrast, a film about the men who fought, and about the ships that sank and those that survived, need not be all action. The limited but authentic footage of the attack and its aftermath, along with interviews with survivors, could have made a film even more compelling than Ford's Midway documentary.

Badly misjudging his audience, Toland tries to make an action film and fails miserably. *December 7th* was shelved for a time, and a chastened Toland sought exile in a South American branch of Ford's photography unit.[35] Eventually, Ford and Robert Parrish drastically reedited the film. What was ultimately released earned an Oscar, and perhaps proved Ford and Parrish to be cinematic sorcerers, turning the leaden original, if not into gold, at least into something presentable. Despite his wizardry, however, Ford was still held responsible for Toland's original. It had been filmed by Ford's chosen staff, and this led to Ford's temporary exile from Field Photo. Unfortunately, even the shorter version still contained much of the fabricated footage, and so not only had Ford underwritten questionable documentary practices, he had also put his name behind substandard footage.

Ironically, although the authentic images from the Midway film sometimes appear in later documentary films, and as stills in history texts, the visual imagery of Toland's film, fabricated as it may have been, has had far greater influence. American documentary films about Pearl Harbor forever quote sequences from *December 7th*, so much so that these have become visual commonplaces. Particularly iconic are the establishing shots of the Aloha Tower, the nearly empty Honolulu street at early morning, and the gate to Hickham Field. Others include two flyers walking toward a line of patrol bombers, sailors playing catch on the dock beside their ship, a ground crew working on a B-17 in a hanger, and the Catholic Mass interrupted by the attack. Countless documentaries have repeated these images to the point that most Americans assume their authenticity as a film record. These segments have thus established for us the visual context of Pearl Harbor as a place at ease about to be attacked. In the aggregate, they create tension in an audience waiting for the bombs to fall. Here, visual legends become their own kind of facts.[36]

In the wartime films of Ford, Capra, and many others, the narrative structures and visual images of World War II's "legends" were conceived and crafted to show why we were fighting the war. Traditions and forms already popular in Hollywood combined with the historical material from the war to create new legends. The images we recall from that war, even the authentic ones, are still those that the culture had prepared itself to receive. The legend existed before there was a story to tell, and once events provided the narrative content, the legend transformed that narrative into the legend's own image. The process began in the early years of the war, and after many decades, we continue to witness the ever-evolving results.

CHAPTER THREE

How *We Fight: Campaigns of Sacrifice and Service*

"Submitted for Your Inspection"—No Question of Mercy

In December 1961, twenty years after Pearl Harbor, *The Twilight Zone* aired an episode called "The Quality of Mercy."[1] Using an idea originally proposed by Sam Rolfe, series creator Rod Serling had written the script himself, based on his own experience fighting in the Pacific. Though set in the Philippines during the war's final days, the story depicts a timeless conflict. A green officer, Lieutenant Katell (Dean Stockwell), feels he must prove himself in the short time before the war ends, so he orders his platoon to attack half-starved Japanese soldiers holding out in a cave. The veteran Sergeant Causarano (Albert Salmi) sees the attack as needless, asking Katell to rethink the order. Katell remains adamant until he experiences a classic "Zone" event. Suddenly, he finds himself on Corregidor in May 1942, in the last days before the American surrender, but transformed now into a Japanese officer, Lt.Yamuri. As Yamuri, Katell tries to persuade his own commanding officer not to attack a cave of wounded American soldiers, but the Japanese C.O. is as determined as Katell had been before. Transformed back into himself in 1945, Katell has learned the necessary lesson in mercy. The pause for his "vision" has also left sufficient time for word to reach the troops—the atomic bomb has been dropped on Japan, and the platoon is told to fall back.

Ironies abound in the episode, not the least of which is that the "mercy" has been made possible, at least in part, by the use of the atomic bomb. More central to the story is the contrast between two "last stands," one

Japanese and one American. At different times in the Pacific, both the Americans and Japanese had fought such battles, and Serling insightfully uses his story to demonstrate the continuity of experience on both sides—the desperation of men driven into a corner, and the intensity of men driven to achieve honor in combat. Although both sides displayed these qualities, Americans tended to interpret the two sets of experiences in different ways. When American and Filipino forces, though starving and disease-ridden, held out for months on Bataan, America praised their "heroic" efforts. Later in the war, when we confronted desperate Japanese defenders on island after island, we labeled their behavior "suicidal" and "fanatic." Dying in a last stand for the emperor seemed lunacy to us, but dying in a last stand against Axis aggression we deemed noble.

Though later than the other material covered in this chapter, this *Twilight Zone* episode provides an excellent example of our divided interpretation of how the war was fought. When our soldiers sacrifice themselves, we claim that they do so out of courage, whereas we assume that our enemies' similar acts reveal their fanaticism—such are the simple commonplaces of propaganda. America's combat soldiers and marines, living in the same jungles and suffering from the same diseases as the Japanese, recognized that such simplistic dichotomies were false. Yet this more direct knowledge did not lead to their showing mercy, for our troops saw that their own survival depended on destroying the enemy. Also, though brutal experience, not propaganda, formed the opinions of combat soldiers, their minds did not offer a tabula rasa. Rather, the troops entered combat with complex cultural frameworks through which they interpreted their experiences. Racial, ethnic, and cultural differences influenced their interpretations. Thus, U.S. veterans of the Pacific theaters often claimed that their enemies exhibited a different cultural psychology, a different pattern of group dynamics that led to seemingly fanatical and suicidal tactics. While this observation was not necessarily inaccurate, the fact remains that Americans who fought to the last and refused to surrender were revered by our country, just as the Japanese revered their kamikaze pilots later in the war. To a certain degree, fanaticism is in the eye of the beholder.

★　★　★

This chapter examines American representations of the war from 1941 to 1943, especially those concerning the first six months, when Americans fought desperate holding actions at places like Wake Island

and Bataan. Although the actual fighting demanded courage and self-sacrifice, Hollywood's fact-based fictions still reflected its standard formulas and clichés. Suicide missions or final acts of self-sacrifice sometimes provide the closure for such stories. Falling on the enemy grenade to save others was becoming a cinematic commonplace, and diving one's crippled aircraft into an enemy ship offered a glorious ending for a Hollywood hero. We think of such acts so differently when Americans have done them that we miss their similarity to banzai charges and kamikaze attacks. Nonetheless, our first representations of World War II on film show many examples of Americans sacrificing themselves in ways that, a few years later, we would call fanatical when done more extensively by the Japanese.

Related to sacrifice is the idea of service, and period war films examine two aspects of this idea. First, they show the *service* of individuals who join and fight or who support the fight on the home front. Second, films often concentrate on a specific branch of the armed *services*, highlighting that service's identity and esprit de corps. Combat films often celebrate a particular service branch by focusing on its contributions in an individual battle or campaign, as *Guadalcanal Diary* (1943) concentrates on the Marine Corps. The same pattern repeats through many films. Other examples from 1943 include *Bataan* representing the Army, *Destination Tokyo* representing the Navy, and *Air Force* representing the Army Air Force. Such films illustrate Hollywood's ongoing construction of story, character types, and commonplace themes and sentiments in the World War II genre. Here, we will consider a few influential films, while touching on others in passing. For every major film that helped establish a typical World War II formula, many others copied the pattern. In this respect, Hollywood has not changed much in the intervening sixty years.[2]

The Alamo, Again

For all its symbolic resonance, the Alamo would seem the wrong image to rally troops. Outside of Hollywood, few American soldiers would be inspired by the message that they are about to be expended as a glorious sacrifice. So in the aftermath of defeats at Pearl Harbor, the Philippines, and elsewhere, one would expect the military to avoid the name Alamo. However, in 1943 General Douglas MacArthur chose "Alamo Force" as the codename for the U.S. Sixth Army in the Southwest Pacific Area.[3] Although possibly reflecting the Texas

origins of that Army's Commander, Lt. Gen. Walter Krueger, the name
may also have had a symbolic association with MacArthur's pledge to
"return" to the Philippines, where Americans had suffered defeat in
another heroic last stand. It is also likely that MacArthur and his staff
were influenced by a broader tradition of American cultural narrative:
in our first defeats lie the honorable images of our eventual victory.
So we remember... "the Alamo," "Fort Sumter," "the *Maine*," and
of course, "Pearl Harbor" and "Bataan." By linking early World War
II defeats to the Alamo, American leaders could connect those losses
to the traditional narratives of American comeback victories in other
wars that had also begun badly. Furthermore, calling up the image of
martyred warriors from earlier battles sends the rhetorically powerful
message, to soldiers and civilians alike, that the survivors must struggle
even harder so that the honorable sacrifice will not have been in vain.
Thus, "Alamo" does provide an effective image with which to rally
support and to build morale. Likewise, it offers a useful designation for
America's World War II films that represent heroic last stands; the two
films that best represent this category are *Wake Island* (1942) and *Bataan*
(1943). Each invokes the heroic mythology of self-sacrifice in the face
of overwhelming odds. Although acknowledging American defeats,
the films also proclaim that we have "not yet begun to fight," honoring
those who had died in the early battles.

★ ★ ★

In December 1941, Wake Island was a small but strategically significant outpost in the Central Pacific.[4] Serving as a way station for Pan
American's clipper flights, the island also possessed an important military airfield with a small Marine Fighter Squadron. An understrength
Marine Defense Battalion of about four-hundred men defended the
atoll, while over a thousand civilians worked at constructing both Pan
American and military installations.[5] On the day of the Pearl Harbor
attack, Japanese aircraft also raided Wake, destroying seven of twelve
marine aircraft.[6] When the Japanese first attempted an amphibious
landing on December 11, marines repelled the invaders, inflicting
heavy losses. A week and a half later, a second, larger Japanese force
successfully assaulted the island, forcing the marine garrison to surrender after a day of intense fighting. The American survivors, military and civilian alike, were shipped to China and Japan to work in
labor camps, where many perished from inhumane treatment.[7] Some
100 civilians, kept on the island as forced labor, were later executed by

the Japanese.[8] Back in America, however, the very fact of the stubborn marine resistance seemed a moral victory, and the story of the battle helped boost civilian morale.

The film *Wake Island* was released in late summer 1942, while the battle was still fresh in the minds of the American public.[9] It provides an interesting melding of peacetime service films with the more serious tone of the Alamo genre. In addition, it combines elements of accurate docudrama with significant mythologizing. Despite its obviously propagandistic elements and standard Hollywood characterizations, the film does provide some sense of realism, especially in scenes of marines in bunkers, sweating out the shelling and bombing. Yet even this limited realism works in the service of myth, providing obvious links to the Alamo tradition.

Action begins at Pearl Harbor, with the introduction of three principal characters about to fly to Wake: Marine Corps Major Geoffrey Caton (Brian Donlevy), Marine Corps aviator, Lieutenant Bruce Cameron (MacDonald Carey), and civilian construction contractor, Shad McClosky (Albert Dekker). Shifting to Wake itself, the film introduces a perennial pair of tough, squabbling marine veterans, drawn from the "Flagg and Quirt" tradition of the Laurence Stallings/ Maxwell Anderson play *What Price Glory?* (1924).[10] Here, the figures are two privates, Joe Doyle (Robert Preston) and Aloysius K. "Smacksie" Randall (William Bendix). As with the original Flagg and Quirt, this pair reveals something of the intimacy and male bonding of military life. They are tied to the life and to each other in a kind of "male marriage" blessed by the military, and they bicker like stereotypical comic couples. While such dramatic relationships are not meant to imply homosexuality, they still may suggest an unacknowledged, underlying homosocial element found in a number of such films. The pair is set to break up, however, because Smacksie plans to leave the corps and get married when his enlistment ends, prophetically, on December 7.

After arriving and reporting to the U.S. Navy officer in charge of Wake, Major Caton takes over the Marine detachment and prepares for battle. The first third of the film alternates between his conflicts with the uncooperative McClosky and the already active squabbles of Doyle and Smacksie. Threading through these two conflicts is background commentary about the growing threat of war with Japan. Action intensifies with news of the Pearl Harbor attack, followed by a Japanese air raid on Wake. Despite the film's limits, the attack sequence conveys some sense of authenticity, comparing reasonably well to John Ford's footage of the actual attack on Midway.

After the attack, circumstances and relationships have changed. The mortally wounded Navy commander puts Caton in overall command of the island. Already mustered out, Smacksie decides to rejoin the Marine Corps, rejecting the chance to leave on the last clipper flight. Likewise, McClosky forgoes his hostility, volunteering to work with Caton to defend the island. Reports have also come from Pearl Harbor, and we learn that Lieutenant Cameron's wife has been killed in the bombing there. A widower himself, Caton breaks the news to Cameron, counseling the younger man that they are now alike—men left only with memories of a beloved woman. It is for such men as these two, the major asserts, to fight on for all the others. The scene also reinforces the male camaraderie offered by the military, a place for men who have lost their women. In three cases—Caton, Cameron, and Smacksie—we see that death or circumstance has severed their bonds to women. They are liberated to be fully military because no wife or lover at home has a claim on them.[11]

The film continues by depicting the first Japanese assault, and as in the actual battle, Caton orders marine coastal guns to hold their fire until the Japanese ships are well within range.[12] When the marines do fire, they decimate the Japanese forces. Despite winning this first engagement, the marines recognize that the odds are against them. Daily Japanese air attacks continue, and soon a stronger Japanese invasion force returns. After heavy bombardment, they begin landing, while the surviving marines, with their artillery out of action, prepare to fight with small arms. Japanese troops "hit the beach," many falling to machine gun fire. Two years later, both reality and film will have reversed the situation: an island's desperate defenders will then be Japanese, and the assaulting troops American. Here, however, it is the Japanese who charge forward and ultimately overwhelm the diehard defenders. Doyle and Smacksie die together, and the other marines are killed while fending off the invaders. Jointly manning a machine gun, Caton and McClosky turn back one attack, but then a series of explosions obscure them in smoke. We know the end has come.

The actual Wake Island battle was not literally an "Alamo" because the defenders were captured, not annihilated.[13] The outnumbered marines surrendered, spending the war in horrific slave-labor camps. The film does not reveal this fact, employing instead the tropes of cinematic hagiography—these men were "lost," obscured by battle smoke in the last scene. They are gone, but we remember them by celebrating their indomitable spirit. Closing with the joint deaths of civilian McClosky and marine Caton, the film also asks civilians to share the burden of war with those in uniform. As the first real American combat film of the war, *Wake Island* was very well received. *New York Times* critic Bosley Crowther called it "A realistic picture about heroes who do not pose as such... with never a big theatrical gesture or a comment that doesn't ring true."[14] Today *Wake Island* seems as clichéd as Crowther's praise. In 1942, however, the film was relatively timely and accurate. More significantly, it would exert a major influence on films to follow.

★ ★ ★

The fighting on Bataan was clearly different from that on Wake, continuing for about four months in malarial jungles. After Japanese forces invaded the Philippines in December 1941, American and Filipino troops on Luzon withdrew from positions elsewhere on the island, retreating to the Bataan Peninsula.[15] While some still hoped for reinforcements, Washington military planners had already written off the Philippines as expendable. In addition, inconsistent prewar planning had left too few supplies on Bataan itself, and troops had little to fight with or survive on. Thus, they endured the burdens of starvation and disease while also trying to defend themselves with a limited supply of obsolete weapons. They finally surrendered in early April; their comrades on the island of Corregidor, in Manila Bay, held on for another month before surrendering.

The film *Bataan*, released when the Allies had finally gained the initiative on all fronts, serves as an important moment in the representation of the war.[16] Americans could finally acknowledge the early defeats without losing heart. Like other Alamo films, *Bataan* depicts a heroic last stand by an outnumbered force, but it also uses the ancient image of the defenders of the bridge. Rather than representing the entire campaign, it concentrates on one symbolic action and one small group. The patrol's thirteen volunteers come from different units, but all are committed to delaying the Japanese so that American forces can withdraw to secure defensive lines. In one respect, this is the classic small-unit movie, with broad demographic representation of typical American groups. At the same time, it is a "special mission" film, in which a group of soldiers from different units, usually volunteers, combine to carry out a difficult assignment.

Central to the story is veteran infantry Sergeant Bill Dane (Robert Taylor), who joins the patrol with his old friend, Corporal Jake Feingold (Thomas Mitchell). The inexperienced leader, Captain Henry Lassiter

(Lee Bowman), wisely allows Dane to take charge unofficially. There are two engineers, the Polish American F. X. Matowski (Barry Nelson) and the African American Wesley Epps (Kenneth Spencer), who share a strong sense of comradeship. Such close friendship across racial lines is exceptional in films of the period as is the presence of the African American fighting alongside whites in the still-segregated Army. The ethnic diversity is rounded out by an Irish American cook/truck driver, Sam Malloy (Tom Dugan); a California Latino tank crewman, Felix Ramirez (Desi Arnaz); and the Filipino Scout, "Yankee" Salazar (Alex Havier). Also in the group is Matthew Hardy (Phillip Terry), a medic and a conscientious objector. Corporal Barney Todd (Lloyd Nolan) seems familiar to Dane. Todd will turn out to be a former murder suspect, Dan Burns, who had escaped Dane's custody years ago.[17] Attached by circumstance are an Air Force pilot, Lieutenant Steve Bentley (George Murphy) and his Filipino mechanic, Corporal Juan Katigbak (Roque Espiritu), repairing Bentley's aircraft so they can rejoin their squadron. Last comes Leonard Purckett (Robert Walker), a band member from a sunken Navy vessel and also an archetypal innocent. Having been a movie usher in civilian life, his imagination overflows with stories of "when I was a . . ."—a series of different fictitious roles he recalls from viewing films.[18] As the innocent youth, Purckett also carries the rhetorical burden of changing the attitudes of an uninitiated audience. Just as combat teaches and toughens him, so the film overcomes the innocence and naiveté of viewers. All together, this polyglot force symbolizes the diverse American culture that opposes the attacking Japanese army.

After American troops have retreated, the patrol dynamites the bridge and remains to keep the enemy from rebuilding it. The inevitable process of attrition begins when Lassiter falls to a sniper's bullet. Dane takes official command, since the remaining officer, the pilot Bentley, has no knowledge of ground fighting. Scene by scene, attrition continues in the soundstage jungle, a setting made oddly chilling by the ever-present mists and ground fog. Such imagery gives *Bataan* qualities of the horror genre, a feature accentuated by the fact that the Japanese are rarely seen until later in the film. Yet day and night, Japanese patrols silently infiltrate the area, and one by one, the Americans and Filipinos die.

The film implicitly contrasts the Japanese with the Filipinos—the "good" Asian people who embrace American cultural values, as illustrated in Salazar's first name, "Yankee." Yet almost because of their shared racial identity with the Japanese, the Filipinos become a special kind of victim, murdered and mutilated in secret. Katigbak is killed in the night by an unseen enemy patrol, and Salazar is captured and tortured to death. Visually and symbolically, the film uses these deaths to suggest that the Japanese represent a kind of preternatural evil. They are something monstrous that moves and kills during the night, preying on the "innocent natives," the Filipinos. This association of the Japanese with monsters or vampires is also evoked by the persistent fog. So the "Good Asians" become special victims of this invading force of Japanese—the "Monster Asians" who are mysterious, clever, cold-blooded, and alien. Consistent with much racist wartime propaganda, *Bataan* argues that *we* fight to liberate the Asians from the evil Japanese. Ironically, Japanese propaganda reversed this same message 180 degrees, in its own racist and self-serving fashion.[19]

As with *Wake Island*, *Bataan* climaxes with a major Japanese attack. The Americans wait until the last moment before opening fire. When the attackers withdraw, only Dane, Todd, and Purckett are left to prepare for what will be the final battle. Soon a sniper's bullet kills Purckett, and Todd is stabbed as he and Dane try to kill the sniper. With Todd dying in his arms, Dane is willing to forget the man's murderous past, but resistant to Hollywood's usual sentimentality, Todd dies cynical and unrepentant.

The final sequence opens just after Dane has buried Todd along with the others. A row of graves with markers extends behind him. Feverish with malaria, he awaits the end. He has also dug himself a machine gun pit, above which he has placed a cross with his name, so that when he dies fighting, he will fall into his own grave. When the Japanese attack, Dane rallies himself for one final effort, firing with his Thompson submachine gun. As many Japanese fall, he shouts, "Come on, suckers.... Ya dirty, rotten rats. We're still here, we'll always be here. Why don't ya come an' get us?" Throughout, he is wide-eyed and laughing maniacally. He discards the Thompson after exhausting its magazine, switching to a heavy machine gun. The camera pulls back until we see only the gun barrel, and all is lost in the jungle mist and smoke of battle. A statement scrolls up: "So fought the heroes of Bataan. Their sacrifice made possible our victories in the Coral and Bismarck Seas, at Midway, on New Guinea and Guadalcanal. Their spirit will lead us back to Bataan!"

Despite these lofty-sounding sentiments, the imagery of the closing scene is ambiguous and disturbing. The usually controlled Sergeant Dane is now reduced almost to madness as he takes as many of the enemy with him as possible. In its original context, this closing may have inspired Americans, but now it haunts us. We see Dane with his crazed expression, defiantly shouting, "Why don't ya' come an' get us?" and firing away with his submachine gun. Where have we seen this image before? In the figure of the defiant gangster, the icon of lawlessness, shouting "Come and get me, copper!" Dane even fires that classic Chicago gangland weapon, the Tommy gun, with the distinctive round magazine from 1928. How did this imagery surface in an attempt to inspire us to fight for justice against overwhelming odds? Counterintuitive as it may seem, the film's rhetorical connection between crime and war has a logic of its own. *Bataan* tells its audience that they must abandon innocence when facing an implacable foe, just as the naïve, movie-saturated Purckett evolves from innocent youth to killer. But the film's argument is even starker than the required loss of moral innocence during war. It suggests that Americans must be willing to join with criminal killers (as Dane does with Todd) to eradicate the monstrous, "inhuman" enemy—only if we kill without mercy can we survive and save our freedom. What better models might we have than killers we have known in our own culture?[20]

Although *Bataan*'s filmmakers were probably unconscious of the ending's full implications, they still created an iconography of desperation that could be shared by Bataan's defenders and gangsters alike, and in desperate moments, murderous violence becomes acceptable, if not laudable. Implicitly, films like *Bataan* try to persuade viewers that criminal violence is absolutely necessary in war and so remains beyond moral question. Indeed, *Bataan*'s underlying logic suggests that war is "necessary murder," a stark view that no film could advocate openly. So beneath the image of a heroic last stand lurks an almost sociopathic acceptance of murder, an acceptance that the film encourages the audience to share. Fear, desire, and anger underlie many representations of World War II, especially in the Pacific Theater. To give free reign to that anger, to "cry 'Havoc!' and let slip the dogs of war," we loosed as well the mad-dog image of our most violent social outcasts.[21] Beneath the surface of rational order, which must marshal its citizen-soldiers to fight, also lie the destructive and self-destructive qualities of the most violent and dangerous of those citizens—unrepentant criminals.[22] In this way, criminal characters—even sociopaths—subtly influence some constructions of the American soldier on screen.[23] In *Bataan*, the asocial truculence of the gangster thus becomes one source of power for the heroic dying warrior. Later, when the last survivor of a Japanese garrison shouted out his equivalent of "come and get me," he was unintentionally mimicking the character of Sergeant Dane, just as Dane unintentionally reflects our own cultural construction of criminal desperation.

American Kamikaze

The word "kamikaze" usually brings to the American mind images of Japanese pilots relentlessly diving their planes into U.S. Navy ships during the later stages of the Pacific war. Such desperate acts of self-destruction are also associated with the fanatical last stands by Japanese troops at places such as Iwo Jima and Okinawa. Witnessing this apparently irrational death wish reinforced Americans' cultural stereotypes of the Japanese as alien from normal human society. In response, our military felt compelled to wage an unusually merciless form of war against the Japanese, one that would culminate in massive bombing attacks on the Japanese home islands, killing hundreds of thousands of civilians even before the atomic bombs were exploded over Hiroshima and Nagasaki. We assumed that only extreme acts of destruction could force the Japanese nation to surrender. Ultimately, the policy looked almost like one of eradication, continually justified by our assertion that the enemy was fanatical and unwilling to accept defeat.

These assumptions grew, in part, from actual experience. The Pacific war created circumstances where the Japanese military culture emphasized far more strongly its "death before dishonor" principles than Americans were likely to do; the Japanese military's fulfillment of this ideal was achieved with an intensity unprecedented in our experience.[24] Also, the Japanese military often showed unprecedented brutality in its treatment of captured soldiers and civilians, especially in China. Yet even acknowledging these facts, we must also recognize that Americans generally viewed the Japanese people as fundamentally different from Americans, both racially and culturally. This view supported our whole approach to fighting Japan "without mercy." We saw the Japanese people as brutal, suicidal fanatics, and we felt justified in using every means to destroy them.

Ironically, the acts of American soldiers early in the war sometimes undermined that assumption of fundamental difference. Our troops also demonstrated a willingness to fight to the last man, to die instead of surrendering, and to sacrifice themselves to oppose an overwhelming enemy. Indeed, before there were Japanese kamikazes in World War II, there were at least some American precedents for such desperate acts, though more often on screen than in actual fact. If we define the kamikaze as a pilot who deliberately dives his plane into an enemy ship, plane, troop concentration, or installation, then American films early in the war show several incidents of American "kamikazes." If we also add "suicide missions," we can expand the range even further, both on film and in historical fact. Of course, films showed Americans acting as free agents when engaged in such self-sacrifice, rather than as members of a specific "suicide corps." While in the "Alamo" film we have the besieged unit fighting to the last man, in the "kamikaze" film (or film sequence), we have the individual who sacrifices himself to save others and/or to destroy the enemy. In *Bataan*, we have a bit of both, since the mortally wounded Lieutenant Bentley chooses to dive his plane into the bridge held by the enemy. The Bentley sequence clearly demonstrates the patterns of Hollywood mythology, not of historical probability. Still, the plane goes down, the bridge goes up, and the story goes on, with the suicidal warrior remembered as a hero, not a fanatic.

Several other films during the same time period as *Bataan* allowed major Hollywood stars to immolate themselves in acts of desperate self-sacrifice. Prominent among these is *A Guy Named Joe* (1943), focusing on the romance of American pilot Pete Sandidge (Spencer Tracy) and Dorinda Durston (Irene Dunne). Early in the film, Pete accepts a dangerous mission to sink a German aircraft carrier. When his lone bomber is severely damaged, he bravely dives at the carrier to ensure a direct hit, destroying it but also killing himself in the subsequent explosion.[25] The film not only assumes the morality of such an act (Pete enters the equivalent of "Pilots' Heaven"), but also suggests that such extreme acts can be expected even of men who leave behind wives or lovers.

The often-overlooked *Pilot #5* (1943) focuses on Allied pilots stationed on Java, just prior to the Japanese invasion. Pilot #5 is George Collins (Franchot Tone), who volunteers to take an aircraft, with an ad hoc bomb-release mechanism, on a desperate mission to attack the Japanese ships. Most of the film is told as flashbacks of civilian life, narrated by George's best friend, Vito (Gene Kelly). A promising lawyer, George became involved with a crypto-fascist politician. Finally realizing his mistake, he exposes the man, ruining both careers (career suicide). Returning to the present, George's bomb-release fails, so he must once again sacrifice himself for the good of others. Like Pete in *A Guy Named Joe*, George dives his plane at the ship and destroys it. In *Pilot #5*, the suicidal act is part self-sacrifice and part atonement for earlier wrongs. Thus, we have a double moral justification for a suicide attack—saving others and saving face. Certainly, any Japanese kamikaze pilot in 1945 would have found these motives appropriate.

Yet the "American kamikaze" was not merely something developed as a Hollywood plot device. At least two somewhat similar historical incidents occurred during the first year of the Pacific war. Most famous of these was the case of Army Air Force Capt. Colin Kelly, a young

B-17 pilot in the Philippines.[26] When the Japanese invaded Luzon in December 1941, Kelly and his crew went on a desperate mission to attack Japanese shipping off the island's northern coast. They bombed what seemed to them a "battleship," but Japanese fighters critically damaged the bomber on its return leg. Kelly stayed at the controls while the crew bailed out, but he died in the crash. While involving no "death dive," Kelly clearly sacrificed his life for others. The Army, however, needing both a hero and a victory, took Kelly's genuine heroism and added the assumed victory. He posthumously received the Medal of Honor, not only for his actual efforts to save his crew but also for his alleged sinking of the Japanese battleship *Haruna*. Actually, Kelly's bombs had missed their intended target, which was only a small warship (reports from high-altitude bombing of ships were usually as inaccurate as the bombing itself). These errors did not change the fact that Kelly had died while on a near-suicidal mission. His story, while not that of an "American kamikaze" per se, was one of heroic self-sacrifice. It offered a historical template for further narratives, both factual and fictional, of those who die so others might live. In this context, and because Kelly was one of the first such heroic figures of the war, his identity took on far-reaching iconic status in support of acts of self-sacrifice. A genuinely courageous young man, Kelly was changed into a posthumous icon of "death before dishonor."

In 1942, a more kamikaze-like incident occurred during the Battle of Midway, when Marine Corps Captain Richard Fleming led his dive-bomber squadron in attacking two Japanese cruisers.[27] Fleming's plane appeared to have been hit during its dive, and after releasing its bomb, it plunged into the cruiser *Mikuma*. It remains uncertain whether Fleming's crash was accidental or intentional, but this dive stands out as a real instance when a crippled American aircraft crashed into an enemy ship, perhaps deliberately.

The cases of men like Kelly and Fleming make us recognize that Americans were willing to take on suicidal or near-suicidal missions, and even to dive their planes into enemy ships, long before the actual Japanese kamikazes were organized. Moreover, the American public viewed these men as heroic martyrs. Thus, the Japanese kamikaze corps was not an example of an essential difference between the two cultures as much as a difference of degree (though that could be a considerable difference at times). Both sides accepted the idea of self-sacrifice in attacking the enemy, but for Americans, this was always an individual act, whereas for the Japanese it was more frequently a socially reinforced and/or militarily organized group action. Still, despite our assertions to the contrary, just like the Japanese, we also accepted as righteous a war-rior's suicide to defeat his enemies and protect his friends. We were not as different from one another as we had assumed.

Service, Services, and Campaigns

The word "service" has a dual meaning during war, referring to the specific branches of the military but also denoting what citizens, whether in the military or in private life, give to their country. During both peace and war, each military branch seeks to promote a unique "service identity" to ensure its survival. Likewise, citizens also seek acknowledgement of the efforts they offer their country. Giving credit both to military branches and to private citizens, wartime news media and filmmakers often focused on this dual concept of service. Many war correspondents were connected with a particular service branch and theater of war, as Ernie Pyle was associated with the Army and its G.I.s in Europe. As filmmakers in uniform, Frank Capra and John Ford created the official wartime film record of the Army and Navy, respectively. Yet Hollywood feature films did the most to define ser-vice identities to the general public, and in turn, each military branch gave active support to feature films highlighting that service's achieve-ments. In the process, Hollywood and the military jointly created a template for the World War II "service film," a template that continues to shape many contemporary war films.[28]

Even before the Pearl Harbor attack, Hollywood had already begun developing the service film genre, as both comedy and serious drama. Numerous films had used the military setting as background for estab-lished comedians, such as Abbott and Costello's *Buck Privates* and Bob Hope's *Caught in the Draft* (both 1941). Many serious service films dealt largely with training, the most popular focusing on aviation, such as *I Wanted Wings* (1941). In addition, service training films usually used a *bildungsroman* structure, with a naïve, troubled, or brash young man coming of age, usually under the guidance of a paternal sergeant or officer. Romantic subplots were often interwoven with the service story. Thus, as the American military began preparing for war, the film industry mobilized the service film by blending a number of traditional Hollywood formulas into a genre celebrating the military services and the service of citizens.

When war came, Hollywood expanded the service-film genre, as dictated by simple pragmatics. War stories were usually set in a particular unit of a specific service, so individual war films necessarily focused on a single branch. Moreover, each military service competed for government funds and public attention, and every service worked diligently to encourage films specifically about itself. Regarding the second meaning of the term, Hollywood also celebrated the service and sacrifice of individual Americans, whether they were in uniform or just ordinary private citizens "doing their part." Any service film about the military offered opportunities to show the sacrifices made by its individual characters, while films such as *Joe Smith, American* (1942), *Tender Comrade* (1943), and *Since You Went Away* (1944) gave American audiences a view of their fellow citizens serving as war workers, as waiting families, and even as grieving widows.

★   ★   ★

In closing this chapter, I briefly examine three 1943 films of the combat-service genre that became so important during the war: *Guadalcanal Diary*, *Air Force*, and *Action in the North Atlantic*. In addition, I mention in passing a number of other examples, illustrating the genre's overall scope and influence. *Guadalcanal Diary* is perhaps the most significant of the three because it helps establish the focal narrative of a pivotal campaign and the role of the Marine Corps in that campaign. The first U.S. offensive in the Pacific began in August 1942 at Guadalcanal, with only the minimal resources available in the area. Concerned about the island's strategic importance, the Japanese counterattacked our landings with large naval and air forces, pushing American units to the limit. In the struggle to control surrounding waters, the U.S. Navy suffered a number of defeats that interrupted the flow of supplies to the island. Despite these obstacles, the marines' dogged defense of the airfield, along with the navy's persistence in the face of terrible losses, eventually turned the tide. Throughout the campaign, the disease-ridden island itself became the principal enemy of both sides, causing far more casualties than the actual fighting.

War correspondent Richard Tregaskis landed with the marines at Guadalcanal, staying through the first two months of fighting. After leaving, he quickly converted his reportage into an influential book, *Guadalcanal Diary* (1943). With its concise and unornamented style, the book represents some of the era's better war correspondence. Released the following November, the film builds on the book's basic structure, but it offers an essentially fictional and sometimes highly inaccurate account of the campaign. It also inserts a number of fictional characters who represent the standard small-unit demographics of the World War II combat film. These include the tough but compassionate Irish Gunnery Sergeant "Hook" Malone (Lloyd Nolan), always playfully sparring with his "Flagg/Quirt" companion, Brooklynite Corporal "Taxi" Potts (William Bendix). Jesus "Soose" Alvarez (Anthony Quinn) is the stereotypical "ethnic" character, also providing comic relief as a "Latin Lover." The "baby-faced kid" is Johnny "Chicken" Anderson (Richard Jaeckel), desperately trying to grow his first whiskers, and the unit's earnest, young C.O. is Captain Don Davis (Richard Conte). Clustered about the principal combatants are a number of subsidiary characters, including a war correspondent, loosely based on Tregaskis himself (Reed Hadley), whose voice provides background narration. Most important of all is the Roman Catholic chaplain, Father Donnelly (Preston Foster). A graduate of Notre Dame and a former football star, Donnelly incarnates the concept of "muscular Christianity" as he provides dramatic focus for the film, guidance for the men, and moral justification for the war itself.

Today, this film feels distinctively unrealistic. Not only does it fictionalize too many of its characters and events but it also never communicates any sense of the debilitating effects of attrition warfare. We see little suggestion of the diseases that ravaged troops throughout the campaign. Like the upbeat war bond posters from the same period, it shows determined but optimistic American troops fighting toward inevitable victory, without being changed significantly by the violence and deprivation they experience. Shot in Southern California, the film also fails to convey the oppressive sense of menace that pervaded jungle campaigns. Tregaskis' book does not reflect the worst of the campaign because he left the island too early. Yet his book still tells its story with greater intensity than does the film, which often seems almost lighthearted in depicting what had actually been a deeply traumatizing campaign. *Guadalcanal Diary* closes with the marines leaving the island after having been relieved by reinforcements. As they march away, they seem almost as hale and hearty as when they had arrived months earlier. Throughout the film, characters fight battles, and sometimes they die, but the experiences do not traumatize the survivors. They gripe, joke, and play games, but they are neither cynical nor bitter. These characters seem locked in late-adolescent male innocence, looked after by the tough but affable Fr. Donnelly. They also appear to suffer no lasting psychological scars from their losses. *Guadalcanal Diary* thus offers the sanitized and superficial view of combat consistent with the expectations of Hollywood, the government, and even the general public.

Only near the war's end would similar small-unit films even suggest the true costs of combat. Yet *Guadalcanal Diary* helped establish the standard features of the American service/campaign film of World War II, with its small unit of representative American types. Likewise, it served to mythologize the Guadalcanal campaign as one in which the endurance, good humor, and resourcefulness of the "lovable" marines won out over a dangerous, "inhuman" foe. Finally, in creating the character of Fr. Donnelly, the film provided audiences some religious sanction for waging war.[29] The image of such moral support made *Guadalcanal Diary* unusually powerful propaganda.

Although the tone of *Guadalcanal Diary* is comparatively light, that of *Air Force* is a good deal darker (though in many respects, more fantastic), partly because the film depicts just the first days of the war, a time of disaster for Americans. The characters themselves reflect the grim circumstances by their appearance. Indeed, once the fighting begins, they look tired, unshaven, and dirty—often more begrimed than the typical muddied ground troops. Directed by Howard Hawks, *Air Force* is a classic service film, celebrating a military branch in the very title. Beginning pointedly on December 6, 1941, it traces the first desperate weeks of the war through the experiences of one B-17 crew and their aircraft, nicknamed "Mary Ann" after wife of the pilot Captain "Irish" Quincannon (John Ridgely). The crew includes the tough, old chief, Sergeant Robbie White (Harry Carey). Also present is a temporary replacement gunner, Sergeant Joe Winocki (John Garfield), an embittered flight-school washout. Contrasting with Winocki's brooding character is the irrepressibly optimistic New Yorker, Corporal Weinberg (George Tobias). Bill Williams (Gig Young) is the co-pilot and friend to bombardier Tommy McMartin (Arthur Kennedy). Several others fill out the crew and add additional personal conflicts to the story.

Each plot conflict is brought into focus by wartime action that occurs during the long journey from California: first to Hawaii, then to Wake and the Philippines, and finally to Australia. The journey's various segments provide time for character development and exposition, also allowing the audience to become familiar with the interior of the plane, itself a major character. Occasional shots of actual B-17s in flight give a powerful visual image to underscore the word "force" in *Air Force*. Many difficult take-off sequences give added tension, but as the plane leaves Wake, we see smoke swirl in the prop wash, an image both realistic and visually poetic.

Finally reaching the Philippines, the crew receives a warm welcome from comrades, amid the desolation of Clark Field. They must leave almost immediately, however, to attack a Japanese invasion convoy. Some earlier plot complications are now resolved. Most importantly, Winocki has changed and become a team player because he has witnessed actual combat. The "Mary Ann" attacks the invasion fleet, but afterward, it is harassed by enemy fighters (cf. Colin Kelly, above). With two engines shot out, Quincannon orders the crew to bail out just moments before he is hit and starts to lose consciousness. Winocki, the last man remaining, rushes to the cockpit, seizes the controls, and levels out the plane for a belly-landing at the field. His heroism compensates for his former bitterness, and the unity and commitment of the remaining crewmembers are confirmed in a scene at Quincannon's deathbed.

After the captain's death, the crew manages to repair the badly damaged plane, gas up, and take off just as the Japanese troops attack the field. Flying toward Australia, they spot another Japanese fleet. They radio its location, and then join in an attack with a large group of Air Force and Navy bombers. At last we see a major battle, witnessing ship after Japanese ship explode and sink. Afterward, the "Mary Ann" manages to make another wheels-up landing in Australia. The film closes with the scene of a pre-mission briefing, at some undisclosed future date, where all the surviving principals can rejoice in the news that the night's target will finally be Tokyo.

Critics at the time praised the power of *Air Force*, and even today's film historians sometimes proclaim it a classic. Certainly, the film communicated the Air Force service message with unique persuasive energy. As Williams says before the bombing commences, "Now you'll see what the Air Force can do." Yet it does not stand the test of time. The flight into the war seems, on the surface, to be a journey into the gritty reality of combat, with exhausted crews, devastated airfields, and major characters killed or wounded. As we move further into a register of visual violence and destruction, however, we also move away from reality and into hyperbole. Incredibly, Winocki succeeds in belly-landing a bomb-laden B-17 on a cratered runway, a nearly impossible feat. Our credulity is further strained by the overnight repair of the damaged craft back to fighting trim. The final encounter with the Japanese fleet further disconnects us from the action with its studio tank-shots of all-to-obvious models. The problem is not just the poor quality of the special effects but also the excessive nature of the story itself. Within what must have been a week of Pearl Harbor, the Japanese fleet seems to have gone down to decisive defeat, and the war has turned in our favor. Had the film been made in January 1942, such fantasy might be forgivable as an effort to raise morale, but over a year later, when so many actual battles had been fought, the story seems absurd. The most galling realization is that a genuinely effective film could have been made if Hawks had stuck to a more realistic story of the Air Force in the Philippines. The 1945 John Ford film *They Were Expendable*, based on a factual book about PT boats during the fall of the Philippines, manages to provide gripping drama with far less exaggeration. Using the powerful image of a B-17 to heighten intensity, Hawks could have accomplished so much more with the story had he tried to do far less.

Action in the North Atlantic (1943) focuses on America's Merchant Marine and Navy in the Battle of the Atlantic. It begins on the tanker SS *Northern Star*, with a voiceover by first officer, Lieutenant Joe Rossi (Humphrey Bogart). Bogart's gruff tone links this monologue to the detective genre with which he was already associated. We soon meet Captain Steve Jarvis (Raymond Massey), an old sea dog with thirty years experience. The remainder of the crew includes standard Hollywood character actors in typical roles: Alan Hale as "Boats" O'Hara, a philandering, Irish chief bosun's mate; Sam Levine as Abrams, a philosophical, Jewish ship's carpenter; and Dane Clark as Johnnie Pulaski, an emotional, argumentative Pole.

Adapted from a novel by maritime writer Guy Gilpatric, the John Howard Lawson script neatly divides the film into four sections, with a closing coda.[30] First comes a sequence on the tanker, which is torpedoed and abandoned. The German submarine surfaces and rams the crew's lifeboat, leaving the survivors to spend eleven days on a raft before being rescued. Section two covers the crew's homecoming and subsequent preparation to return to sea. Jarvis visits his wife, and Rossi meets and marries a young singer. The crew quarrels in the union hall because Pulaski is reluctant to ship out again, but all is resolved quickly. The principals, along with a new Navy gun crew, reassemble aboard the new Liberty Ship SS *Sea Witch*. The third section includes the *Sea Witch*'s joining a convoy to the "Russian" port of Murmansk (in the film, the Soviet Union is always called "Russia"). This third segment closes with the attack of a submarine wolf pack, and the fourth begins as the convoy disperses, with the *Sea Witch* trailed by one of the submarines. The cat-and-mouse game between the *Sea Witch* and its would-be attacker provides the most suspenseful portion of the film. After several attacks by both the submarine and German aircraft, the segment climaxes as the *Sea Witch*, torpedoed but still seaworthy, rams and sinks the attacking submarine—recalling the earlier scene of the lifeboat being rammed). The ship also repels several air attacks before "Russian" planes arrive to shepherd it into port. In the brief closing coda, the crippled *Sea Witch* limps into Murmansk, to the cheers of the "Russians."

While *Action in the North Atlantic* is an engaging film, it also focuses on issues of personal and social commitment. Three characters grow and change throughout the film, becoming ultimately more committed to their shipmates and to the Allied cause. Early on, Joe Rossi tells his dour but affectionate skipper, "You remember the pain, but I remember the fun." Though qualified to captain his own ship, the uncommitted Rossi avoids taking the responsibility. Mr. Parker, a cadet from the Merchant Marine Academy, suffers the scorn of Jarvis, who disapproves of "book-trained" sailors; Parker struggles to prove himself throughout the film. Pulaski, angered by America's failure to protect endangered shipping, would prefer a shore job to the wartime risks of the seas. He fears he will leave his wife a widow and his yet unborn son an orphan, but his mates shame him into going out. In the course of the film, each of these characters matures. Rossi develops a sense of personal responsibility, finally taking over the ship when Jarvis is wounded. Rossi also counsels Parker when the young man confesses his fears. Reassured by Rossi, Parker gains new confidence. When the Navy gun crew on board is incapacitated, he and Pulaski take over the gun and shoot down an attacking aircraft, but Parker is mortally wounded in the effort. Later, as Pulaski assists Rossi in collecting Parker's personal effects, the formerly reluctant warrior examines one of the Merchant Marine textbooks, wondering aloud what it takes to become an officer. He, too, has clearly changed course. Thus, the film reveals its *bildungs-roman* substructure—each of these characters comes of age. Parker faces his fears though he dies as a result of his heroism. Pulaski conquers both his fear and his embittered social isolation, picking up Parker's fallen standard. Rossi, though the eldest of the three, changes the most; from the reliable but happily uncommitted first mate, he grows into the new husband who is finally ready to command his own ship.

By focusing on character development, Lawson's script also manages to give the film an ideological edge.[31] *Action in the North Atlantic* shows the war as a genuine international struggle against fascism and for freedom. In this context, men performing their ordinary duties accept new levels of social responsibility. It is not enough to preserve a safe haven for one's wife and child unless the rest of the world is also safe. It is not enough to sail the oceans; one must be willing to fight and even die to defend the freedom of the seas. It is not enough to be a reliable first officer; one must shoulder the burdens of command and take full responsibility for the welfare of others. Such acts of social responsibility show the basically laudable Allied motives for fighting the war—a commitment to the good of others, to the "brotherhood of man." Although this theme constitutes a common "democratic" message in much wartime representation, in Lawson's hands, it also reflects his particularly left-wing views.[32] It is significant that the characters' growth in social commitment occurs during a challenging journey to "Russia," a communist state. Both geographically and symbolically, the film shows that, as one grows closer to the left (Russia), the more one sees the need for commitment, and as one sees the need for commitment, one grows closer to the left. Reaching Murmansk is a celebratory event on both practical and ideological levels. The composite effect is to support not only the war in general but also the war aims as seen in the most liberal or even socialist terms. Lawson's politics, as well as those of the left-leaning Maritime Union, underlie the film's ideological message. The convoy itself, with its international character and common cause, represents a socialist vision of a world moving toward greater social justice. Thus, rather than merely celebrating a service, this film invokes a new understanding of the nature of "service," one that transcends personal issues and recognizes a universal ideology that links all such commitments.

Lawson found a home at Warner Bros. because this studio represented the more liberal wing of a generally conservative film industry. Released later the same year, *Sahara* (also a Lawson script for Warner Bros.) once again has Bogart leading a diverse group, representing Allied solidarity in the worldwide struggle against fascism.[33] Both films emphasize the international nature of the Allied effort and the fundamental brutality of the Nazi foe. Disparate personal interests are set aside so that the common goal and common good can be achieved. Those who die in the process are mourned and celebrated while the survivors draw new strength from these examples of sacrifice. Likewise, a good technological device, be it a tank or a Liberty Ship, reflects the combined efforts of a committed industrial work force. In these two films and in *Casablanca* (also from Warner), Bogart created a powerful image of the American identity in response to the war. Indeed, the three films can be seen as a kind of Warner/Bogart trilogy—about commitment to the cause, solidarity with Allies, and sacrifice of personal interests to a greater call of social responsibility. All three films present service in the most idealistic terms: service to the common good of all people. Although advocated by Lawson and the left, such ideals also appealed to a broad spectrum of Americans because they represented what is best about America

★ ★ ★

Studios continued to produce campaign and service films throughout the war. *A Wing and a Prayer* (1944) focuses on Navy aircraft carriers, while *Bombardier* (1943) advocates for strategic bombing. *Gung Ho!* (1943) and *Marine Raiders* (1944) depict efforts of special U.S. Marine units. Films such as *Stand by for Action* (1942) and *Destroyer* (1943) highlight Navy surface units, while *Crash Dive* (1943) and *Destination Tokyo* (1943) show U.S. submarines. The list of similar films, many quite forgettable, goes on at length. In the aggregate, these films combine with poster art, documentaries, and journalism to create the vast social construction of the American narrative of World War II combat. It is a construction that underlies much of how we still understand the war's cultural significance.

Central to that construction is the concept that individuals who formerly saw themselves as isolated—from government, from the international community, and from their fellow citizens at home—are now called to a new role of service. One must freely choose to answer that call, either by volunteering or dutifully accepting conscription because choice is the prerogative of a free people. Refusal to serve, whether in the military or in another way, still constitutes a moral failure. The result of the choice was to change not only one's mind but also one's condition of being—one joined the service, one gave service, and one became part of a larger whole—the unit, the military, the nation, the world. Choosing to serve was choosing a new faith, a faith that linked one with fellow citizens at home and with fellow peoples across the globe. Such was the message, and in 1943, it was compelling.

This same concept of service was reflected in the motives and efforts, if not always the results, of the OWI and of the FDR administration in general. In service, we combine the values both of *why* and *how* we fight, and in 1943 that could still be viewed idealistically. Americans could be called to serve and fight, believing that they would do so in the cause of universal freedom. In that cause, they would fight fiercely but fairly. In Europe, the obvious evil of the Nazis offered a clear contrast to American ideals; in the Pacific, we characterized the war as protecting the "outposts of civilization" from a barbaric and uncivilized enemy. Even as late as 1943, the war's cost in human lives and suffering still seemed something that Americans could endure without becoming as brutal as our adversaries. By the war's end, such idealism was in much shorter supply, largely exhausted by our efforts to wage a total war on a truly global scale. Our energy had gone instead into developing a wide array of weapons, including atomic bombs. We also had come to accept the mass bombing of civilian targets—an enemy tactic that had horrified us in 1939 and 1940—as just one more way to achieve victory. Somewhere during the journey of destruction that was World War II, the American psyche gradually shifted from a concern for "the brotherhood of man" to a commitment to "exterminate the brutes." The soul of the nation, along with the bodies of its young men, had suffered the inevitable wounds of modern, total war. We bear the scars to this day.

CHAPTER FOUR

"The Great Crusade"

> Soldiers, Sailors and Airmen of the Allied Expeditionary Forces:
> You are about to embark upon the Great Crusade, toward which
> we have striven these many months. . . . Good luck! And let us all
> beseech the blessing of Almighty God upon this great and noble
> undertaking.
>
> Dwight D. Eisenhower,
> Address to the D-Day Forces[1]

"Warriors for the Working Day"

The long-awaited Allied offensive against Nazi-occupied Northern
Europe began with the invasion of Normandy on June 6, 1944. For
the Western Allies, 1944 was a year during which they brought the
battle to the enemy on an unprecedented scale. To some, the word
"crusade" seemed an apt label, not only for the Normandy invasion but
also for Allied offensive operations across the globe. "Crusade" carries
deep cultural significance, interpreted by many as the Christian equivalent of the Islamic term jihad. Yet the epic proportions of Operation
Overlord, along with the subsequent battles that raged across northwest Europe, seemed to call for expansive terms. Indeed, the Nazis
were a demonic foe, and the Allies sought to liberate Europe's millions
from that oppressive regime. We can understand, then, what prompted
Eisenhower's "holy war" rhetoric. Fighting so brutal an enemy called
us to live up to our own highest ideals. Make war on the devil and,
certainly, one fights on the side of God's true angels—so the narrative
suggests.

Yet if World War II was a crusade, then it also shared the kind of mixed motives that propelled the original crusades. Combat veterans such as novelist Kurt Vonnegut and cultural historian Paul Fussell have acknowledged this complexity. Vonnegut gave *Slaughterhouse-Five* (1969) the subtitle "The Children's Crusade," while Fussell alludes to this in titling one study of World War II, *The Boys' Crusade* (2003). Both recognize that the crusading images of wartime rhetoric were often constructed by a generation too old to shoulder weapons while very young men, often mere boys, fought the actual battles. Theirs were the bodies and minds that endured the shock and scars of combat. Far from the bright-hued recruiting posters, these young men lived, fought, killed, suffered, and sometimes died in conditions that resembled an artistic collaboration between Dante and Hieronymus Bosch. As Vonnegut and Fussell attest, those lying in the mud and blood of places such as the Huertgen Forest usually felt more crucified than crusading.

Still, genuine evil was loose in the world, evil that had to be stopped. The Nazi menace had become undeniable even long before we opened the gates of the death camps and directly viewed the horror for which we scarcely had language. Afterward, the Allies could point to the Holocaust/Shoah and claim that to oppose such genocide was truly "why we fought." This claim was valid, in part, but for the nation and for individuals, motives at the time of the actual fighting were far more complicated. Certainly, many American soldiers gave serious thought to the issues behind the war, issues highlighted in such government productions as Capra's *Why We Fight* films. Yet others did not think so deeply about the war's politics. Some fought from unquestioning national loyalty and patriotism, some from a desire to experience the dangerous and unknown, and some because it was what everyone else seemed to be doing; many fought because they had little choice, and many others shared in all these motivations.[2] Whatever their original reasons, all who fought were changed by the process, sometimes discovering additional motivation only during or after the experience of combat. Indeed, almost all combat veterans came to believe they were fighting for survival—their own and that of the other members of their small units. Yet some Americans who fought against the Axis powers indeed did so as an act of ethical responsibility and moral commitment. They came to answer what they believed was a call to bring freedom and justice, not only to the subjugated lands of Europe but also to all peoples, even those groups back in the United States who had yet to share in genuine freedom. For these idealistic soldiers, the "crusader" image may have seemed most appropriate, whether or not the religious reference carried weight.[3] Crusaders or not, America's fighting men in World War II rarely proclaimed their ideological views. They usually came with no splendor and little heraldry, except for the iconic shoulder patches on their uniforms—rather poor livery for crusaders. As Shakespeare's pragmatic Henry the Fifth says of his bedraggled troops:

> We are but warriors for the working-day;
> Our gayness and our gilt are all besmirch'd
> With rainy marching in the painful field. . . .[4]

Thus it was with America's citizen soldiers who, despite often-ragged appearances, were still described in the mythic terms of medieval warriors, seeking to rescue something sacred from the clutches of infidels. Yet these were also the ordinary G.I.s, who landed at so many beaches, who marched through countless miles of mud, who slept in holes, and who ate food that often tasted little better than the cardboard or metal in which it had been packaged. They were the ones who, like their counterparts in World War I, suffered from countless diseases such as trench foot and dysentery; who endured shelling, machine guns, and snipers; and who saw far too many friends not just killed but torn to bloody shreds in the abattoir of total war. Although the word "crusade" might come readily to those with grandiose, historical imaginations, the role seemed quite distant from actual life and death on the modern battlefield. So these soldiers lived two lives, or at least, lived in two different registers of life—on the one hand called to see themselves as crusading warriors out to set the world right, and on the other hand, made to live in the squalid conditions of a "combatant underclass." Now, at a distance of sixty years, the phrase "Great Crusade" may strike us as everything from inspiring to ironic. In the minds of many who were actually fighting, however, inspiration and irony coexisted in that problematic word "crusade." In combat, crusading often meant merely the effort to survive for another day while maintaining a small hope that something might exist beyond the drudgery and pain of modern war.

Warrior as Everyman—The Evolution of G.I. Joe[5]

During World War II, over 17 million Americans served in the military, more than 12% of the total United States population, and more than one-third of the eligible males.[6] Mobilizing such an army requires that individual concerns be abandoned in favor of order and discipline, but America marshaled its army from a traditionally idiosyncratic people, deeply committed to their individual rights. So while dictatorships could more easily raise enormous forces, America depended on its untested citizen-soldiers—citizens first and soldiers only for the duration of the crisis.[7] These soldiers drew strength from their sense of common citizenship, but what was *most* common about soldiers was their resistance to military regimentation. Thus, the character of the American soldier in World War II was an uneasy amalgam of conformity and idiosyncrasy, of shared identity and expressed individuality.

We called this amalgam "G.I. Joe." Although a warrior, he had not emerged from a medieval epic. If we were to associate him with a medieval text, it might be the morality play *Everyman*. G.I. Joe was Everyman in uniform, John Doe with a rifle and helmet. What was similar or repeatable about the "citizen-soldiers" was that, as citizens, all Americans ideally shared common rights and obligations, despite their diverse backgrounds and identities.[8] This common legal and constitutional identity, transcending other identities, allowed for greater range of individuality as well. Ideally, in the military one G.I. was like every other G.I—an ordinary person answering the call to serve the nation; however, every G.I. also retained a strong sense of his own personal identity.[9]

The term "G.I." encompasses the citizen-soldier's uneasy relationship with the military. To be "G.I." was to conform to regulations and to be like the masses of materiel stamped as "G.I."[10] At the same time, to be "G.I. Joe" was to endure, but not necessarily to accept, such regimentation. Having lost his accustomed freedom of action, and being caught up in the great bureaucratic machinery of war, the new citizen-soldier came to identify with the term "G.I." Thus, in their own self-deprecating and self-asserting way, the troops reclaimed the term and reinscribed it with a sense of American informality, irony, antiauthoritarianism, and democratic directness. Everyone is the same, all G.I.s together. Like their weapons, their food, their clothes, and even their toilet paper, the troops were "general" or "government issue." Likewise, they were also expendable in the war effort. A kind of gallows humor permeated the term G.I., an acceptance of this fate. Yet, by adopting the term, the soldiers were indirectly expressing their basic annoyance with authority. They might be loyal to the country and even to the Army but never to the Army's bureaucracy, with its humiliations and petty authority. The G.I. knew that there was little he could do about his situation, but by claiming the term as his identity, he made common cause with his fellow sufferers, and he also thumbed his nose at the petty tyrannies of military life.

Thus, in our epic war, in our "Great Crusade," we sent forth a mass army of what seemed individualistic, common men. It was an army where heroism was not uncommon, but where heroes themselves were otherwise ordinary individuals who made some extraordinary effort, largely on behalf of their fellow soldiers. The small unit was like family, and for the infantry, it was the squad, platoon, or company that constituted the unit. So in actual combat, soldiers fought not for ideology but to save themselves and their buddies. Furthermore, they were often willing to sacrifice themselves for other members of their close-knit unit because they knew their squad mates would do the same.[11] The "G.I. War" was one in which soldiers in countless small units fought to keep themselves and their comrades alive in the face of brutal enemies and the overall impersonal machinery of war. This was the "crusade" at the direct and personal level.

★   ★   ★

If we consider the G.I. crusade as an "Epic of the Common Man," then one of its chief "poets" was war correspondent Ernie Pyle. Pyle spent most of the war covering campaigns in the Mediterranean and northwest Europe, publishing hundreds of articles. Many were collected in two volumes: *Here Is Your War* (1943) and *Brave Men* (1944), the second earning a Pulitzer Prize in 1944. Late in the war, he went to the Pacific and was killed covering the Okinawa invasion.

Not before or since has anyone expressed so well, through the simple prose of the journalistic feature story, the attitudes, ideals, and personalities of a broad range of American fighting men. At the war's outset, Pyle was already an experienced journalist, well known for syndicated travel columns.[12] Yet the war called Pyle to what seemed a higher purpose—making Americans aware of the struggle and sacrifice of the ordinary G.I. To accomplish this, Pyle had to suffer many of the same rough and dangerous conditions, and so he achieved a special intimacy with soldiers, allowing him to write with insight and authority. The draft of an unpublished column, found on his body, refers to his time covering the campaigns in Europe: "[T]he companionship of two and a half years of death and misery is a spouse that tolerates no divorce."[13]

Pyle's war writing grew from the journalistic conventions of "human-interest" feature writing. He combined the keen observational and descriptive skills of a reporter with the stylistic insights of a personal essayist. He had a gift for capturing a person's salient qualities in the briefest of passages while conveying a strong sense of place and circumstance. Whenever possible, he included the full names and hometowns of his subjects. These elements allowed him to profile soldiers in an honest, compelling fashion that brought out the uniqueness of each soldier and put an individual human face on the vast impersonality of war. Pyle helped his readers see that every life risked in war was precious, every loss was personal, not only for the man's family and his unit but also for the nation. Though no one could adequately convey the full traumatic impact of the war, Pyle communicated to ordinary Americans, more powerfully than most other journalists, the experiences of the common G.I.

As both man and writer, Pyle took inspiration from the youth and courage he witnessed in so many of his subjects. Moreover, covering the war up close allowed him to deepen his writing, but he paid a price for this experience. With each stay at the front, he suffered an increasing sense of loss because men he had grown to know and respect lay dead across the battlefields—by ones, tens, and hundreds. The words of that final column capture the profound trauma he had witnessed and shared, speaking of the indelible images of the almost countless dead men: "Dead men by mass production....Dead men in such monstrous infinity that you come almost to hate them."[14] Darker by far than many of his pieces, this column reveals the gradual erosion of the high spirits with which Pyle had originally greeted the opportunity to cover combat zones.

Among Pyle's many war columns, "The Death of Captain Waskow" (January 10, 1944) particularly stands out.[15] Eulogizing a company commander, the piece grew so well known that it became the basis for a fictionalized film about Pyle's experiences, *The Story of G.I. Joe* (1945). Understated and solemn, the column transcends our usual assumptions about war correspondence, revealing as well a powerful sense of the writer's craft. Its structure conveys the assurance of classical rhetoric, with a brief opening comment followed by three quotations from Waskow's men about his value as a leader and as a man. Then Pyle sets the scene: on a moonlit winter night, he and the troops huddle in a cowshed at the bottom of a hill, as others bring the dead down from the heights. Each corpse is strapped to the back of a mule. The simple statement "I was at the foot of the mule trail the night they brought Capt. Waskow's body down" says much in its direct, unornamented form. Pyle has already revealed that Waskow inspired unusually deep devotion in his men, so the dead captain seems like a martyred saint.

Pyle carefully describes the process of bringing the dead down the hill—how the men slowly unload the mules and leave the bodies in a row along the roadside. David Nichols, editor of *Ernie's War*, appropriately observes that the repetition and concreteness in the passage reveal Hemingway's influence.[16] This is, after all, a highly ritualistic passage that serves as a kind of G.I. funeral service. Its ritual and repetition indeed echo Hemingway, as do many stylistic features of the better World War II reporting. After a brief pause, the men individually speak parting words to the dead officer. One says merely, "God damn it," while another, probably an officer, says, "I'm sorry, old man." A final soldier has no words, but he sits down briefly and holds the dead captain's hand before returning to the others to sleep in the cowshed; despite the losses and poignant farewells, sleep must still come. Given his martyred condition, the fact that Waskow has ridden a mule down the mountainside vaguely recalls Christ arriving in Jerusalem, shortly before the crucifixion. Ironically, the fact that the men huddle in a cowshed suggests the Christmas nativity scene, but here they grieve rather than rejoice.

"The Death of Captain Waskow" stands as a testament to those other G.I.s whose deaths haunted Pyle with the enormity of their loss. Like each of Pyle's portraits, Waskow is an individual—in this case, an endearing man who cared for his company as a father for his sons. "'He always looked after us'" captures how his men remember him, and because of Pyle's article, so many others would remember him.[17] Such a stark reality at the end—the corpse in the cold winter night, the men returning like orphaned children to sleep in a cowshed—conveys powerful emotion while largely avoiding sentimentality.

The Waskow column also reflects a new trend emerging in the representation of the war during the fall and winter of 1943 and 1944: an acknowledgment of just how costly modern war can be.[18] American corpses begin to appear in news photographs as well as in the poster and advertising art supporting bond drives or encouraging increased production. Despite its prior censorship of such images, by mid-1943 the OWI was allowing the public to see them. The smiling face on the recruitment poster or the laughing soldiers in the Coca-Cola ad would still appear frequently, but next to them, in silent testimony, would also be the photographs or drawings of dead men. Photographers still avoided showing faces—because it seemed too much a violation of the dead man's privacy, and also because it would convey too negative an image. Columns such as Pyle's, however, gave an identity, a personality, and a memory to those who had died, reminding readers that each of those bodies had been a distinct individual. Each death was a hole torn in the fabric of the nation.

★　★　★

Complementing and contrasting Ernie Pyle's reportage about G.I.s was the work of Sgt. Bill Mauldin, the cartoonist and writer who was also a combat veteran. Pyle once featured Mauldin in a column, calling him "the finest cartoonist" of the war and describing the cartoons as not only "funny" but also "grim and real."[19] Interestingly, Pyle's column on Mauldin dates from the same month as the Waskow piece, a time when Pyle was particularly aware of that grimness. Pyle also gave the youthful Mauldin credit for being unusually mature in his work, high praise coming from a veteran journalist.[20]

At the time of the Pyle article, January 1944, Mauldin was working for the G.I. newspaper *The Stars and Stripes*. His cartoon series, *Up Front*, featured two of the more enduring representations of the American soldier in World War II: Willie and Joe. So bedraggled, wrinkled, muddied, and bearded were these two that they were natural comic images, and like the best comic figures in art and literature, they could humorously convey a very serious message. Willie and Joe often appear about to collapse from exhaustion, but their irony and pathos keep them standing, holding up the weight of army life and the drudgery of the dogfaces' existence.[21]

The visual rhetoric of these images is obvious. Mauldin constructs Willie and Joe as classic clown figures, adopting the iconography of circus and vaudevillian comedy (already apparent in some prewar comic strips) to the specific circumstances of war. The sad expression, the slightly caved-in posture, the beard-darkened face, and begrimed and torn clothing—all these come from a preexisting theatrical pattern for portraying clowns. In addition, the down-and-out nature of such clowns derives from class-based comedy, and Mauldin employs a dialect that indicates Willie's and Joe's lower-class origins and unrefined, though highly perceptive, intellects. Expressions such as "ya," "th," "yestiddy," "wot," and "fer" provide linguistic class markers that parallel the visual ones. In theater, such clowns burlesque upper-class manners by wearing the tattered remnants of once-elegant clothing and by using expressions that both imitate and mock class distinctions. *Up Front* burlesques the Army hierarchy by representing a uniform that is almost unrecognizable for its wrinkles and dirt, while the language satirizes both class pretensions and military protocol. Thus, Willie and

Joe are the perpetually downtrodden, powerless to change their circumstances and able merely to endure them. Yet from their underclass position as dogfaces, they can comment ironically on the painful lot of the infantryman. Although the dangers of combat plague them, the unpleasant circumstances of daily life often cause them more immediate grief. Lack of proper food, clothing, and shelter throws them back into a comically primitive existence. In addition, the Army's persistent "chickenshit" causes the greatest irony for the long-suffering pair. Power without reason or sensitivity, hierarchy without respect for community, and the combination of arrogance and ignorance that seem to govern the worst of those in authority become the focus of the simple ironic comments of the two weary veterans. Servicemen took great pleasure in this celebration of their own woes, making Mauldin quite popular with his G.I. readers. Mauldin's work also reached a stateside audience when his book *Up Front* was published in 1945. His insight into the G.I. life, his gift for comic characterization and ironic situations, and his direct experience with the war, all led to the complex achievement of his cartoons. He places Willie and Joe in numerous situations, sometimes in combat, often in discomfort, and always with some appropriate quip or comment.

Yet death is never far from the margins of these cartoons. *Up Front* offers a great deal of gallows humor, jokes attempting to take men's minds off constant discomfort and danger. In one representative cartoon, as both men crouch in a foxhole, with shellfire and bullets all around, one quips, "I feel like a fugitive from the law of averages."[22] The caption sums up the tone of much of Mauldin's work as well as the quality of G.I. experience. Its honesty and ironic bite speak directly to the experience of the combat veteran, for whom death or injury seems inevitable. Staring into the sad, hang-dog expressions of Willie and Joe, we see them as ennobled clowns, but we also know that, as with all such clowns, those sad eyes have seen a great deal—perhaps far too much.

★   ★   ★

While Ernie Pyle wrote the G.I. narratives and Mauldin presented the cartoon images, others provided the photography. Many photographers covered the war, and each gave it a particular sense of style and emphasis, but one in particular comes to mind whose work for *Life* created some of the most enduring images of the American G.I. This was Robert Capa, the Hungarian-born photographer already known for his coverage of the Spanish Civil War. Of all Capa's photographic accomplishments, one set of images stands out: capturing the first day of the "Great Crusade" in Europe, D-Day. Capa landed on Omaha Beach, the site of some of the bloodiest fighting and some of Capa's best-remembered black-and-white photographs. We see ordinary G.I.s, their drab uniforms a shade darker because they are soaked with sea-water. We see the leaden sky and almost feel the chill of the water, in the unrelieved gray halftones that blend land, sea, clouds, and smoke into a depressing background. The photographs also seem blurred by the speed of soldiers, and the photographer, rushing to the beach under fire. They become even more compelling for seeming to capture that fleeting quality of the experience.

Yet intent was only part of the picture. Capa wanted to take as many photographs as he could, as clearly and sharply as he could. After all, Omaha Beach was not the place for fuzzy-focus art photography.[23] Very active that day, he took 106 shots before using up his film and securing quick transportation back to England. There, the photo lab bungled the developing process, and only eight photographs survived, with several of those blurred. Yet these imperfect images, conveying a sense of wild confusion, helped shape the historical memory of the fight for Omaha Beach. We see both artistic intent and realistic representation in what was actually a technical failure. We remember that G.I.s, soaked to the skin before landing, were dumped into water that was too deep. If they made it to the beach, they found it a hell of artillery and small-arms fire, littered with shattered equipment, corpses, and body parts. The whole plan had come apart, the whole invasion seemed about to collapse, but out of this blurred "fog of war," individuals and small groups finally struggled forward to secure objectives and to open up the beach exits. Capa's seemingly rushed and frantic pictures capture for many the essence of those first moments on the beach.[24] These images, too, construct for us the iconography of G.I. Joe in the context of the "crusading" mission demanded of him. Determined though temporarily confused, persistent though almost in shock, and ultimately, victorious, despite enormous casualties caused by planning errors and circumstances—that is how we remember G.I. Joe on D-Day. A handful of Capa's photographs have done much to shape our cultural memory of what that Day, that War, that "Crusade" meant—to those who fought and to later generations.

Along with many other journalists, Pyle, Mauldin, and Capa helped fashion for our culture the iconography, identity, and narrative of the U.S. fighting man in World War II. It would be this image, character, and story that would provide the fundamental material of films and books for decades after the war—some attempting a genuine representation of the war, and many sanitizing and sentimentalizing the experiences. And given that the G.I. was seen as "Everyman," most who witness such representations feel capable of sharing in their meaning, whether or not that feeling is justified. What we have perceived is neither a clear picture nor an image deliberately blurred for purposes of art or obfuscation—rather, it is the uncertain imagery that grows from many different, often competing attempts to represent some part of vast and complicated events. With such material as Capa's D-Day photographs, our inferences become more influential than either historical fact or artistic intent. Likewise, our cultural knowledge of "G.I. Joe" comes not only what his authors constructed but also what we have refashioned through multiple readings, viewings, and interpretations. Ultimately, G.I. Joe is as much a product of his audiences as of his artists and writers.

Crusade on Film—G.I. Joe on Screen

Perhaps the most compelling cinematic representations of G.I.s came from wartime documentaries by talented Hollywood directors in uniform. Such films not only helped shape American perceptions of the war at the time but also prepared audiences for the visual iconography and narrative structures of later Hollywood war films, many of which incorporated combat and documentary footage to heighten their authenticity. Two of the more important among these documentaries are William Wyler's *The Memphis Belle: A Story of a Flying Fortress* (1944) and John Huston's *The Battle of San Pietro* (1945).

Wyler was another Hollywood luminary who brought his directing talent into the service, and his documentary *The Memphis Belle* is one of the more effective representations of the air war in Europe. Filmed in 1943, it supports the Air Force's unproven strategic doctrine of precision, daylight bombing of industrial targets. Its advocates dominated the Army Air Force, but other Army leaders believed that aircraft should be used largely in direct support of ground troops. Moreover, U.S. strategic bomber losses over Europe throughout 1943 were becoming prohibitively high, and some American leaders wanted to end the campaign.

Wyler's film focuses on the B-17 bomber named *Memphis Belle* and its crew as they are about to go on their twenty-fifth mission.[25] A tour of duty for bomber crews was then twenty-five missions, but no single plane and crew based in England had yet completed all twenty-five. Airmen knew the statistics, and many questioned whether they could survive a full tour. In response, the film would celebrate the first crew to reach the twenty-five-mission milestone and so be rotated home. Serving as an Air Force officer and filmmaker, Wyler stationed himself and his film crew at an English bomber base. They not only spent time with the bomber crews on the ground but also accompanied the *Memphis Belle* on bombing missions.[26] Along with building Air Force morale, the film sought to persuade home-front audiences to maintain support for America's daylight, strategic-bombing campaign in Europe. Despite the film's obvious propagandistic intent, it still conveys a sense of authenticity, both in representing the crewmembers and in its use of actual combat footage. The sequences showing enemy fighter attacks give the film a unique visual power, and for its time, *The Memphis Belle* did not shy away from confronting the gruesome realities of air war. We see bombers going down during the mission, and we see wounded crewmembers afterward. Audiences realize that the deaths on screen are real, and that a B-17 spinning out of control is no Hollywood special effect.

Crafting a film to support a radically new form of warfare, Wyler chooses to begin with the visual dissonance between the peaceful English countryside and the harsh realities of the adjacent bomber base. The dissonant effect is enhanced in an early, continuous panning shot that leads directly from the landscape to a bomber, heightening surprise and underlining the idea that this is a new kind of war. This, we are told, is an "Air Front." Another sequence focuses on the nose section of a parked B-17, looking from below, with the bomber in silhouette and light coming through the transparent Plexiglas nose and its aluminum framing. In the visual field of this shot, the fuselage and portions of the wing form a partial cross, perhaps reinforcing the symbolism of the war as a crusade.

We move quickly from the introduction to exposition about the ground crews preparing for a mission. The voiceover tells us that this is a mission to "deliver" the bombs to "specific" points in Wilhelmshaven, Germany, ironically labeled as a "hauling job." From ground crews, Wyler shifts to the briefing for aircrews. Their youth is acknowledged as the voice over uses a direct address: "Not too long ago, you were sitting like this in a college or a high school classroom." The film will make starkly clear, however, that failure in this "school" is deadly. Moving out to the planes on the hardstands, Wyler shows the crew going through a last-minute discussion before boarding. On the plane's nose, we see the

Vargas-like image of a woman in a strapless, one-piece bathing suit—the aircraft's symbolic namesake. This "Memphis Belle" is the kind of erotic image often painted on aircraft, though. For the crewmen, her image connects the plane to a nostalgic world not only of the overtly erotic and feminine but also of the romanticized past. The image suggests the lines from Randall Jarrell's poem "Losses": "In bombers we named for girls, / we burned the cities we had learned about in school."[27]

The subsequent takeoff sequence in *The Memphis Belle* provides some of the film's most dramatic moments. Bombers line up on the runway, engines running, and then one begins rolling forward, its engines roaring at full-throttle. We see the process repeated, with each aircraft moving from a slow, lumbering motion to the point where it lifts off and begins to soar like an enormous bird of prey. Throughout, Wyler cuts effectively to balance side, forward, overhead, and rear shots of the different planes.[28] In subsequent years, other documentaries, and also fictional feature films such as *Twelve O'Clock High*, would borrow from Wyler's specific takeoff, landing, and in-flight footage to add credibility to their stories.

During the early part of the mission, Wyler provides impressive shots of the bomber formations while the commentary explains the purpose of these missions to attack the enemy's industrial heartland. This exposition serves as indoctrination, for the film misses no opportunity to proclaim the strategic-bombing doctrine. No mention is made of "collateral damage" although the close proximity of civilian housing to industrial targets meant that even so-called "precision bombing" would kill many civilians. As the mission proceeds, the film also introduces us to each member of the *Belle*'s crew, providing name, hometown, and former occupation (just as in Ernie Pyle's columns). Several had been in college while the others had worked in a variety of occupations. At their various crew stations, the men appear focused on the business at hand, sometimes smiling for the camera to break the tension. When the aircraft climbs above 10,000 feet, the crew dons oxygen masks, making them look strangely alien. Throughout, Wyler crosscuts from shots of the plane's interior to ones of the bombers in formation, and viewers see an overwhelming force that will not be deterred from its objectives. Yet the film also reveals the dangers and the strangeness of high-altitude combat, commenting that men see "reflections in Plexiglas," images they have seen nowhere "but in a dream"—language that Jarrell echoes in "The Death of the Ball Turret Gunner."[29]

When the planes finally cross the German coast, the narrator makes additional attempts to justify strategic bombing. Though the German cities seem just like our own, the film notes that they are home to a people who have "twice within one generation brought unprecedented suffering upon the world." The film implies that, should our bombs accidentally fall upon the homes of this destructive people, then they have only themselves to blame. Like so much wartime propaganda, the film's rhetorical strategy is to eliminate the distinction between the enemy military and the enemy people. Even so, it consistently supports the strategic assumption that the "precision" bombing will hit only "specific" targets, limiting civilian casualties.

The film reaches its climax with the attack sequence, as enemy flak and fighters try to stop the American bombers. When the group finally drops their bombs, we see explosions and subsequent fires caused miles below. Then the planes turn for home, and enemy fighters attack again. Voices of crewmembers on the interphone, sometimes excited and sometimes calm, point out the positions of attacking planes. Of course, the voices would have been recorded after the fact, so they sound more restrained than during actual combat. The camera work, however, is stunning, capturing the overwhelming speed of fighters attacking at 300 to 400 miles per hour. Barely glimpsing the rushing fighters, the audience gets some sense of how difficult it is for the B-17's gunners to hit them. The camera often shudders from the vibration of the heavy machine guns in the aircraft. Over the years, many viewers have grown familiar with this footage, in documentaries and fictional films alike, but the original audience must have found this an extraordinary experience. We also see several B-17s hit. Some fall away slowly, trailing smoke, but one spins out of control. In the last case, we hear of only five parachutes from the ten-man crew, and we know that five men are trapped in the doomed bomber.

Wyler crosscuts back to the base, where he reinforces a commonplace in so many films about the air war: ground personnel waiting and watching. Finally, the planes begin to arrive, and we see them land one by one, some untouched, but many damaged and carrying wounded or dead crewmembers. As aircrew emerge, we witness their full range of reactions—relief, joy, anger, and grief. Tension builds as we wait to see if the *Memphis Belle* is among the surviving aircraft (though we know it will be, or there would be no film). At last, "she" appears and buzzes the field before landing to the cheers of all on the ground. As the plane stops, the crew emerges, and one kisses the ground—he and his fellow crewmembers have survived to go home. Wyler tells the story of strategic bombing through the experience of one aircraft and crew successfully completing their final mission, and despite his film's

propagandistic elements, it is both cinematically and rhetorically powerful, establishing much of the standard imagery and structure of later
films about the air war.

★ ★ ★

John Huston, though an experienced screenwriter, was relatively new
to directing when he joined the Army Signal Corps to make films during the war. Best known of his Army documentaries is *The Battle of San
Pietro*, a powerful representation of the bitter cost of modern combat.
Huston brought his tough, unrelenting vision to the film, so much so
that, although his original fifty-minute version was shown to American
troops, the later commercial release was significantly trimmed.[30] Shot
from October through December 1943, the film focused on the U.S.
36th Infantry Division, which had fought almost continuously since
landing at Salerno in early September. These troops were now at the
edge of the Liri Valley, whose road was essential for advancing north
to Rome. The battle-weary infantry battalions of the 36th now faced
another set of hills before and around the village of San Pietro, where
fighting would be even grimmer than what had come before.

A faux "travel guide" sequence opens the film, with Huston's grav-
elly voiceover describing the history, people, and points of interest with
understated irony. Even more ironic are shots showing the obvious
devastation. In contrast to the travel guide clichés, the camera reveals
the shattered church, the rubble-strewn streets, and ultimately, a child's
dead body. The voiceover acknowledges that this is not a normal year
because the war has come to San Pietro. As in this opening sequence,
images of dead bodies get a great deal of attention throughout the
film—bodies of Italian peasants as well as bodies of both German and
American soldiers. The pictures carry a terrible honesty and need little editorial comment. Huston wisely keeps the commentary lean and
focused, allowing the images to tell the story by showing actions and
their results.

Before the attack, a map sequence traces out the positions of the
opposing troops relative to the village and surrounding hills. Though
the graphics are rather primitive, they convey the feel of a military
briefing. Now that we know what the men have been ordered to do, we
see them alone and in groups. They sit and stand, talk and keep silent,
smoke and laugh nervously, awaiting the inevitable. Again and again
we see the faces, each distinctive, yet all sharing the common misery
of frontline combat troops.[31] Here and throughout the film, Huston

creates the kind of visual sequences that will be fundamental to combat films, documentary or fictional, for the next two decades. Effective use of light intensifies the film's depressing tone, especially because the skies seem permanently overcast, belying the image of "sunny Italy." What sun does shine seems pale, as if shining through a haze of smoke, so bringing little light and less warmth. The soldiers look as if they are never warm, always bundled in their uniforms.

After a spectacular bombardment, the attack goes forward, soldiers burdened with heavy overcoats and equipment. The iconic G.I. helmet identifies these men as American. As they advance, they move cautiously but steadily, up the forbidding slopes or across the valley floor among orchards and olive groves.[32] They know their jobs and the risks, and they go forward nonetheless, appearing more like workmen than warriors. Then they hit the minefields, and enemy machine guns pin them down as mortar rounds come crashing in. The troops run, scatter, fall, and hug even the smallest depression or cover they can find. One, standing by a tree, is hit and falls like a broken toy. Follow-up attacks gain no more ground, and the pattern repeats itself, again and again.[33]

The film visually links the actions of this campaign with those of World War I—ceaseless and often pointless attacks that went nowhere, leaving survivors huddled in holes. Such imagery would be familiar to Americans from Lewis Milestone's influential film *All Quiet on the Western Front* (1930), and Huston builds on that legacy. After the attacks, we see dead American soldiers being collected and placed in white body bags. We even glimpse their bruised, scarred, dirty faces, with eyes closed and sunken.[34] The motions of the graves' registration troops are not reverent or elegant, merely workmanlike. They, too, have a job to do, and they want nothing more than to get it over with. Despite terrible losses, the process of attack and retreat continues through several cycles until the American troops finally capture flanking positions in the hills. Then the Germans evacuate San Pietro, and the Americans cautiously occupy the abandoned town.

The film closes with the Italians returning to their shattered homes. Huston offers a montage of scenes showing the people resuming their daily routines while both grieving over their losses and celebrating their new freedom. We see many images of rehabilitation and rebuilding as the people reconstruct both their town and their lives. Represented in a patronizing tone, the Italians are shown as a primitive people who, in their simplicity, believe that the battle was fought merely to liberate them. Of course, the Americans "know" this liberation was merely the secondary consequence of strategic necessity.

These final scenes also introduce a religious element to the film, amplified by a score using the Mormon Tabernacle Choir and St. Brendan's Boys Choir. As the chorus swells, we see a woman doing her wash in a fountain while an American medical truck with a red cross drives by, suggesting both mercy and divine purpose in this fight. These images, along with those of a religious procession and the broken statue of San Pietro, clearly link the film to the crusading theme articulated in so many representations of the campaigns in Europe. The sense of the struggle and the cause, the arguments of *Why We Fight*, still pervade this film, as they do all such military releases, despite any skepticism that Huston might suggest.

The final segment seems the film's weakest point. One wonders if this resulted from Huston's own lapse, or from the influence of an Army command that wanted to justify its actions. In either case, it is disappointing to see an otherwise powerful documentary film add a superficial veneer of religious authority as if to justify the irredeemable loss and trauma of combat. Just prior to the return of the villagers, however, we witness the digging of graves for the Americans. We learn that one regiment alone required over 1,100 replacements as a result of the battle, over a third of its effective combat strength. We see the surviving Americans, again smoking and relaxing, but Huston notes that many we see on screen have since died at places such as Cassino. He also tells us that there will be a thousand more San Pietros before the war ends. It is easy enough to work out the grim statistics—that would mean over a million Americans killed and wounded in this war, a relatively accurate estimate in the end.

Despite lapses, *The Battle of San Pietro* offers a starker representation of the war than do most documentaries of the time. Its combat footage is compellingly realistic, revealing the tension, terror, pain, and death experienced by the troops. We see the dead—Italians, Germans, and Americans—and we learn that many more will die before the war ends. Crusades call their ranks to service, to sacrifice, even to martyrdom, which may sound clean and uplifting when taken out of the context of actual death and suffering. Huston's film gives a face, first alive and then dead, to that martyr's role, and so we see the war's cost in very concrete terms. Few directors can claim to have represented World War II combat with this level of stark honesty.

★　★　★

Although American audiences viewed documentaries about the war in Europe, Hollywood struggled to complete major feature films on the subject. Two of the better wartime combat films—the only two that focused on American ground combat in Europe—were completed during 1945 and were released in the months just after the war ended. These were William Wellman's *The Story of G.I. Joe* and Lewis Milestone's *A Walk in the Sun*, and each established a new level of gritty realism in portraying the war. Moreover, each showed American soldiers, in leadership positions, who break down psychologically under the prolonged stress of combat.

Wellman originally turned down *The Story of G.I. Joe*, but Ernie Pyle convinced him to take the project.[35] The director then threw himself whole-heartedly into the production, using actual soldiers as extras and forcing actors to live with the troops so they would understand their characters. As a result, *The Story of G.I. Joe* became one of the more effective and accurate films about ground combat made during the war. The central character is war correspondent Ernie Pyle (Burgess Meredith) since the film is based on Pyle's writing. Using Pyle's character as a narrator, the film traces the progress of one infantry company from the early campaigns in North Africa and through the Italian campaign, culminating with the Battle of Monte Cassino.

The Story of G.I. Joe is a small-unit story, with its standard Hollywood microcosm of the American melting pot, including a Polish American (Sergeant Warnicki) and an Italian American (Private Dondaro). At the center, along with the reflective Pyle, is Captain Bill Walker (Robert Mitchum), based on the actual Captain Waskow of Pyle's column (see above). Mitchum plays Walker with a quiet, youthful intensity, creating a character who is tough on the surface but deeply committed to his men. Meredith's version of Pyle accurately evokes a sense of fatherly affection for the men of whom he writes. He observes far more than he talks, and his narration echoes passages from the actual columns. Freddie Steele as Warnicki and Wally Cassell as Dondaro are both effective in their supporting roles. As a platoon sergeant, Warnicki provides steady leadership for his men and consistent support for Walker. Private Dondaro is the platoon goldbrick as well as its "dame-crazy" Latin character—here an Italian American but not unlike the Hispanic "Soose" Alvarez in *Guadalcanal Diary* (see chapter three). Dramatically, Warnicki's reliability balances Dondaro's clownishness, but each ultimately proves more complex than might be assumed at first.

The story begins when Pyle joins C-Company before its first battle in North Africa, and it concludes in Italy, after Walker's death, as the surviving members of C-Company are finally marching toward Rome. The North African segments serve to establish characters and relationships while the combat sequences occur mostly in Italy, during the film's second half. Joining both halves is a brief montage with narration by Pyle. He rejoins C-Company as it is marching down an Italian road, learning that Walker is now the company commander. The film then shifts to a relatively convincing attack sequence as C-Company assaults a town that resembles the rubble-filled San Pietro of Huston's documentary. Though Wellman represents the house-to-house fighting with few clichés, some Hollywood exaggeration persists, as when Dondaro ducks into an abandoned cafe and meets an Italian woman who quickly responds to his advances. In a parallel sequence, Warnicki and Walker try to root out German snipers from a shattered church. With two snipers dead, the obviously Catholic Warnicki kneels to pray, but a third sniper's bullet knocks off his helmet. Walker cuts down the last sniper, and the town is now "secure." Despite the clichéd qualities of these two scenes, the overall attack sequence still has an authentic feel to it.[36]

After the town sequence, the film becomes more static visually but more powerful emotionally. As the men reach the base of Monte Cassino, their advance stalls, and the action begins to resemble World War I. Opposed by entrenched Germans on the high ground who can call down artillery on the hapless Americans, C-Company is reduced to burrowing into the hillsides. In endless rain and mud, men hunker down to avoid shelling. They must also engage in patrol after fruitless patrol. We see little actual combat, only the men shuffling forward and then returning later, stumbling with fatigue, always missing one or two more men. The film does not flinch from showing the painful conditions of everyday life in muddy holes as well as the horrific cost of the fighting. Both Walker and Warnicki feel the strain, but the latter still does more than his part, going on extra patrols to look after his men. During this sequence, the film frankly confronts the psychological trauma of combat, trauma that eventually overwhelms Warnicki. After returning from one particularly bad patrol, he finally manages to listen to the "victory record" from his family, using a Victrola he had earlier taken from the town. Upon hearing the voices of his wife and son, he breaks down completely. The voices open him emotionally, leaving him vulnerable to all the pain he has felt and witnessed. He goes on a rampage, striking out wildly at the other men. When finally subdued, Warnicki must be turned over to "the medics," as much a casualty as any of the wounded or dead.

The final attack on Cassino makes liberal use of footage (both actual and reconstructed fighting sequences) from Huston's San Pietro film, spliced with shots of the principal actors. The film ends at a different location, with the troops resting by a road, at the bottom of a hill. Once again, Pyle joins them. We see mules being led down the hill, each carrying a corpse that is removed and laid on the ground. One final mule is led by a limping Dondaro, and when men lift the corpse, we see that it is Captain Walker. Now the scene faithfully replays the impromptu memorial service depicted in Pyle's "Waskow" column, but afterward, the troops once again shoulder their packs and march forward, up the hill. Pyle follows them as his words eulogize the dead and honor those still in the fight.

Despite the obvious sentimentality and the expressed confidence in final victory, this is still a somber ending in many respects. *The Story of G.I. Joe* differs from most war films of its time because it not only shows that men die but also that the "unscathed" survivors may be casualties as well. To use words from Pyle's final, unpublished column, they have the images of dead men "burned into their brains."[37] The weight of this psychological burden cannot be lifted easily; it must be shared, in one sense, by the whole nation. With some degree of honesty, the film shows that not just weak or untrustworthy men break down in battle, an old Hollywood convention, but reliable men such as Warnicki also succumb to combat trauma. A rather grim message underlies the film's overt support for the war—not only will this be a hard and costly war to win but it will also scar a generation.[38]

By 1945, a growing number of Americans had begun to realize that the reality of the war was not as suggested in the early newsreels, advertisements, or public-service announcements.[39] The war was a living hell, and many more men would die or be permanently disabled than had been originally anticipated. It was only in the last eighteen months of the war that the true cost became evident because only then were truly large numbers of Americans engaged in combat. Once censored by the OWI, representations of physical and psychological losses were allowed in films because the government knew it could no longer hide these images. People needed to recognize what the war would really cost if they were to support it fully. *The Story of G.I. Joe* provided, for its time, an unusually dark vision of these costs. This material would never have seen the light of day in 1942, but in 1945, it was necessary if the government's war efforts were to remain credible.

★   ★   ★

Another grim film made as the war ended is *A Walk in the Sun* (1945), directed by Lewis Milestone, well known for *All Quiet on the Western*

Front. While action in *The Story of G.I. Joe* covers a year and a half, *A Walk in the Sun* adheres to Aristotelian dramatic unities, limiting its action to one place on a single day. Indeed, the entire action takes little more than six hours, from the predawn darkness of the landing to the final assault on a German-occupied farmhouse a few miles inland. Based on a novel by Harry Brown, *A Walk in the Sun* explores the personalities and relationships of the men in one platoon, all revealed under the stressful conditions of the day when Allied troops landed at Salerno, Italy. Using this microcosm of the war, the film attempts to convey the essential character of the American G.I. in his multiform variations.

During the process of this ironically named "little walk in the warm Italian sun," the troops often find themselves cut off from both higher headquarters and other units. The lieutenant and platoon sergeant die before the men leave the beach, so the unit must depend on its own resources to carry out a mission that may still be important, or which events may have made irrelevant. Such isolation in the vastness of the overall battle is quite consistent with the recollections of actual combat veterans. For combat soldiers, war is experienced road by road, ditch by ditch, and meal by meal. It is an eternal present, often spent waiting, without a clear sense of what will happen next. There is also the deadening perception that this process, barring serious wounding or death, will go on forever. Platoon scout Private Archimbeau (Norman Lloyd) captures such fatalism by repeatedly saying, "All I know is that in 1958, we'll be fighting the Battle of Tibet." The war will go on because it is so large as to constitute a universe, with its own laws and powers far beyond the grasp of one small group of G.I.s. This view is the basis for what will become, in the hands of writers like Norman Mailer and James Jones, the neo-naturalism of war fiction (see chapter seven).

The film opens with stock framing devices, including a disappointing "folksong" score. In the darkened landing boat heading for the beach, we see a close-up of a watch showing 6:00 a.m. We also hear the voice of Private "Windy" Craven (John Ireland), who serves as an internal commentator on the film's action. Windy is engaged in two ongoing discourses: sometimes he speaks to himself aloud, but often he mentally pens letters to his sister Frances, writing them in his head and sometimes vocalizing as well. It is not always clear when he is talking to himself or when he is composing the imaginary letter, and perhaps it makes no difference. Whoever the intended audience, Windy's running monologue offers insights into a soldier's life and reflections on the actions of the platoon.

While some characters stand out more fully, the platoon as a whole seems the real main character. However, we experience the platoon as small subgroups who reveal their personalities and relationships through ongoing patterns of interaction. The most serious and central group is focused on Sergeant Bill Tyne (Dana Andrews), one of the platoon's three squad leaders. Connected to Tyne is Sergeant Eddie Porter, third in command behind the dead lieutenant and platoon sergeant. Having assumed command after the others are killed, Porter is clearly uncomfortable. Although willing to go into danger himself, he seems unable to handle responsibility for the whole unit. He consults frequently with Tyne, who remains calm and helpful. Porter's psychological breakdown will force Tyne to take over during a crisis—a central aspect of the film's story.

Contrasting the serious conflicts of platoon leadership is the cluster of relationships built around the machine gun section, mostly focusing on the Italian American gunner, Private Rivera (Richard Conte), and the Jewish assistant gunner, Private Jake Friedman (George Tyne). The ongoing banter between these two not only establishes them as a classic "Flagg/Quirt" comic pair but also provides another ironic commentary on the action of the film.[40] Though Milestone uses these ethnic stereotypes as comic relief, Rivera and Friedman are more complex than mere clowns. Their sarcastic repartee reveals an intense bond between men who constantly fight side by side and have learned intuitively to depend on one another. Moreover, by shifting from the tension of the Tyne-Porter relationship to the wisecracking of Rivera and Friedman, Milestone achieves an unusually effective tonal balance between the deadly seriousness of combat and the absurd ironies experienced by those who must fight.

Milestone also uses the Rivera/Friedman pair for a pattern of repeated linguistic ironies. The most common is ironic repetition that "Nobody dies," an expression that the novel itself identifies as the "platoon cliché."[41] The first man to utter the expression is Private Trasker, shortly after the lieutenant has been mortally wounded by a shell fragment. Ironically, Trasker will be one of the first killed after the landing—shot in the mouth, in mid-sentence, his language edited by a cruel fate. Windy, Rivera, and others use this expression often, usually shortly before or after someone's death. Each man who says it knows this statement to be contrary to fact. Everybody dies sometime, and combat infantrymen know that many of them will die, perhaps their whole platoon, before the war is over. But irony is the men's only defense against the constant assault on their psyches; it is the verbal/psychological "body armor" against the trauma of witnessing death after death. It is also a transgressive statement against the institutional powers of destruction, against wars and armies (theirs and ours), and against the power of death itself. It asserts the force of life even if only ironically. In this use of intricate verbal irony, both novel and film prepare the way for another form of postwar writing: the bitterly satiric, absurdist fiction of Joseph Heller's *Catch-22* and Kurt Vonnegut's *Slaughterhouse-Five*. In the contrary-to-fact use of language, the verbal act denying reality, we have the fundamental source of all "Catch-22s" (see chapter seven).

While Rivera and Friedman keep up a dialogue that superficially lightens the action, Tyne and Porter confront serious issues, especially Porter's decline into a psychotic state. On the road toward the farmhouse, the platoon is strafed again, resulting in more casualties. At a subsequent rest stop in a patch of woods, Porter finally cracks, sobbing and huddling on the ground. Windy comments that Porter has been wounded as much as if he had been hit by a bullet—a perceptive analysis for the time. But there is little opportunity to sympathize with Porter. German forces are coming down the road, and Tyne, whom Porter asked to take charge, must quickly rally the platoon to attack a German halftrack. The platoon successfully ambushes the vehicle and suffers no casualties, confirming Tyne's leadership ability.

As they march on, eventually reaching the farmhouse, Tyne himself begins to suffer the burdens of command. Yet he also demonstrates an ability to work with the other men, taking advice as well as making decisions, and so making the burden more bearable. Tyne accepts Windy's plan to outflank the farmhouse and to blow the bridge behind it. The assault on the house itself will proceed as soon as the exploding bridge distracts the defenders, but while waiting, Tyne still experiences the nervous tension that leadership imposes. As the platoon begins crawling through high grass to reach the house, Tyne sees the whole landscape swirl surrealistically. He seems about to break down himself until he finally hears the explosions at the bridge, and then he rises to lead the men in their successful assault. The farmhouse captured, Windy checks his watch—it is noon, and a mere six hours have passed. Throughout the film, he has been writing to "Dear Frances" in his imagination, and now he pulls paper and pencil from his pocket and begins writing: "Dear Frances, we just blew up a bridge and took a farmhouse. It was so easy—so terribly easy." Again the grotesque irony of his construction is obvious to both the character and the audience—nothing was easy.[42]

A Walk in the Sun is a moving film about the experience of ordinary soldiers. Despite the annoying folksong score, Milestone still provides an insightful depiction of World War II ground combat. The film is an exceptionally strong character study, made more forceful by its dramatic concentration of time and place and its effective pacing. In a varied and complex style, the cinematography captures both the tension of waiting and the sudden shock of battle. The imagery, cutting, and simple but ironic dialogue emphasize the psychological isolation of each soldier and the social-psychological dynamics of the entire unit. Windy's comments reveal a keen awareness of the motives and feelings of others, and sometimes they offer insightful reflections on whatever simple image or object catches his eye. Much of what the men say is openly satiric, as when Rivera quips, "Life in the army is simple: either you live or you die." By focusing on simple conversations, cutting from group to group during lulls in the action, Milestone allows the idiosyncrasies of character and relationship to emerge naturally, conveying the character of the platoon as a whole.

Film scholar Bernard Dick has criticized *A Walk in the Sun*, accusing Milestone of having abandoned the realism of *All Quiet on the Western Front* for a tonal "pictorialism"; in contrast, he applauds Wellman's *The Story of G.I. Joe* as a better and more authentic film.[43] Yet Wellman's film does have considerable flaws; for example, the wedding sequence seems forced and sentimental, while Dondaro's characterization is uneven and heavily clichéd. The film's pacing and development also leave something to be desired. After its first defeat, we never see what converts C-Company into a real "outfit"; we just catch up with it about nine months later in Italy and are told that they have become "killers." In fact, no one seems much different. It is not until the Cassino sequence, whose depiction is historically inaccurate, that we see the psychological strain on the troops. *The Story of G.I. Joe* combines both social and sentimental realism, but it succeeds largely because of the power of Meredith and Mitchum in their roles of Pyle and Walker, respectively.

In contrast, Milestone and scriptwriter Robert Rossen worked closely with Harry Brown's understated and ironic novel to make *A Walk in the Sun* into a tense and powerful film. Subtly expressionistic photographic techniques, interwoven with more realistic ones, suggest the difficulties of translating war onto the screen. In many ways, the film is strongest in the sense of its own fissures and fragments, a quality that even its director may grasp only intuitively or subconsciously—much as the tonal features of *All Quiet on the Western Front* suggest an intuitive grasp of how to visualize fear and anguish. Indeed, *A Walk in the Sun* is about the combined verbalizing and visualizing of complex emotional responses to combat. It is rife with contradictions and ambiguities: constantly being in a group, but always being alone; being part of a major battle, but being a unit cut off and confused; focusing on the immediate pleasures and pains of life, in the midst of the equally immediate and constant threat of death; confronting the fact of death with the impossible statement, "Nobody dies"; and facing trauma with the comment that "It was so easy—so terribly easy." Whereas Wellman's film leaves us with the completely un-ironic speech by Pyle, Milestone's film closes with odd and inconsistent juxtapositions. We see wounded Americans in the field around the house, crawling forward like dying animals. We see no faces, for they look downward at the anonymous earth over which they crawl. Even when the fighting ends, no one rushes to aid the wounded. Indeed, the uninjured act as though nothing has happened, and we see most of the principals leaving the farmhouse with some form of victory trophy. This inconsistency may be a flaw in Milestone's sense of realistic visual continuity, but we may also regard it as an intuitive insight into combat soldiers' psychological defense mechanisms. In his novel *The Thin Red Line* (see chapter seven), World War II veteran James Jones describes the soldiers assembled on the beach, looking at the wounded and dying laid out before them. The two groups seem to exist in totally different universes—the dead and the wounded have become part of another realm, and those who remain untouched physically seek also to remain unscarred psychically—walls come up, and shields cover the mind. Such barriers are always present but never spoken of directly. Milestone's G.I. is not whole, but fragmented; his fissures and cracks covered over, not to disguise them but to highlight them. The very covering is so obviously ironic, in word or image, that the fissures become even more apparent. Indeed, although *The Story of G.I. Joe* and *A Walk in the Sun* deserve praise for their willingness to confront some of the war's brutal realities, Milestone's film is by far the darker work. While Wellman's film leaves us with a statement of purpose and value, Milestone's leaves us with ambiguous images and statements that consciously deny the reality we see, thus leading us into the far more tortured psychology of the deeply traumatized. In postwar writing, such as the poetry of Randall Jarrell and Howard Nemerov, as well as in the fiction of Mailer and Jones, this kind of brutal irony will be merely the starting point for various descents into hell. In the satirical novels of Heller and Vonnegut, such irony will be the governing principle of an increasingly absurd universe. But in Milestone's film, perhaps subconsciously, the director has recognized the fundamental fact that modern war traumatizes so deeply that identity, relationships, perception, and our very language are called into question. Nothing can ever be quite what we say, quite what we mean, and yet in our attempts to avoid saying the obvious, we reveal it.

The Story of G.I. Joe and *A Walk in the Sun* must also be recognized as important films that break through a major barrier—the revelation of psychological casualties. Unlike most films made during the war, these show American soldiers who break down and become incapacitated as a result of "combat exhaustion." Moreover, these are not just any soldiers but platoon sergeants, the old reliable war horses of combat films. By 1945 the government had already relaxed censorship regulations about showing U.S. combat dead, but only at the war's end was it willing to accept the representation of something that, for many viewers, was even more troubling: the psychological casualty. Those who grew up with post-Vietnam-era films may find it difficult to understand the significance of *The Story of G.I. Joe* and *A Walk in the Sun*; they showed that the ordinary soldier in the "great crusade" was often beset by demons.

"This Is Where I Came In"—Crusade in the Film Canister

No war had ever been represented in so many ways, for so many audiences, as was World War II. Along with traditional written reportage and the work of visual artists, photography and film recorded almost every battle. Radio broadcast news also came of age at this time, giving a voice and real-time coverage to the war's events. Film, however, has exercised the greatest influence in shaping our collective cultural memory. In millions of feet of exposed film, we can see everything from the earliest acts of the German Blitzkrieg in 1939 to the Japanese surrender aboard the battleship USS *Missouri* in 1945. By seeing just a few seconds of film, a few hundred frames, many of us know already that we are in the context of World War II, and we can often recall the general situation being depicted. When Americans think of the war, they usually have films running in their imagination.

Just as the war produced a great surplus of materiel, it also produced a great surplus of images that could be appropriated for multiple uses. Documentary film footage, especially combat footage, helped to influence Hollywood's style of making feature films about the war.

Moreover, the footage could be integrated directly into those films, giving them an unprecedented sense of authenticity. The combat sequences of such 1949 films as *Sands of Iwo Jima* and *Twelve O'Clock High* would be impossible without the aid of actual combat photography. True, films were made both before and after the war that made no use of combat footage, but they often strained credibility when portraying large battles, especially if the battles involved aircraft or ships.

From the 1940s into the 1960s, the World War II combat film became a unique cinematic experience because it used so much actual historical footage that fiction and history became inexorably intertwined. This quality amplified the mythic power of film, allowing it to take on the authority of history while retaining the imaginative power of fiction. Also, this blended style became particularly important in shaping America's mainstream representations of the war for more than twenty years after the war's end. After all, full access to combat footage, as well as to authentic equipment and settings (e.g., actual ships) was available only to those filmmakers whose work was acceptable to the branch of the military portrayed in the film. Those offering contrary views had fewer resources necessary to make a realistic-looking film. Films that followed the mainstream narrative of the war were "synoptic," telling parallel stories from parallel viewpoints, thereby mutually reinforcing each other's narratives. With more and better combat footage, military equipment, and technical advice, such films appear more authentic, thus making their messages more believable. In contrast, those films made without extensive military help often lose credibility because they seem to lack authenticity. This process intensified with each film that reinforced the mainstream narrative, making it ever more difficult to change the process until external political and cultural forces of the late 1960s caused a shift in the attitudes and perceptions of the American audience.

The creation of literature is quite different, and early criticism of the mainstream war narrative appears in novels, poetry, plays, and personal narratives. The resources in the hands of the more critical or skeptical writer were usually never less than those in the hands of one who wished to support the mainstream story. The only problem was that, successful as the literature might be (e.g., Norman Mailer's critically acclaimed, 1948 novel *The Naked and the Dead*), it had nowhere near the influence and power of film. For every American whose understanding of the war was shaped by a book, there were perhaps a hundred others whose attitudes were shaped by film. What is more, within a few years of the war's end, television extended film's influence further, with broadcasts of wartime and postwar films. During any one week, numerous World War II films might be shown as either local or network presentations. Throughout the two decades following the war, Americans were thus saturated with images of the war on film, primarily from films that supported a mainstream perspective on the war. A whole generation of Americans grew up with that process of saturation, and certainly some of the filmmakers among them, such as Steven Spielberg, were profoundly influenced by what they saw.

But it is not merely the filmmakers who have been affected. On March 29, 2003, Chuck Stevenson, a reporter for *48 Hours*, was embedded with marines who were bridging a river in Iraq. In describing the events before him, he felt dependent on allusions to film. "The war grew real to me as we came into the city of Nasiriyah," he said. "With choppers screaming overhead, it was like a World War II movie."[44] Though Stevenson here conflates an iconic image of Vietnam (the helicopter) with World War II, his association of combat with film hints at the powerful influence the cinematic representation of war has had on our culture. It seems we come not "trailing clouds of glory" but reels of film. In the past sixty years, the American imagination has been shaped not so much by what happened in World War II as by how it played out on screen. The "Great Crusade" may have begun as combat, but it has been kept alive as film.

CHAPTER FIVE

"Saddle Up! Let's Get Back to the War."

The Shot Seen 'Round the World

It was just another patrol.[1] An earlier one had reached the summit but
had yet to secure the area completely. Enemy soldiers still hid in undis-
covered bunkers, but the first patrol now needed more supplies. And
then there was the matter of a flag. That first flag probably seemed sufficient to the men, but once raised, it came to the attention of others.
Secretary of the Navy James Forrestal, observing the operations from
a ship offshore, wanted the flag as a souvenir. But it was the battalion's
flag, and battalion headquarters wanted to retain its own souvenir. So
someone at battalion gave the second patrol a replacement flag, a larger
one. Still, it was just another patrol.

Already at the summit was Associated Press photographer Joe
Rosenthal. He had missed the first patrol and flag-raising but had
climbed to the summit to take pictures of the invasion fleet. When
the second patrol reached the top, they hunted for a piece of pipe
to use as a flagpole. Though raising the flag always had symbolic
value, this was just one more job for a small group of exhausted
marines. As they set to work, they caught Rosenthal's attention,
and he prepared to take pictures. First Lieutenant Harold G. Schrier,
officer in command, organized the effort so that the first flagpole
would come down just before the new one was lifted into place. One
man attached the new flag to the pipe, others gathered around, and
five helped lift while a sixth positioned the bottom. During the few
seconds it took to raise the flag, Rosenthal quickly took his shot,
without even time to look into the viewfinder. It was all in a day's

work—the day being February 23, 1945, and the work site being Mt. Suribachi on Iwo Jima.

★   ★   ★

Later, some would claim that it had all been posed—such was the effect of the image.[2] Certainly, a veteran photographer such as Rosenthal knew what made for an effective photograph, but here he was shooting targets of opportunity. Moreover, he would neither see the film that was developed on Guam nor join the AP photo editor, John Bodkin, in deciding which photo to dispatch by wire. This classic image resulted from collective effort—tired marines at their jobs and Rosenthal snapping a sudden action—all focused through the discerning eye of an editor, without whose judgment the photograph might have remained unknown. Yet this image and its fame grew from an even more complex process, beginning with the simple fact that there were millions of men fighting a global war and thousands of photographers snapping hundreds of thousands of pictures. But the cultural constructs of preferred form and content had grown over time in the practices of the photographers themselves and in the minds of editors and publishers. This image-making process was intricately interwoven with the rhetoric of cultural icons and national myths. American identification with this image was not created *ex nihil*; rather, it grew from the patterns of cultural production that shaped and were reshaped by our ongoing attempts to represent a war in progress.

Of course the flag is a commonplace icon of patriotism whether as an actual picture or as a verbal reference. Always common in American public life, flags became even more ubiquitous during World War II—represented in poster art, photography, and motion pictures. Even the new medium of radio could evoke the flag verbally and musically by playing the national anthem. Yet one of the most popular representations of the flag during World War II came on a U.S. Treasury Department poster in support of War Bonds.[3] Artist Carl Paulsen had designed this 1942 poster, under the direction of the Outdoor Advertising Association of America. Its "landscape" format image shows only the flag and a portion of the flagpole. The flag is at an angle, as if being carried forward or being raised. Like many World War II government posters, its style recalls World War I poster art, like designs by James Montgomery Flagg and Howard Chandler Christy. The flag ripples in the wind, suggesting a restless energy, and combines with the pole's angle to distort the flag's shape into the appearance of a pennant. The image, though still, appears to be in motion, and as our eyes move from left to right, we sense the power of the wind. In the lower left-hand corner are the words "WE CAN...WE WILL...WE MUST!" followed by the name "Franklin D. Roosevelt." "*BUY* U.S. WAR SAVINGS BONDS & STAMPS *NOW*," the principal message, runs across the bottom. This traditional flag imagery apparently touched a deep emotional chord in the American people, and in 1942, this flag's rippling energy also caught both the nervousness and impatience of a people anxious to get the war going and over with.

While the Iwo Jima flag-raising photograph does not consciously imitate the 1942 Treasury Department poster, it is clear that flag imagery was a powerful commonplace in the American cultural psyche. When Bodkin saw the Rosenthal shot and proclaimed it "one for all time," he was perhaps unconsciously responding to the basic flag-raising iconography that had made the earlier poster so successful.[4] Careful visual analysis shows that the flag in the Iwo Jima photograph is at a similar angle and rippling in a similar fashion to the one pictured in the poster. Both convey a sense of energy moving from left to right in the image—in the poster, through the suggestion of the unseen wind, but in the photograph, through the implied motion of the six men, who are also moving from left to right. Their postures, besides creating a classic triangular composition in relation to the tilted pole, suggest as well the determined and forceful release of pent-up energy. Rosenthal did not know what kind of image he had captured, and even the editor was not likely conscious of any connection to the earlier poster. The restless, active, mobile quality in both images may very well be what makes each so compelling, though the Rosenthal photograph, given its inherent human element, is by far the more dramatic. Both images reflect a cultural pattern broader and deeper than either can encompass. The historical moment of the Rosenthal photograph, however, gave it an influence beyond its formal aesthetics because it seemed to symbolize the coming of an American victory. Within days, wire services spread the photo across the world. Soon a sculptor was at work on a model, and shortly thereafter, the image (as a painting) was featured on posters for the 7th War Loan, accompanied by the words, "Now—all together." It would eventually be translated into the bronze colossus that stands as a monument to the Marine Corps. It would also become the climactic tableaux of what very well may be the most influential American film ever made about World War II.

The Postwar Quartet: Four Films Define the
Mainstream and the Message

By late 1945, the movie industry sensed that the public was tired of war films, so Hollywood started retooling for peacetime work. Some films about returning veterans did appear, such as William Wyler's *The Best Years of Our Lives* (1946). With a few notable exceptions, however, the studios went back to their stock-in-trade—entertaining films for a broad popular audience. Increasingly, that audience included America's citizen soldiers, sailors, and airmen, who were returning to their civilian lives as quickly as possible. Within a year of Japan's surrender, our vast military force was dissolving back into the national population from which it had been drawn. Most veterans wanted to resume their lives where they had left off, but many had been irrevocably changed in ways they would not fully recognize for years. Some seemed to move easily beyond the horrors of war as if energized by their own survival, vigorously pursuing professional and personal lives. Some lapsed into a haunted, shadow existence, isolated from a society otherwise buoyed by unexpected prosperity. Most, however, began leading productive lives while still being burdened with some unspeakable memories. Like the duffle bag gathering dust in the basement, something was stowed and locked deep in veterans' collective consciousness, something so indescribable that they often felt incapable of sharing it. Those few veterans who did not conform to the national narrative of triumphal return were largely dismissed as either flawed or weak. Most civilians believed that, despite the war's terrible human tragedy, conditions in America had actually improved because of the war. Now they wanted to move into a bright future, not dwell on a painful past. Indeed, America had never been so powerful, either militarily or economically, and so Americans resisted the idea that combat trauma, whether physical or mental, had long-lasting consequences. Our national story was that we had endured the war, recovered from its losses, and now assumed our rightful, hegemonic place in a new world order. For the subsequent two decades, this became the underlying message of America's mainstream cultural narrative of World War II—what we came to call the "Good War."

For the military, the war's end brought a relatively swift change from unprecedented expenditures back to greater economic restraint. While it was unlikely that the armed services would ever be reduced to the small size of the interwar years, considerable reduction was inevitable. Without the personnel to use and maintain all of it, vast quantities of equipment stockpiled at home and abroad became more a liability than an asset. Some was scrapped, some given away, some stored for future use, and some sold wholesale (spawning that commercial phenomenon of postwar America, the military surplus store). Thousands of planes, once so vital to victory, stood wingtip to wingtip, assembled not on an airfield preparing to take off but waiting to be dismantled for their parts and materials. Ships that only recently had wrested control of the oceans from the Nazi U-boats and the Japanese Combined Fleet were now to be "mothballed" or sold for scrap metal. In a sense, Isaiah's words were being fulfilled—we were beating our swords, if not into plowshares, then into Plymouths and Studebakers.

In this new environment, the traditional services competed for honor, recognition, and in the case of the Marine Corps, institutional survival (some efficiency-minded politicians thought that the Marines could easily be folded into the Army). In contrast, the high-tech Air Force had grown even more powerful by war's end, with its Superfortress bombers carrying that most mysterious of payloads, the atomic bomb. With this "big stick," it seemed America could talk as loudly or softly as it pleased, and it could also intimidate the Soviets' numerically superior ground forces. In this new atomic age, some even wondered whether traditional armies and navies were not obsolete. Facing these challenges, each service sought to enshrine itself in the new military pantheon constructed from the National Security Act of 1947. The act created an independent Air Force, retained an Army of significant strength, and conceived of a Navy built more around submarines and aircraft carriers than around "old-fashioned" battleships and cruisers. It ultimately retained the Marine Corps, in part because the Corps stood as an icon of American fighting spirit, epitomized in that photograph from Iwo Jima. The act also established a new military organization, the Department of Defense, that replaced the old War and Navy departments.

By 1947 international relations once again grew tense as the wartime alliance with the Soviets began to deteriorate. Events in Eastern Europe and elsewhere expanded the fissures between East and West, leading to a realignment of powers—the now-familiar pattern of NATO versus the Warsaw Pact. In the pivotal year 1949, the Soviets exploded their first atomic bomb, while in China, Mao Zedong's Communists toppled Chiang Kai-shek's Nationalists, who then retreated to Taiwan. Across the world, some saw these events opening a long-anticipated "people's revolution," the rising tide of history itself. Many Americans, however, perceived a growing "Red menace," a surge of despotism sweeping away the fruits of the victory that had seemed so secure only four years earlier. Many wondered if the United States and its Western Allies had fought the bloodiest war in history, stemming the tide of fascism, only to have it replaced by communism. So emerged the Cold War, too dangerous to begin, yet seemingly impossible to avoid.

As the events of the late 1940s reemphasized America's need for a strong military, Hollywood responded with new and influential war films. Among these were *Sands of Iwo Jima, Task Force, Twelve O'Clock High*, and *Battleground*, all of which appeared in 1949. Each film of this quartet focused on and promoted a specific service and its principal strategic doctrines, almost as if produced specifically to give testimony before the Senate Appropriations Committee. Each film used its World War II story to show how that service continued to be essential in the new, Cold War environment—sending a Cold War "message" through a World War II story.[5] The films argued implicitly that we could no longer afford to let our guard down or to appease our global enemies. The consequences of having failed to confront Germany or Japan early enough were obvious to all. Since we faced a new communist threat, the films argued that we must maintain a powerful military deterrent or risk a "nuclear Pearl Harbor."[6]

Therefore, this generation of World War II films embedded the Cold War argument for military preparedness in what had already become the standard American narrative of the war. That narrative told how, once taken by surprise, Americans united and made the necessary sacrifices to create, supply, and deploy the overwhelming military force necessary to defeat the Axis. Our allies play only supporting roles in this story while America—with its industrial might, its commitment to individual freedom, its high-tech military, and its citizen soldiery—is the star. That we had emerged from the war with our national infrastructure intact, unlike any other major power, seemed to confirm our role as "Leader of the Free World." So our mainstream story of World War II told how the "sleeping giant" awoke, armed, fought, and ultimately stood across the world like the Colossus. This narrative thus extended the theme of "manifest destiny" from America's subduing of a continent in the nineteenth century, to its achievement of global hegemony in the twentieth. It also confirmed that the "American Century" was the product of American arms, so we used this narrative during the Cold War to persuade ourselves that only by becoming and remaining the most militarized nation in history could we maintain our "rightful status" in the world.

"But When You Do Stand Up, You'll Be Marines"

Sands of Iwo Jima is perhaps the most influential American film about World War II combat. That is not to say it is necessarily the best, even for its time. More than any other, however, it shaped the iconic imagery and mythic structures that would underlie America's mainstream narrative of the war for most of two decades. It was released in 1949 as the Cold War was heating up and Americans were growing more fearful of communists both here and abroad. The House Un-American Activities Committee hearings led some Americans to feel that our laxness in confronting political "radicals" at home had now endangered our democracy. It seemed time again for figures of strong leadership, be they real or mythic. Enter John Wayne, stage right.

In 1949, Wayne was already over forty years old and an established star, associated largely with Westerns. His greatest successes had come when directed by John Ford, a man whose paternal leadership both inspired and intimidated Wayne.[7] Ironically, the actor best known for playing the mythic figure of the American soldier in World War II had never donned a real uniform during that or any other conflict.[8] Of course, he had "served" in films like *Flying Tigers* (1942) and *Back to Bataan* (1945), but until 1949, viewers were still more accustomed to seeing Wayne on a horse than in a jeep.

The history of the making of *Sands of Iwo Jima* also reveals some interesting conflicts. Leonard Maltin's 1993 documentary *The Making of* Sands of Iwo Jima claims that the producer and director had wanted Wayne to play Sergeant John Stryker from the outset. Lawrence Suid, however, provides detailed evidence that they originally wanted Kirk Douglas, perhaps giving very different qualities to both the character and the film.[9] When he learned of the role, Wayne pursued it with a vengeance, even when producers at first rejected the idea; Wayne was chosen, however, because Douglas was not yet available. The original script by Harry Brown (*A Walk in the Sun*) did not quite fulfill Wayne's desires, and so the star brought in his friend James Edward Grant to do the rewrite. Although Allan Dwan directed the film, Wayne actually took charge behind the scenes. The actor felt that he knew this role instinctively, and in the process of filming, he became the character, or the character became him. In the end, the marriages of actor with character and cinematic image with cultural icon were both fruitful, and the result was the classic American World War II film.

Sands of Iwo Jima remains an oddly distorted, idiosyncratic treatment of the war, however. Critic Jeanine Basinger praises Wayne for making

Stryker a three-dimensional, tragic figure, but this apparent depth is achieved largely by diminishing the other characters.[10] As Wayne pushed to create a vehicle for himself, his supporting cast retreated into two-dimensionality. Moreover, *Sands of Iwo Jima* is a deeply unsatisfying film in its treatment of the war itself and of actual experiences of the marines, especially as we now understand those experiences from the writings of veterans such as William Manchester and Eugene Sledge (see chapter eight). Like a Shakespearian history play, the *Sands of Iwo Jima* turns real history into popular myth to serve the ends of contemporary politics and artistic fame—in this case, Cold War politics and John Wayne's image. Prior to *Sands*, Wayne had been a star, but he had yet to become an icon. By merging himself with the character of Stryker, by clothing himself in the now sacred uniform of the battle-scarred marine, he elevated himself to mythic status. Wayne does not become Stryker as some have argued; rather, he manipulates Stryker to create a "John Wayne" character whom he can transfer into future roles.[11]

Of course, Stryker is an interesting character, powerful and compelling in his own right, but having little to do with the war as such. The character's essence lies in the issues of paternal authority and responsibility. A failed and conflicted father figure, he demands loyalty because he loves his children so intensely, be they literal or figurative, but he cannot express his love directly. This character is not so much John Wayne playing Stryker as he is John Wayne playing, of all people, *John Ford*—the Hollywood "daddy-dearest" figure who had encouraged and rejected Wayne at the same time.[12] We may analyze this in terms of Freudian father-son conflicts, or we might apply a range of other psychological theories. Regardless, the classic, postwar John Wayne character is a troubled father figure, a character he developed by working with both Howard Hawks and John Ford. Given Wayne's intense but awkward relationship with Ford, this character type likely shows the actor trying to emulate, satisfy, and in some ways, supplant the old director who so thoroughly shaped his career.[13]

Some credit Wayne and *Sands of Iwo Jima* with "saving" the Marine Corps, but such claims for the film's impact are considerably overstated. While a few in Congress wanted to merge the Corps with the Army for reasons of efficiency, Americans held the image of the flag-raising at Iwo Jima to be a sacred national symbol. Such symbols are powerful enough on their own, without the help of John Wayne. Yes, the Marine Corps gave the film its vigorous support because it provided excellent public relations.[14] However, that still does not make John Wayne into a savior of the Corps. Though *Sands of Iwo Jima* accomplished something for the Marines Corps image, it did much more for the actor. Once an icon is established, we view it as inevitable, and assume that John Wayne lent his powerful image to help the Marines. Yet before the film was made, his image was not nearly so powerful. In *Sands of Iwo Jima*, Wayne borrowed the Marine Corps, flag and all, to help reconstruct his screen image into the archetypal American fighting man of World War II. In the process, however, he unconsciously shaped that character's personality in the likeness of John Ford—himself the tough, flawed "father" of so many cultural icons.

★ ★ ★

Structurally, *Sands of Iwo Jima* fits the mold of previous World War II combat films. It focuses on a single marine rifle squad and covers a period from mid-1943 to February 23, 1945—the day of the Iwo Jima flag-raising. Indeed, the film builds toward this event and co-opts it, even using the three surviving flag-raisers to help recreate the action. During the story's two-year time span, the action includes both training and combat. Two major Marine battles, Tarawa and Iwo Jima, provide the combat segments, and while the film devotes less than half its screen time to battle sequences, they are the strongest portions of the film.

As in other small-unit films, Stryker's squad is a composite of Hollywood's standard character and demographic types. Stryker, however, seems to transcend any ethnic identity—his demographic group is the Marine Corps, nothing more or less. His tough and uncompromising behavior stems from a desire to help his men survive the ordeal of combat. His inner life is conflicted because his wife left him years before, taking their young son with her. Estrangement from the boy, who never answers his father's letters, leaves Stryker alternately angry and depressed. He compensates by an even greater devotion to the Corps, and to his men, though he shows that devotion through his severity. When on leave, he gets desperately drunk to forget his desolate personal life. At such times, Private First Class Charlie Bass (James Brown), Stryker's only close friend in the squad, keeps the sergeant out of trouble.

Among the squad's newcomers is Private Pete Conway (John Agar), who becomes Stryker's principal foil. A reluctant marine, the educated and reflective Conway feels that he was never accepted by his late father, a career Marine Corps officer who had been Stryker's C.O. on

Guadalcanal. Conway's love-hate relationship with his father immediately puts him at odds with Stryker, who admires the dead officer. Both men are attracted and repelled by one another, with Conway seeking to prove himself to a dead father, and Stryker trying to reach out to an estranged son. This mutual surrogacy is symbiotic, and its energy drives the film.

The remaining squad members are familiar types. Pfc. Al Thomas (Forrest Tucker), a veteran marine but a goldbrick, has had prior trouble with Stryker that resurfaces during the course of the film. Other newcomers reveal standard ethnic stereotyping. The ever-quarreling Flynn brothers, Eddie (Bill Murphy) and Frank (Richard Jaeckel), are the "fighting Irish" of the group, while "Ski" Choynski (Hal Baylor), the Polish character, is slow both with his wits and on his feet. George Hellenopolis (Peter Coe), known as "the Greek," is the most ethnic since he speaks with an accent. Benny Regazzi is the classic Italian-American stereotype, played by Wally Cassell (*The Story of G.I. Joe*, see chapter four). Just as the Flynns are always fighting, Regazzi is always talking. Although he becomes an effective member of the squad, he is the most obviously comic figure. He also adds a note of comic sexual ambiguity, laughably drawing attention to the "beefcake" features of his stronger squad mates. When he is drunk, he calls men, as well as women, "beautiful, beautiful, beautiful." In one scene, he tells Thomas, "If I was a girl, I'd marry you." The film uses this comic gender-bending to defuse any possible audience concerns, however unconscious, about male sexual identity in a story where the intense emotions of strong male bonding must energize the plot.

The film devotes its lengthy opening segment to character development during the training in New Zealand. The Stryker and Conway conflict emerges here, and the friction between Stryker and Thomas also resurfaces. We witness Stryker's toughness, expressed in such refrains as "Saddle up." He tells the squad, "I'm gonna ride ya 'til ya can't get up. But when ya do stand up, you'll be marines!" Stryker's strengths and weaknesses are more than features of personality; they are hyperbolic elements in the film's construction of his character. In one scene, he breaks Choynski's jaw with a butt-stroke from a rifle because of the recruit's incompetence on the bayonet course. Later, Stryker teaches him the bayonet drill by using a record of the Mexican Hat Dance, literally dancing Choynski into the proper rhythmic motion. The image of the hardened sergeant dancing with the awkward recruit is certainly unusual in the pantheon of American war films. Yet both the jaw breaking and the dancing are gross exaggerations, lacking credibility as anything other than on-screen gestures. During the film's opening portion, we also follow Conway's awkwardly sentimentalized romance with Alison. The romance and subsequent marriage are necessary only because Conway must have his own son so that he can finally understand Wayne as a foster father.

The action accelerates with the invasion of Tarawa Atoll. Dwan effectively integrates actual Tarawa combat footage into his film, also carefully preparing his shooting location to look like the original battle sites seen in documentary footage. During the beachhead sequence, Stryker demonstrates his effectiveness as a fighting man and a leader. Amid the chaos and death, he keeps his cool and, at the right moment, single-handedly risks his own life to knock out the main enemy pillbox. In contrast, the next sequence shows the cost of Thomas's irresponsible behavior. Having returned to the beach to get more ammunition for himself, Bass, and the Greek, he stops to get coffee. He returns too late, and in his absence, the others have been overrun. The Greek is dying, and Bass is missing.

That night Stryker's mere squad must hold a sector normally requiring a whole platoon, while awaiting an unseen enemy. No attack comes because the marines never reveal the weakness of their position, but even without combat action, this is still the most effective sequence in the film. Wounded and delirious, Bass cries out for help from no-man's land, specifically calling for Stryker, who shares a foxhole with Conway. Conway wants to rescue Bass, but Stryker knows that doing so could reveal and jeopardize the company's position. He threatens to shoot Conway if the young man ventures out. The camera focuses on Stryker's darkened, grimy face, streaked with sweat, and perhaps with tears, as he listens to his best friend call for him. Here Wayne communicates the personal cost that comes from total devotion to duty, making this scene not only into the dramatic high point of the film but also one of Wayne's best scenes in any production.

After Tarawa has been secured, the unit sails to Hawaii for retraining. While there, Conway learns by letter that he is now a father, replaying the commonplace scene from mail calls in so many films. New recruits join the squad, while Bass returns, so Stryker finally learns of Thomas's neglect of duty at Tarawa. He confronts and attacks Thomas, who finally accepts personal responsibility and acknowledges Stryker's authority. For his part, the sergeant forgives the "sinful" Thomas, admonishing him that "When we make a mistake, someone don't walk away—forevermore, he don't walk away." Despite the stilted language, the scene still has emotional resonance, in part because Tucker plays the guilt-ridden Thomas with some conviction.

In the next liberty sequence, Stryker is again drinking alone, when a prostitute named Mary (Julie Bishop) tries to pick him up. Mary patiently gets through his tough hide, and they return to her apartment. Out of liquor, she asks for money to buy more, and while she's gone, Stryker discovers a baby boy in a crib in the next room. When Mary returns, he finds that she has bought formula as well as whiskey, and though she fears that he will be angry, he helps prepare the bottle. "You know about babies," she says, and he replies, "Yeah, I know about babies." The boy's father had left, and Mary must survive as best she can—classic Hollywood sociosexual pathos. Stryker smiles, throws his money clip of cash to the infant, and goes on his way. The scene shows that, given the chance, Stryker could have been a good father, just as he could have rescued Bass, but he is married first to the Corps, and such a marriage brooks no rivals. In this sequence, however, Stryker finally realizes that he need not feel sorry for himself—a revelation that he shares with Bass when they meet shortly thereafter.

With the Iwo Jima operation, the action intensifies again. The landing and battle scenes once more demonstrate effective integration of combat footage with live-action. The Iwo Jima sequences are also enhanced by the contributions of hundreds of actual marines and a large quantity of heavy equipment provided by the Marine Corps. The scope of the beachhead scenes makes for a powerful re-creation of the battle, appearing consistent with the combat footage. During the subsequent battle sequences, Conway finally proves himself by saving Stryker's life, and the two men complete their reconciliation when Conway shows Stryker the photo of his new son, named Sam to honor Conway's father. Conway has finally accepted paternal authority—his dead father's and Stryker's. He has also accepted the Marine Corps as his greater family. For his part, Stryker has demonstrated that, even if a failure with his biological son, he has succeeded as Conway's surrogate father.

The final assault on Suribachi is the film's closing sequence. During the attack, Stryker's squad suffers further casualties, and only a handful remain when the marines reach the top. With the crest achieved, the film prepares to restage the flag-raising, with actual flag-raisers John Bradley, Rene Gagnon, and Ira Hayes participating. Now, just as Stryker begins to loosen up and share a pack of cigarettes with the squad, a shot rings out, and he falls. Bass kills the sniper, but that act is too late to help Stryker. Thomas then discovers the proverbial letter home in the dead sergeant's pocket—an unfinished letter to Stryker's son, expressing his love and his sense of personal failure. After Thomas reads it, a tearful Conway volunteers to finish it for him. The music swells, drawing our attention to the flag-raising, which is paused in mid-action to create a dramatic tableaux. The strains of the "Marine Corps Hymn" are now heard softly as the squad looks on. Conway briefly stares down at Stryker's body, then lifts his gaze, tenses his jaw, and growls, "Awwright. Saddle up. Let's get back to the war." It seems that Conway has taken on Stryker's role and even his voice, barking out commands and leading the men back into combat. As the squad disappears into the smoke of battle, the music and words of the hymn swell to the closing.

Certainly *Sands of Iwo Jima* has some strengths, especially in the battle sequences. Wayne creates in Stryker a convincing character, one torn between personal relationships and loyalty to the Marine Corps. In addition, the structure, pacing, and tone of the film are carefully balanced realizations of Hollywood commonplaces, designed to please an audience without fail. The film's success is thus not surprising. Yet the film is still disappointing, and in many ways, disturbing. The acting among the supporting cast is generally weak, and Agar especially has difficulty expressing emotion without seeming exaggerated. The squad itself is constructed of stereotypes, and the scenes allow them to play out their predictable behaviors with little genuine character development. Even though these are not exceptionally strong actors, many are still capable of better performances than either the script or direction allows. Together, their main effort is to make Wayne look good and to make his character seem larger and deeper by comparison.

Perhaps the most disturbing aspect of the film, however, is the use of the Iwo Jima flag-raising as an iconic image of closure. There is something shameless in co-opting both the image and the sacrifices that it stands for (even though the government had already done so to sell bonds). Likewise, using the three actual survivors insults the genuine heroism and sacrifice of those who made up the original patrol and raised the flag. Of course, this tactic was good for the picture and for Wayne, and it seemed good to the Marine Corps, who persuaded these veterans to work on the film.[15]

Subsequently, *Sands of Iwo Jima* has come to be known for its tough portrayal of the war because the main character and many of his squad are killed during the course of the film. Upon closer scrutiny, however, it is not really a film about the war as it is about the new prototypical John Wayne character, the flawed but heroic father figure. It is also a film about the sentimentality of male bonding and father-son surrogacy, and it shamelessly uses every possible cinematic gesture to elicit emotion from its audience. It is not a realistic representation of the war or of marines in combat—such a representation would have to wait for a later period. It did please the Marine Corps authorities because it portrayed the service in a highly positive light. Perhaps the most telling judgment on the film, however, comes from John Bradley, one of the flag-raisers who had agreed to be in the film. In a letter quoted in the memoir, *Flags of Our Fathers*, written by Bradley's son, the veteran says

> They didn't get us out to California to help make the picture. All that was a cheap publicity trick to get a little free advertising for the movie. . . . Chief Hayes says they have the picture so f——d up he isn't even going to see the movie.[16]

While many critics have praised this film and Wayne's part in it—both his acting and his bringing it to the screen—the project, despite its influence, seems ultimately unworthy of the veterans it sought to portray.

The Fleet Comes to Stay

In support of Cold War appropriations for the U.S. Navy, director Delmer Daves' *Task Force* attempts an epic depiction of how carrier aviation developed, from the 1920s through 1949. It focuses this story through the experiences of the fictional Rear Admiral Jonathan "Scotty" Scott (Gary Cooper), who also narrates. Contained within the frame of Scotty's 1949 retirement, the main story is told in flashback, beginning in 1922, when both the young officer and carrier aviation have yet to prove themselves. The film presents multiple narratives: Scotty's career in the Navy and his romance with and eventual marriage to Mary Morgan (Jane Wyatt); the Navy's struggle to develop carrier aviation; and Scotty's combat experience with carrier task forces during World War II. Naturally, the U.S. Navy gave ample support to the film, including access to ships, planes, and documentary footage; *Task Force* made an effective case for Navy appropriations. As Lawrence Suid has pointed out, Daves even advanced the release date to make sure the film could influence congressional appropriations hearings. Unfortunately, the Daves' broad scope results in an unwieldy film as well as one whose propagandizing is all too obvious.

The World War II sequences in *Task Force* are the most important for this discussion. War is foreshadowed early in the film when Scotty predicts Japanese aggression, yet neither this view nor his support for aviation endears him to the Navy hierarchy, so he is exiled to "fly a desk" at a distant base. Obviously, Scotty is meant to stand for all military officers who warn us of impending danger from an aggressive global power. Thus, *Task Force* provides an excellent example of using the World War II narrative as a vehicle for a 1949 Cold War message: we must be both strong and suspicious to protect ourselves against international communism.

Wartime portions of *Task Force* begin with a brief Pearl Harbor sequence, but most of the World War II material is divided between two lengthy sequences about the battles of Midway and Okinawa.[17] The Midway sequence centers on the bridge of the USS *Yorktown*, where Rear Admiral Richard (Walter Brennan) and Scotty, air operations officer, must plan and then sweat out the mission to attack the Japanese carriers. Daves effectively builds the tension in the small, cramped room, and Brennan and Cooper play their scenes in a powerfully understated style. Interspersed are brief scenes of the American strike force of bombers and fighters searching for the Japanese. After hours of waiting, the air group commander breaks radio silence to announce the sighting and to commence the attack. Battle scenes cut between actual combat footage and close-ups of actors in studio mock-ups, also crosscutting back to the *Yorktown*'s bridge. American planes destroy the Japanese carriers, but not soon enough to prevent a Japanese counterattack that cripples the *Yorktown*, requiring it to be abandoned. Throughout the Midway sequence, Daves reveals the inherent drama of men waiting in a cramped space, something he had demonstrated in his earlier submarine film *Destination Tokyo* (1943). Rather than a submarine crew sweating out depth charges, *Task Force* shows the admiral and his staff "sweating out" the long attack mission on which the course of the war may depend. Some critics find such scenes too static because they fail to "open up" the film to the full possibilities of cinema; however, contracting the scope actually heightens the intensity of the interspliced attack scenes in *Task Force*, making the Midway segment the film's strongest.

Following a reunion in Honolulu between the rescued Scotty and his wife, the film returns to Washington for an encounter with the domestic enemy, Senator Bentley (Stanley Ridges), who sees the loss of several carriers as reason to end funding for these new capital ships. This scene dramatizes the U.S. Navy's perennial fight for necessary appropriations, and it clearly addresses itself to politicians, few of whom would want to be identified with the short-sighted Bentley. Subsequently, Scotty's voiceover tells us that "We got the carriers, and I got one of them."

The action jumps from 1942 to 1945, moving directly to the final battle sequence at Okinawa, where the American fleet suffered horrendous casualties from kamikaze attacks. Since these attacks stretched out over days, instead of mere hours, this second sequence lacks the intensity of the Midway scenes. It maintains dramatic interest by focusing not only on the bridge of the carrier but also on CIC (Combat Information Center), hub of air defense for the whole task force. Daves provides a realistic representation of the CIC crew, men who calmly fight the war by radar scope while knowing that a kamikaze may destroy their ship at any moment. Yet Scotty and Richard provide a stronger sense of dramatic tension as they wait on the bridge, tension amplified by Daves' frequent crosscuts to the ever-turning radar antennae. After days of waiting, the raiders come. Once again, Daves blends actual footage of kamikaze attacks with staged shipboard scenes. Though numerous attackers are shot down, some break through with devastating results. Daves includes actual film of the USS *Franklin*, the most badly damaged ship to survive the war. Of course, Scotty refuses to abandon his severely damaged carrier, and he rallies his crew to save the ship. The sequence ends with shots of the real *Franklin*, its flight deck a tangle of wreckage, sailing majestically into New York harbor, the Statue of Liberty at one point framed between torn metal deck spars. From the bridge, Scotty announces to the crew the news that the war has ended. The restrained but obvious emotion in his voice communicates something of the cost of that victory.

Task Force ends with Scotty, in civilian dress, leaving his ship and riding a small boat to shore. Richard, already retired, and Mary are there to greet him. "The Navy's losing a good man," says Richard. "And I'm getting one back," quips Mary. The film closes with Scotty's voiceover. As jets fly over, he thinks of the future when something new and better will come, implying that such progress will depend on congressional appropriations. Obviously, the film aims to keep the U.S. Navy afloat, and by the film's closing, we know that the Navy floats on an ocean of dollars. Daves wants viewers to leave the theater believing that those future dollars should be guaranteed and that they will be well spent.

Elegy for the Eighth Air Force

In bombers we had named for girls, we burned
The cities we had learned about in school—
Till our lives wore out; our bodies lay among
The people we had killed and never seen.
                                   Randall Jarrell, "Losses"[18]

Jarrell's postwar poem about the death of bomber crews serves as an elegy for all who die in war, whether a young man in a bomber or an old woman in a Berlin apartment. *Twelve O'Clock High* elegizes only the bomber crews of the U.S. Eighth Air Force, who from 1942 to 1945 flew their missions in the stratosphere over continental Europe. For the first two years of U.S. involvement, they were often the principal American force in direct battle with Nazi Germany. Although the point is not without controversy, many historians argue that the Eighth and its sister Air Forces were largely responsible for the defeat of the Luftwaffe, though long-range fighters ultimately had to help the bombers accomplish that task. Until those fighters became available in 1944, the bombers alone fought the American air war over Germany, suffering great losses.

Unlike the ordinary G.I.s, aircrews tended to live better if not longer. Of course, bomber crews had to fly all the way to and from Germany, suffering almost continuous attacks from enemy fighters. Over the target, flak erupted, but bombers could take no evasive action until they dropped their bombs. In the freezing skies, 30,000 feet over Europe, men died by the hundreds in almost every major raid. These men are the focus of *Twelve O'Clock High*'s elegiac treatment of the air war in Europe. Although this film defends the U.S. Air Force doctrine of strategic bombing, it still offers a compelling psychological drama about the strain of both combat and command in modern air warfare. It also reunited Darryl F. Zanuck (producer), Henry King (director), and Leon Shamroy (cinematographer), who had worked together on *A Yank in the RAF* (1941), but the later film reveals how the war had matured their style. The opportunity to use actual combat footage, from films such as *The Memphis Belle* (1944), also allowed them to portray air combat realistically, eliminating the clumsy use of models. The script was by Beirne Lay Jr. and Sy Bartlett, who had also collaborated on the original novel. An Air Force veteran, Lay based his story and characters on actual events and experiences. Ironically, although the novel sounds like typical Hollywood fare, with a romantic subplot that detracts from the overall story, the film wisely eliminates such distractions, leaving only the gripping story of men in combat and those who command them.

Like *Task Force*, *Twelve O'Clock High* uses a framing structure, placing the main story in the memory of former Major Harvey Stovall (Dean Jagger). In London on business in 1949, Stovall discovers in an antique shop an old toby mug that seems to have great significance for him.[19] After purchasing it, he takes it on a journey to the English country village of Archbury, where he bikes out to an abandoned airfield.[20] As Stovall stares at the empty runways and buildings, we hear male voices softly singing popular 1940s songs, indicating our passage into memory. Suddenly we hear the roar of engines, and the wind blowing through the grass now becomes "propwash." We are back in the war. The framing device is clearly elegiac, calling up the ghostly voices of the young men who once flew from this base, often never to return.

Within this frame, the principal story of *Twelve O'Clock High* is simple but dramatic. Early in the bombing campaign (autumn 1942), the 918th Bomber Group has become a "hard-luck outfit," underperforming on missions and suffering heavy losses. The commander, Colonel Keith Davenport (Gary Merrill), identifies too closely with the men, so he cannot push them to deliver the "maximum effort" needed to pull off tough missions. General Pritchard (Millard Mitchell), Eighth Air Force C.O., relieves Davenport and picks Brigadier General Frank Savage (Gregory Peck), already a veteran combat leader, as the new group commander.[21] The scene where Pritchard asks Savage to take over the group becomes a short sermon on the importance of daylight strategic bombing. The still fledgling Eighth Air Force must prove this controversial theory, or Army leaders will abandon the campaign—a decision that bombing advocates feared could lengthen or even lose the war. This is the standard Air Force narrative of the air war in Europe, but even in 1949, the newly minted, independent Air Force still wanted support for strategic bombing, though it no longer practiced "daylight precision bombing." Savage agrees to take over the group because, as a faithful "disciple" of Air Force doctrine, he also believes that strategic bombing is essential to win the war. Yet despite its support for such doctrine, the film still demonstrates that we may find human interest in the story of any disciple's sacrifices, whether or not we share his beliefs.

At the core of the 918th's problem is the issue of the "maximum effort." This ambiguous term refers most literally to Eighth Bomber Command's sending up the maximum number of bomber groups on a raid to achieve the maximum effect on a target. It also refers to the most effort that can be expended by an aircrew before they are no longer capable of flying. Giving a "maximum effort" thus becomes the new, bureaucratized equivalent of giving "the last full measure." At the same time, the very ambiguity and elasticity of the concept unintentionally connects it with the numerous occasions of governmental and military double-speak—vague language that can be manipulated to get the last drop of effort from the men, despite their interests or wishes. "Maximum effort" is not very different from the satirical concept of "Catch-22," Joseph Heller's extreme parody of such double-speak (see chapter seven). Though *Twelve O'Clock High* does not attempt to parody "maximum effort," the concept remains problematic even in this film. It becomes the cross on which some disciples of air power will be crucified.

General Savage arrives at the 918th knowing that he has to shake up the group, a job made more difficult because they were so devoted to their former commanding officer. Savage, however, cannot afford to expend emotional energy on the past even though Colonel Davenport is his friend. So the new commander takes charge aggressively. Addressing the aircrew officers with a blood-and-thunder approach, he tells them to consider themselves "already dead."[22] He also demotes or reassigns lazy or incompetent officers, chief among them the group's air executive officer, Lieutenant Colonel Ben Gately (Hugh Marlowe). The son of a high-ranking officer, Gately has taken his position for granted and done little to ease the command burdens of Colonel Davenport. In a highly dramatic confrontation, Savage relieves Gately as air exec, ordering him to fly every mission in a plane labeled "The Leper Colony" because it will get every deadbeat in the outfit. The chastened Gately must now take his responsibilities seriously, and eventually he becomes one of the group's best officers.

While seeming relentlessly tough in these scenes, Savage is no mere martinet. His blood-and-guts persona allows him to function in command, but since his command responsibilities never let up, Savage lets the persona slip only rarely and briefly. Instead, he lets his actions speak for him. He combs through the group's records, promoting those men who have shown courage and leadership. One is Major Cobb (John Kellogg), whom Savage selects as the new air exec, largely because Cobb showed courage in honestly facing off with the new commander in the officer's club. Savage also quickly earns the trust of the ground exec, Major Stovall, a World War I veteran now too old for combat duty. Throughout the film, the wise Stovall provides calm advice for the younger and more impatient Savage, and Jagger and Peck in these roles convey a deep sense of friendship and mutual respect. In simple conversations with the older man, Savage indirectly reveals his more sensitive side, and Stovall realizes that, although awkward in interpersonal situations, Savage feels as deeply for the men as Davenport had. Stovall comes to know the general most closely and witnesses the price the commander pays to get the "maximum effort" from himself and his men.

As the film progresses, the group begins to develop both competence and confidence. They also come to admire Savage even though he cannot show how much that means to him. As the air war intensifies, the 918th flies more missions, coalescing into a tough, reliable fighting unit. Missions also increase in complexity and distance, finally reaching into Germany itself, not just the occupied countries. Of course, as the missions add up, so do the losses. Each time Savage hears of another dead airman or lost plane, he says nothing, but we see his face tighten and his jaw clench. Stovall witnesses this impact, but few others recognize that Savage has begun to suffer from the same command illness that had plagued Davenport—overidentification with his men. General Pritchard, however, senses this change, realizing that he may have to remove Savage as he had once relieved his predecessor.

A long sequence late in the film covers a raid deep into Germany, with Savage leading the group. This time viewers are not sweating out the mission on the ground but flying it, and they witness every facet. As the group approaches enemy territory, Savage warns about possible fighter attacks, especially those attacking from directly ahead and slightly above a bomber formation (from "twelve o'clock high"), the most deadly form of attack. Emphasizing the intensity of these attacks, the film splices in multiple scenes from actual aerial combat footage, depicting running battles with German fighters. After the group successfully bombs the target, Savage orders them to make a turn so that stragglers can catch up, but Major Cobb radios that the turn will take them over a flak concentration. Savage sees no alternative. Moments later, Cobb's plane is hit and explodes. We see Savage, sweating and seemingly nauseated, turning over control of the plane to his copilot. For a few moments, he cannot continue flying, and we wonder how long he can continue to command the group while suffering the effects of his unspoken loss and guilt.

We receive our answer as the next mission is about to take off. When Savage walks to his plane to lead the group once again, he cannot pull himself up into the hatch. He begins trembling and seems to have lost all strength. His face expresses confusion and dismay as he looks uncomprehendingly at his shaking hands. The "reformed" Gately, now second in command, runs over to assist, and seeing Savage's distress, helps the commander over to the jeep where Stovall and a visiting Keith Davenport are waiting. Gately will lead the mission, but the other two must restrain Savage, who is shouting that "They can't go up again—they can't make it." After the takeoff sequence, we cut to a catatonic Savage, tight-jawed and silent, sitting in his quarters, his hands grasping the arms of his chair. The doctor, Stovall, and Davenport discuss his condition. He's up there, flying the mission, says the doctor, and maybe he'll come out of it when they get back. Ironically, even bitterly, the doctor describes the situation: "I think they call it 'maximum effort.'"

Only when the planes return does Savage come out of his catatonia, calling the tower for the count of returning planes. The mission has been successful, the losses light. Savage relaxes, confesses fatigue, and says, "I think I'll get a little sleep." Almost immediately, he is unconscious on his cot, and Davenport covers Savage with a blanket as one would a tired child. Stovall picks up his coat and walks out of the building, deep in thought. We cut to the sky as the returning bombers fly over, but then the sky is all at once empty and silent. We see Stovall, now in his business suit again, walking the deserted runways while muted voices of the young men return with their ghostly chorus of old songs. He walks away, his face an expression of tender sadness and deep love for the lost men and the lost years, and we are left with the memory of war's costs, a memory that the film, through the person of Stovall, has shared with us.

Like all the other films of the quartet, *Twelve O'Clock High* supports a service and a doctrine, and so it serves as propaganda. Viewing the film, we are again reminded of the U.S. Air Force commitment to strategic bombing and of the argument that this commitment was vital to winning World War II. The film also indirectly justifies the Air Force's new position as an independent service, with all the additional costs that entailed. Moreover, we are reminded not to let our guard down now, for we must never be back in the position of the Eighth Air Force during 1942 and 1943, of having to push men beyond the limit of endurance to make up for our late start in preparing to fight.

At the same time that it fulfills a propaganda "mission," *Twelve O'Clock High* is also a moving story of what happens to the men who fight wars, of the cost in lives and the psychic scars. Directing, writing, photography, and acting work together to produce this memorable experience. Indeed, memory is what the film is ultimately about— memory of the war and of those lost in the war. Its elegiac treatment is not overstated but, like that muted male chorus singing in Stovall's consciousness, subtle and compelling. On screen, Peck and Jagger together create the sense of their complicated and powerful relationship, which lingers for the older man. As he walks the now empty field, he recalls for himself this story, thus allowing us to view it. In the end, his memory becomes our memory—our American cultural memory—of the air war in Europe. The film has this effect because of both its technical and artistic excellence. This is not merely a war story, but a human drama about what duty demands. It is proof positive that, despite the rhetorical support for Air Force appropriations, the film can stand on its own as an artistic achievement.

In all memories, of course, there exist lacunae or spaces yet to be filled. This is a film about pilots and crews, and about their commanders as well. It is a film about the American bombing campaign in Europe from 1942 to 1945. It is not, by any means, the whole story. For every crewman lost, many civilians below died as well. True, the British accounted for the majority of German civilian casualties because the RAF engaged in night area bombing, frequently with incendiaries. Yet even when accurate, our "precision" bombs rained down on factories and warehouses filled with civilian workers, some of them slave laborers. And our bombs were rarely so accurate as to hit only the designated targets. Thus, there are many elegies to sing, many songs of mourning. Jarrell's poem "Losses" comes nearer the mark when he writes "our bodies lay among the people we had killed and never seen."[23] Yet even Jarrell cannot encompass it all. We must remember that for every German civilian killed in the bombings, twenty people died in the camps of the Holocaust/Shoah, totaling nearly 12 million—those are frightful numbers.[24] If *Twelve O'Clock High* can stand as art, it stands because it will help us begin the process of remembering, but not conclude it. It is but one elegy among many.

Battleground

Of all the quartet films, perhaps the most effective and memorable is William Wellman's *Battleground*. Like *Twelve O'Clock High*, it was written by a veteran of the campaign depicted in the film—Robert Pirosh, who had served in the 35th Infantry Division during the Battle of the Bulge.[25] Producer Dore Schary originally conceived of the project at a time when most studios were convinced that war films would fail to attract big audiences. He wanted to demonstrate that the Americans had fought the war for an important cause, one that should not be forgotten. Schary chose the highly dramatic Battle of the Bulge for subject matter, and he contacted Pirosh because the writer had fought in Europe. The final element came into place with the selection of Wellman to direct.

Unlike the other quartet films, *Battleground* achieves unusual intensity and concentration by focusing on one small unit, at one location, during a period of about two weeks.[26] The film makes no attempt to cover the epic scope of the Bulge, the largest battle fought by the American Army during World War II. Instead, *Battleground* shows the fighting from the standpoint of one platoon of the 101st Airborne Division. Also, though the whole battle lasted from December 16, 1944, until the end of January 1945, *Battleground* covers chiefly the period during which the 101st was cut off at Bastogne, roughly 10 days. Clearly, this period of siege offers the most dramatic concentration, and Wellman and Pirosh decided to make the most of the historical facts.

In choosing the 101st Airborne Division, *Battleground* focuses on an elite unit of the U.S. Army, one of only a handful of airborne divisions. Airborne troops received more intensive training and developed more comprehensive survival skills because they knew that they would often have to fight when cut off. Their standard doctrine and tactics were to seize objectives, occupy them, and defend them until the regular ground units could break through. Although other units were already at Bastogne when the 101st arrived, it became the principal unit, and its temporary commander, Brigadier Genenal Anthony McAuliffe, took command of the area.[27] Therefore, the 101st is most specifically associated with defending Bastogne. In part, *Battleground* helped establish the mythic narrative that made the 101st one of the most legendary units in the U.S. Army.

In addition to having a good writing and directing team, *Battleground* is served well by its cast. The popular Van Johnson plays what would be considered the lead—resourceful, somewhat cynical Private First Class Holley. Also central is the intellectual and reflective Private Jarvess (John Hodiak), a former newspaper man who often comments on the action. Private Jim Layton (Marshall Thompson) is the naïve replacement, but his rapid growth into a veteran will provide an accelerated example of what novelist James Jones calls the "evolution of the soldier"—from innocence, to experience, to bitterness, to acceptance.[28] The tough but sympathetic Platoon Sergeant Kinnie (James Whitmore) shepherds the men while constantly chewing tobacco and dispensing occasional bits of laconic wisdom. The film also sets characters into contrasting pairs, such as the worldly wise Holley with the innocent Layton, but Private. "Pop" Stazak (George Murphy) and Private Johnny Roderigues (Ricardo Montalban) make the most compelling pair. Married and in his thirties, Pop serves as a surrogate father for the youthful Johnny, who supplies the principal "ethnic" character in the group. Unlike Hispanic or Latino characters in earlier films, however, Johnny transcends the usual stereotypes. His character could be of any nationality—a young man, deeply attached to his now-distant family, who draws comfort from his close friendship with the older "Pop." A far more stereotyped character is Private Abner Spudler (Jerome Courtland), a typical Hollywood "hillbilly," who provides an unintentional foil for the well-educated Jarvess. Despite Abner's characterization, *Battleground* generally rejects the demographic stereotypes so familiar in earlier small-unit films. Here, the characters transcend their regional or ethnic backgrounds, in part because their most genuine identity comes from being G.I.s in the same platoon. Likewise, the real star of *Battleground* is the whole ensemble of actors. Their unified efforts before the camera evoke the very sense of teamwork that the film attempts to portray in the actions of combat soldiers.

Battleground's story stays relatively close to historical facts. It opens at a camp in France, the afternoon before the platoon is scheduled to go on leave in Paris. The next morning, however, Kinnie rousts the men to leave for the front instead of for Paris.[29] A breakthrough has occurred, and the 101st is one of the few units in reserve, so it will be trucked to the frontlines. After a bone-crunching ride, they end up in another place they had never heard of, Bastogne—a name that provides dramatic irony for the 1949 viewers because the battle had made it famous. The principal characters are billeted temporarily in the house of Denise (Denise Darcel), Hollywood's rather sexy version of a young Belgian woman.[30] But with the next morning comes another rude awakening—out from the billet and into the woods where the real action takes place. Although Wellman filmed *Battleground* mostly on a sound stage, the set design is unusually realistic. As in the actual battle, men are in the woods, which for most of the action are snow covered. At Bastogne low fogs and clouds produced a dark, dreary landscape, and the film emulates this, creating an image of perpetual overcast that suggests the stress of being under siege. Units were isolated and could see only short distances, so in this case, the studio set is not a liability. The inability to see much beyond a few yards also highlights one of the themes of the film—that wars are fought principally by small units of infantry who do not know where they are and who cannot see the "big picture" of the battle.

Also highly realistic is the fact that much of the battle happens elsewhere, delivered either as reports or rumors. The platoon itself spends much of its time digging in, only to be ordered somewhere else, thus having to dig in again. Small groups of three or four men go on patrol or take outpost duty, and the whole group dives for cover when shelling begins. Only in one instance does the whole platoon engage in a firefight with an enemy unit. All this activity is quite realistic and accurate. For most men in combat, there are extensive periods of hard labor and waiting under unpleasant circumstances; there is also relatively frequent shelling. The periods of direct firefights are more limited. Mostly, the men sit, watch, wait, and wonder what will happen next. In this respect, *Battleground* is unusually effective in conveying the actual concerns of combat soldiers.

The cycle of digging in, patrolling, guarding, moving, and digging in again organizes the unit's days and nights. As time progresses, casualties mount, and gradually, the platoon's numbers decrease. We also get to know the men and their relationships, and we see that irony haunts their lives, struggles, and deaths. In a sense, this ironic treatment is itself a realistic feature of an infantryman's life. When it snows, Johnny Roderigues is ecstatic because he has never before seen snow. Of course, it is Johnny who freezes to death after being wounded on patrol. Pop Stazak has been awaiting official word that he can be discharged because his wife is ill, and he must return home to care for their children, but he gets his letter only after the unit is surrounded. Layton, the neophyte, quickly learns the ways of the unit; for a time, he becomes its most cynical member, but eventually, he achieves the ironic acceptance that characterizes the veteran members of his squad.

Further ironies occur when the platoon is posted to defend a railroad embankment, their foxholes running along in front. Holley has become an acting squad leader and has also been teamed up with Layton. When an unexpected attack begins, we can see from Holley's expression that he is panicking, and he finally bolts from his hole and runs up the embankment and down the other side, to where a road passes under a railroad bridge. As he stands there, Layton suddenly appears from behind, saying, "I'm with ya, Holley." Layton's still youthful enthusiasm has led him to assume that Holley is making some kind of flanking movement, and Holley realizes this. He overcomes the panic, and taking his cue from Layton's misreading of the act, Holley leads Layton to the flank. Several other platoon members follow, setting up a base of fire from which the squad kills or wounds most of the attackers. Victory in this small action is the result of a veteran's panic and a neophyte's misreading of that panic as courage. What greater irony could there be in war than that one's failings, having been misinterpreted as virtuous, be changed into the virtue they had appeared to be at first. As Jarvess says, "Things just happen, then afterwards you try to figure out why you acted the way you did."[31]

Interwoven with the daily activities of the squad are events from the larger battle, which later became narrative commonplaces in other films about the Bulge. These include English-speaking German soldiers who, disguised in American uniforms, infiltrate American lines. We also hear of the well-known episode when General McAuliffe responds to a German surrender ultimatum with a single word—"Nuts!" In these and other features, the pattern of action is consistent with the historical facts of the battle, and these facts surface just enough to remind us that, indeed, this is the Battle of the Bulge. At the same time, our focus is still directed toward the experiences of the unit and its men—their gains and losses, their lives and deaths. The human stories and interrelationships of these men remind us that the history of great battles seldom confronts us with such details of life in a foxhole, with its near futile efforts to keep warm, dry, and fed. Wellman and Pirosh effectively blend the facts of history with the unit's drama of survival, deepening viewers' understanding of infantry combat far more than most films do.

As the film reaches its climax, the reduced platoon, low on ammo and food, must pull back from their positions. As Kinnie starts to get the men organized, he realizes that there is nowhere to which they can pull back. Germans are advancing in front and on both sides, and pulling back through the open is now out of the question. They must wait, with the likelihood they will be wiped out in the coming attack. The men grimly prepare in their foxholes, taking out their last clips of ammo and their last grenades, and fixing their bayonets as well. Just then, Kinnie sees his shadow—the weather has cleared. Suddenly, from above come waves of fighter-bombers to decimate the German attack. After those come the supply planes, airdropping the necessary weapons, ammo, and food. The men jubilantly collect their manna, and then a montage follows, showing their counterattacks against the Germans. The montage includes a good deal of actual combat footage, and when it ends, we see the men sitting by the road as tanks of the relief column move up to the front lines.[32] They rest not unlike the men of C-Company at the end of Wellmen's *The Story of G.I. Joe.* A jeep drives up, an officer gives Kinnie orders, and he calls the platoon to form up in the road. They think they are marching back to the front, but then he grins and orders an about face—this time, they are marching out of action. Limping away, they look bedraggled and worn, more like beggars than soldiers. Holley sees a fresh unit coming up and calls it to Kinnie's attention. The platoon changes into their old parade ground step and sings "Sound Off" while marching out of the picture. Even this unrealistic demonstration of unit pride does not overwhelm our credibility because the film's overall authenticity has already persuaded viewers to accept its representations. The film closes with a series of images of platoon members as they looked before the battle, and we know that many of them have not survived.

Battleground's final marching scene reminds us that this is a propaganda film supporting the U.S. Army, especially the infantry. *Battleground* cannot make arguments for high-tech weaponry as one finds in *Task Force* or *Twelve O'Clock High* since this film is about the humble dogfaces. There is some similarity with *Sands of Iwo Jima* because the 101st is an elite airborne unit, thus akin to Marine Corps units in its *esprit de corps*. Still, the men appear just as bedraggled as the ordinary, rank-and-file infantry of *The Story of G.I. Joe.* It is difficult to make a glossy public relations pitch when showing men living and working in conditions worse than those experienced by the poorest of migrant workers. But the message of *Battleground* is revealed in these very pedestrian images—for all the high-tech and glamour of the Navy and Air Force, and for all the mythic quality of the Marine Corps, modern wars must be won by mass armies made up of many individual, expendable units of very ordinary G.I.s. The Army is ultimately more a matter of men than of machines—millions of men in small, often isolated units who, because of their training and commitment, choose to flank the enemy rather than to flee them. Day by bloody day, such units won World War II in Europe. When the chaplain (Leon Ames) gives his Christmas sermon, he asks, "Was this trip really necessary?" He explains that because countries tried to avoid the war, more ultimately died when war came. The only answer is never again to allow appeasement to govern our policies. He continues, saying that:

> We must never let any kind of force dedicated to a super race or a super idea or a super anything get strong enough to impose itself on a free world. We have to be smart enough and tough enough in the beginning to put out the fire before it starts spreading.

The chaplain's speech is another aspect of the film's dual purpose. The speech makes perfect sense in the context of December 1944, in reference to Nazi Germany and to the other Axis powers, justifying our fighting in World War II. Yet in the context of 1949, the speech also seems an apt interpretation of Cold War policy.[33] Describing what we fight for, the chaplain uses the specific phrase "free world," associated far more with Cold War rhetoric than with that of World War II. This is merely one example of a common Hollywood trope—eliding the antifascist message of World War II with the anticommunist message of the Cold War. Many World War II films from the late 1940s to the mid-1960s make direct or indirect arguments in support of such messages. *Battleground* is an early example of this rhetorical strategy, arguing that World War II taught America to remain powerful in the face of foreign threats, such as those posed by communist nations in 1949. We saw what happened in the period between the wars when we had allowed our military to atrophy. Should the Cold War ever get hot, we would not have additional time for mobilization. Thus, we must keep the U.S. Army strong enough to fight at short notice. As goes the Army, so goes defense, and the Army is only so strong as the individual G.I.s in each small unit in the field.

Like *Twelve O'Clock High*, *Battleground* effectively fulfills its "service mission," garnering popular support both for a specific service and for a strong military in general. Yet it also succeeds dramatically because it offers a relatively convincing representation of combat, especially for its time. Written by a combat infantry veteran, it reverberates with the qualities of genuine experience. Although still a Hollywood feature film, it shows unusual faithfulness both to historical fact and to particular experiential details. It is a combat film that can reach a broad audience but still have a special register of meaning for the veterans. In the end, it is one of the better films made about American ground combat in World War II. Like the other quartet films, it not only serves the military but also pays legitimate respect to the actual combat veterans. Subsequent films about ground troops in Europe should have to be measured against it, and even today, few reach its levels of honesty.

Old War Story, Cold War Message

When planning *Battleground*, Dore Schary believed that war films continued to be both marketable and culturally significant. His assumptions proved quite accurate, even prescient. As *Battleground* and the other quartet films demonstrate, the emergent Cold War brought new interest in World War II films as well as new purpose. The Defense Department was eager to support films that advocated increased military appropriations and new Cold War policies. So from 1949 through the middle 1960s, Hollywood released numerous World War II films that proved remarkably adaptable in conveying dual messages—celebrating our victory in World War II and supporting military preparedness in the Cold War. These films, which covered all theaters of the war, most major battles, and many small actions, represented every service. Some are effective and entertaining while others are little more than clichés. Most are mixed efforts, with memorable moments and awkward passages. All built heavily on the foundation of the quartet films, and they helped shape America's sense of itself as a world power during the Cold War era. Many Americans of the generation too young to have fought in World War II, but born before the baby boom, were deeply influenced by the psychology and politics of such mythic representations of the war. Stephen Ambrose, author of many World War II histories, and newsman Tom Brokaw, who coined the phrase "greatest generation," provide significant examples. Likewise, the baby boom generation grew up on such films, shaping their cultural consciousness and leading them, at different times, either to reject or embrace the films' historical vision and political messages. Director Steven Spielberg has revealed this influence, at many levels, throughout his career.

In addition, war films of this era provide a range of unusually elastic images that have influenced America's cultural politics. When we watch marines in films like *Halls of Montezuma* (1950), or when we watch infantrymen in similar films from the period, it is not always immediately clear whether we are watching World War II or Korea. Indeed, sometimes combat footage from World War II was spliced with film from Korea. Uniforms, tactics, and many weapons had remained the same. If the enemy is Japanese, North Korean, or Chinese, audiences still see a "malevolent Asian horde." Sometimes, in the minds of viewers watching such films on television, the intertextuality became part of a general cultural pattern—U.S. troops fighting bitterly in some far-off Asian place. A person turning on the late-night television movie in the mid-1950s, and seeing marines in their classic camouflage helmets advancing up a grassy slope on a hot day, would have had a hard time deciding whether these men are fighting the Japanese in 1945 or the North Koreans or Chinese in the summers of 1950 or 1951. The interchangeability of the action between two different wars suggests a natural progression of history and foreign policy that ultimately acclimated Americans to accept the Vietnam War without question, at least during its early stages. One year, it's Okinawa, another year, it's Korea or Vietnam, and the next, who knows? For many Americans, the mere fact of ongoing and endless war became a reality, as it does for the citizens of George Orwell's *1984*. It seemed that Private Archimbeau, in *A Walk in the Sun*, had been a visionary when he claimed that "...in 1958 we'll be fighting the battle of Tibet." While no hot war brought U.S. troops under fire in Europe as it had in Asia, the stories that told of our sacrifices and victories on all fronts in World War II were used to give us both caution and confidence in facing the Cold War world. We were cautioned never again to allow ourselves to become militarily weak or to be surprised as at Pearl Harbor. We were reassured that, by maintaining both a large military and the same spirit of unity and self-sacrifice with which we fought the Axis, we could emerge triumphant from our conflict with the communist powers. Thus, the themes played by "the quartet" were orchestrated in most of the war films that followed throughout the next twenty years. It was only the obvious failures of the Vietnam War that brought such "martial music" to a halt.

C H A P T E R   S I X

Longest Days in the "Good War"

Arrangements for War and Male Chorus

Mitch Miller's name triggers little recognition for today's moviegoers, but his male chorus was quite popular in 1962 when Darryl F. Zanuck's *The Longest Day* featured the group singing during the final credits. Repeated throughout their song is the phrase "many men." Despite sentimental lyrics and a dated arrangement, this choral theme still conveys the film's underlying assumption—D-Day itself was so vast that one can understand it only as a grand chorus of identities and experiences. Just as no one voice dominates the chorus, no one individual or small group dominates the film's action. All characters share in representing great events that originally involved hundreds of thousands. To manage this scope, the film concentrates its action on approximately thirty-six hours of June 5 and 6, 1944, following the basic structure of the Cornelius Ryan book on which it was based. Maintaining a narrow temporal focus allows the film to portray the complete battle, involving all sides—an effort requiring three directors, with Zanuck supervising all. Clearly, Zanuck's aim was to construct a "choral" narrative, an epic work to represent the war's most important amphibious invasion and, by extension, the war as a whole. Of course, every chorus requires a single conductor, and the more voices involved, the more amplified the conductor's importance. In "conducting" *The Longest Day*, Zanuck wanted to show his mastery of the Hollywood war epic, but as a veteran who had produced wartime Army films, he also wanted to confirm the justice and significance of the Allied victory. His epic acknowledges the painful loss of so many lives while honoring the sacrifices of those who fought, arguing that all this was done to defeat Hitler and the Nazis, a theme also explicit in Ryan's book.[1]

Interestingly, despite focusing on the inherent justice of the Allied cause, both book and film represent the German Army positively, with brave and intelligent officers fighting in a lost cause and for a demented leader. Indeed, Hitler seems as much their enemy as do the Allies, so these loyal Wehrmacht officers fight for their country but regret its Nazi leadership. Such characterization reflects America's postwar effort to rehabilitate the reputations of both Germany and Japan. With the advent of the Cold War, both our government and media increasingly showed these former enemies, now allies, as having been honorable opponents.[2] After all, our Cold War alliance with West Germany would seem greatly suspect if we could not assert that most Germans had not been "like the Nazis." Hollywood therefore constructed a narrative of "good" Germans controlled by "bad" Nazis whereas the actual history is far more complicated. In fact, the Wehrmacht and its leadership shared much responsibility with the Nazi political leaders for the horrors that Germany perpetrated against so many in Europe.[3] Zanuck, however, avoids such political complexities, for to do so would be to introduce dissonance into his choral narrative. Instead, he represents German soldiers as merely doing their duty. Such ideological simplification allows the film to fulfill the traditional role of an epic as a monolithic confirmation of a culture's values—in this case, how the war demonstrated our commitment to personal and economic freedom, along with our opposition to totalitarian regimes. By implication, the same commitment continues in America's Cold War policies, but with our "converted" former enemies now fighting alongside us. In *The Longest Day*, both the Allies and the Germans are thus "harmonized" into the grand cinematic chorus of "many men." Therefore, both book and film clearly stay within mainstream American representations of World War II, confirming the "Good-War" narrative and Cold War policies supported by that narrative.

When attempting the epic form, filmmakers risk losing touch with the individuals whose struggle and suffering constitute the most authentic experience of war. Their personal agonies can be lost in the hyperactive landscape of a battlefield panorama. Thus, in constructing or viewing an epic war film, we may distance ourselves from specific human experience, numbing rather than intensifying our awareness of suffering. Only by careful effort can an artist or audience balance individual experience with the scope of an epic work. This chapter explores how *The Longest Day* uses the epic form both to celebrate and yet, unconsciously, to supersede the narrative of the war as a people's struggle, both individually and collectively. We will examine this film and its cultural context, contrasting it with the alternative epic form used in *Patton* (1970). *The Longest Day* is perhaps the most complete American representation of the war as collective achievement; however, its very epic structure allows viewers such an omniscient vantage point on the war that the experience is somewhat disorienting. As the masses of individual soldiers fade into the fog of battle, the vastness and potential confusion of modern warfare become all the more apparent, arousing in audiences an underlying desire for a godlike, heroic individual whose forceful character seems reassuring. Thus, while completing one cycle of narratives about the war, *The Longest Day* prepares us, unconsciously at least, for the quite distinctive narrative found in *Patton*. Viewers begin the subtle shift from the war of "many men" to the war of the "one great man."

Scope as Purpose—Achieving the American World War II Epic

From the time of D. W. Griffith's disturbingly racist, Civil War epic *Birth of a Nation* (1915), Hollywood has openly embraced the epic genre. Despite his distorted and racist view of history, Griffith was among the first to recognize film's potential for exploring subjects of vast scope, in part building on such nineteenth-century forms as panoramic painting. After World War II, filmmakers reemphasized the epic for both marketing and technical reasons. Competition from television drove the movie industry to invest heavily in large productions, often using new wide-screen technology to surpass what was then available on the "small screen." While cost factors obviously limited the number of epics, these still became increasingly important in the industry's overall marketing mix. *The Longest Day* thus grew from a postwar film industry committed both to the cinematic epic and to America's mainstream narrative of World War II. It also built upon half a century of epic war films. Though *Birth of a Nation* had established the early structural precedents, Hollywood had produced several other influential war epics during the silent era, including King Vidor's *The Big Parade* (1925) and William Wellman's *Wings* (1927), both about World War I. All these films employ extensive outdoor and location shooting, common in silent films but less so in early sound pictures. In addition, these epics cover a span of several years while focusing on a few characters in close relationships, some of them romantic. Shortly thereafter, Lewis Milestone's *All Quiet on the Western Front* (1930) set the standard for depicting modern warfare in the new sound format. Films actually made during World War II, however, were not usually so ambitious, for wartime rationing discouraged such epic scope, and postwar combat films, even when big-budget, generally kept to a narrower range of action.

The Longest Day, however, differed from prior epics in important ways, creating unusual obstacles for Zanuck. First of all, this was largely a male story, with no major female characters or significant romantic subplots. The film's emotional impact had to come from the compelling intensity of each individual soldier's story as well as from the dramatic action of the larger combat sequences. Of course, spreading his representation of D-Day over many episodic stories, Zanuck had to maintain the film's pace while engaging in frequent crosscutting. He used three directors (Andrew Marton, Ken Annakin, and Bernhard Wicki), recognizing that he was really making three films—one about the Americans, one about the British and French, and one about the Germans.[4] With associate producer Elmo Williams coordinating the action scenes, Zanuck then braided the three strands of primary material into a single production. This process demanded unusually effective editing, since no one central group or character could hold the audience's complete attention. Both action and reflection would also have to be interwoven so that viewers could understand the interrelationships among characters and the underlying significance of the many stories being told. Even while depicting complicated events, Zanuck had to avoid slowing the film with dull exposition. Moreover, to tell the story convincingly, he had to depend heavily on location shooting, with all its additional risks and costs. Finally, Zanuck had to secure an unprecedented level of cooperation from the military. No one of these was an easy task, but together, they posed a truly formidable challenge.

★   ★   ★

While it took Hollywood over fifteen years before it produced a truly epic World War II film, novelists had begun publishing epic works soon after war ended. Two of the first came in 1948: Norman Mailer's *The Naked and the Dead* and Irwin Shaw's *The Young Lions*. James Jones' *From Here to Eternity* and Herman Wouk's *The Caine Mutiny* followed in 1951, and Leon Uris' *Battle Cry* was published in 1953.[5] Within just a few years of the war's end, a whole new generation of writers began to tell the war's story in massive novels that achieved popular acclaim and, in a few cases, lasting cultural significance. Former war correspondents also began publishing nonfiction accounts, as did some veterans turned historians. John Hersey's *Hiroshima* (1946) exemplifies the former and Charles B. MacDonald's *Company Commander* (1947) illustrates the latter. Many other works of fiction and nonfiction followed throughout the 1940s and 1950s.[6]

It was in the context of such well-established World War II books that Cornelius Ryan wrote *The Longest Day*. Having covered the European Theater as war correspondent, Ryan remained a successful journalist after the war. As noted by scholar Philip Beidler, Ryan also became one of the preferred writers of *Reader's Digest* publisher DeWitt Wallace.[7] The project that would become *The Longest Day* grew originally from Wallace's offer of substantial financial and editorial support for a worthy book of Ryan's choice. Beidler explores the book's evolution in detail, concluding that the "personalizing" tone of standard *Reader's Digest* pieces (personal portraits, small comic vignettes, sudden crises— all packaged as brief formulaic offerings) influenced Ryan's treatment of the book's material.

What seems to have been Ryan's own counterintuitive insight, however, was to present the massiveness of D-Day itself by focusing on the experiences of many individuals. To accomplish this, he may have drawn, as Beidler suggests, on the standards of *Reader's Digest* features.[8] But this interpretation may reverse cause and effect. *Reader's Digest* conventions were already common journalistic practice, for the publication thrived on repackaging the commonplace. In writing *The Longest Day*, Ryan drew on his own journalistic experience, especially his work as a war correspondent. Time and space constraints demand that correspondents focus on the events taking only a few days or even hours—single engagements rather than whole campaigns. In addition, they often construct brief human interest stories to bring great campaigns down to the level of individual experience with which readers can identify. Some correspondents imitated Ernie Pyle, a master of this form, but many simply drew from the same tradition of journalistic conventions underlying even Pyle's work. It made perfect sense to write feature stories about individuals in the war. Most likely then, Ryan drew on this tradition much more so than on the norms of *The Reader's Digest*. Of course, Beidler is correct that the success of Ryan's project depended entirely on his having the support of *Reader's Digest*.[9] Certainly an independent writer would have had to take considerably longer to research and write even a much more limited account of D-Day. With the benefit

of this robust financial and editorial support, Ryan was able to publish *The Longest Day: June 6, 1944* by 1959, the fifteenth anniversary of
D-Day—a time when Americans still accepted the mainstream narrative of World War II and its implicit support of Cold War policies.[10] One
cannot imagine this book achieving quite the same response had it come
out a decade later, at the height of the Vietnam War.

Principally, however, the book takes shape from Ryan's ability to
balance multiple narratives of individuals with the overall scope of the
battle. To manage this task, he decided to limit his coverage to a mere
three days—June 4 through 6. He frames this period neatly between
two scenes at the headquarters of Field Marshall Erwin Rommel in La
Roche Guyon. The book opens with the town's church bells ringing
the six a.m. "Angelus" on June 4, and it closes with their ringing at
midnight as June 6 ends.[11] This frame evokes a religious theme consistent with the already common characterization of the invasion as
the "Great Crusade" (see chapter four). Ryan divides this short period
into emblematic segments titled "The Wait," "The Night," and "The
Day," suggesting that the D-Day events can stand for all the waiting,
all the nights, and all the days throughout the war. *The Longest Day*
becomes, by extension, the war itself. What is more, Ryan specifically
declares that he is writing something different from the unusual historical accounts of the war:

> What follows is not a military history. It is the story of people: the
> men of the Allied forces, the enemy they fought and the civilians
> who were caught up in the bloody confusion of D-Day—the day
> the battle began that ended Hitler's insane gamble to dominate
> the world.[12]

Thus, Ryan establishes three very important points at the outset. First,
he is writing a human interest story about individuals in the midst of a
great event. Second, he is writing of "the day the battle began" to end
Hitler's attempt to rule the world. The campaign in northwest Europe
becomes the emblematic battle, and D-Day becomes its essential first
assault. Finally, Ryan characterizes this as a fight against "Hitler,"
the story's one essential villain, and not against the German people.
Even German soldiers and their commanders become Hitler's victims,
betrayed by his insanity as well as by their own tragic misjudgment in
originally trusting him.

Serious histories of the Normandy invasion, such as John Keegan's
Six Armies in Normandy (1982) or Max Hastings' *Overlord* (1984), reveal

the campaign's complexity, demanding much more of the reader than does Ryan. Yet Keegan and Hastings cover something that Ryan has no inclination to examine—causality. Historians ask *why* the battle turned out as it did, not merely *what* occurred and *how*. They also evaluate the decisions of leaders and their subordinates. Since every battle is fraught with mistakes, even when all leaders agree on the overall strategy, there is much room for historical argument, a good deal of it acrimonious. What is usually missing from such books, however, is how it felt to be in the turret of a specific amphibious tank about to sink in the Channel, or what it felt like to dangle from a parachute over the Cherbourg Peninsula between streams of German antiaircraft fire. Rarely can a writer, whether a journalist or a historian, place a reader both in the battle and beyond it.

Ryan chooses to write only about what happened and how. Yet by focusing on a period of only sixty-six hours, he effectively gains the space to cover the whole range of what happened on all sides— American, British, French, and German. He can show the vastness of the invasion while also introducing a number of individuals and small groups whose experiences he can trace throughout the day's events by crosscutting among episodes. He thus achieves dramatic concentration, epic scope, and individual human interest. Consciously or unconsciously, he also suppresses controversy. His narrative depends on unquestioned assumptions about the invasion's leadership and planning. The Allies always appear powerfully *allied* in every sense of the word. Little is said of the intense bickering that often went on among leaders. The weather, with a kind of Greek tragic uncooperativeness, threatens the plan, but the Allies' decision to invade even under poor conditions, proves correct. Although that risky decision causes greater difficulties in the short run, it is ultimately vindicated. So by suppressing controversy, Ryan makes interpretation easy for readers who do not wish to bother with nagging historical or ideological questions. Deep critical analysis seems beyond the point since the Allies succeeded and won not only the battle but also the war. Of course, military historians will continue to argue about causality so that the next generation of soldiers might learn lessons for future wars. To Ryan, however, those are problems for war college faculties, not for a journalist who wants to make a major battle come to life for mass-market readers.

Representing the Germans, Ryan explores the internal conflicts dividing the German high command, specifically arguments between Rommel and Field Marshall Gerd von Rundstedt. German confidence that the Allies would invade only in good weather, and across the narrowest part of the Channel, is also shown as fatal arrogance. Yet because of his unstable personality, Hitler himself causes the greatest problems for German commanders. The German generals and their staffs are thus portrayed as competent but tragically flawed in their strategic rigidity as well as beset by a tyrant whom they must serve but can barely tolerate. Indeed, of all the German generals depicted by Ryan, not one seems to have any interest in the Nazi party or its goals. They are professional soldiers doing their duty without responsibility for the overall policies of their country. Again we see the pattern of historical rehabilitation of former enemies that Lawrence Suid and others have identified in a number of films.

Ryan's Germans thus become honorable enemies for their Allied counterparts—respectively, the Trojans and Greeks of this modern *Iliad*. Of course, Ryan still portrays the Allies as having the higher cause of liberating Europe from Nazi tyranny. What therefore amazes the critical reader is that, even while the German Army's implicit "cause" is to maintain that evil Nazi control, Ryan's representation of its leaders never suggests that they support such oppression. This inconsistency remains under the narrative's surface, but it still raises troubling questions. It is inherently contradictory to claim righteousness for the Allies while failing to confront the moral responsibility of the Germans. Obviously, most readers will not ask those questions of Ryan's book. He is telling the interrelated, often poignant stories of ordinary individuals swept up in vast events, so he replaces both historical and moral judgment with personal interest. Rhetorically speaking, *The Longest Day* appeals to us on the basis of emotion (pathos) and personality (ethos).[13] Ryan wishes to persuade us merely to share in the powerful feelings of the moment, and having shared those feelings, to preserve a sense of awe about what we have witnessed. Furthermore, his book is consistent with America's mainstream narrative of the war, a narrative found more than anywhere on film. In short, this book offers a simplified account of a complex event for a movie-going audience in a movie-made culture. The next step should be obvious.

★   ★   ★

Writing a book suitable for the screen is one thing, but getting it there is quite another.[14] Like Ryan's book, Zanuck's film is composed of many interwoven stories. The compelling sketches of individuals caught up in the vast events of D-Day capture our attention and touch our emotions. In addition, we know that these are real people, many of whom were still alive when the film was made. We think of Private Arthur "Dutch" Schultz (Richard Beymer), the lost American parachutist who cannot seem to find the war no matter how hard he tries. We think of Major Werner Pluskat (Hans Christian Blech), a German artillery officer who is suddenly aware, in the early dawn of June 6, that the invasion is pointed directly at him. These and so many other stories come to mind as we recollect the film. Indeed, it is an extraordinary accomplishment that the characters and their stories make such a lasting impression. Like so many epics, Ryan's book is filled with commonplaces, and on screen, those commonplaces become visual as well as verbal. Nonetheless, both book and film manage to convey, through such formulaic patterns, some of the individuality of those involved and the uniqueness of their experiences.

To be sure, there are weaknesses. For example, many of the exposition scenes sound unnecessarily forced as even the best actors have trouble breathing life into lines that have little dramatic content. Given the surface-level attempt to imitate a documentary style, Zanuck might have used voice over narration to good effect. This approach, used briefly and successfully in *A Bridge Too Far* (1977) and in the Civil War epic *Gettysburg* (1993), can clarify a complex situation without encumbering the dialogue. The acting is also rather uneven and sometimes quite clichéd. Scenes with John Wayne and what appears to be his Hollywood entourage—Steve Forrest, Tom Tryon, and Stuart Whitman—make us feel as if we were watching a group of wandering actors looking for a movie in which to play soldier. Zanuck also cast his then-mistress, Irina Demick, as a French resistance fighter, even though she looks more like a fashion model than a member of the Maquis.[15] Of course, casting such a large film demands many compromises, such as when Zanuck chose teen-culture idols Paul Anka, Tommy Sands, and Fabian to play American soldiers, despite their limited acting abilities. At least their youthful appearance is refreshingly realistic in a film where a number of actors, such as John Wayne and Robert Ryan, are clearly too old for their roles.[16] In contrast, Robert Mitchum was an excellent choice to play Brigadier General Norman Cota, not only because he bears a striking resemblance to the original but also because he effectively conveys Cota's forceful personality. Still, we are seeing celebrity actors typecast in roles that fulfill our expectations. Audiences are willing to accept this fact because they want to connect with the stories of the people whom the actors represent. In a sense, the actors *stand for* more than *play* the people from Ryan's book, becoming symbols even in their attempt to portray actual people.

In so vast a film, structure is always a challenge.[17] Keeping all the disparate threads of story consistent and coherent in a cinematic epic is even more challenging than in a book. The structure of Zanuck's film, despite some adaptations to suit a visual medium, still maintains Ryan's basic pattern—the preinvasion wait, the night airborne assault, the dawn landings, and the beachhead combat. To keep the audience from becoming confused by the frequent crosscutting, Zanuck labels scenes with at least the place and sometimes the date and time. This process begins with the first scene, where we hear the familiar opening notes of Beethoven's *Fifth Symphony* that correspond to the Morse code for letter *V*, which stood for victory. We hear waves rhythmically hitting the shoreline as we see an American helmet, bullet hole in the side, upended on the beach. That the helmet is there at all makes no logical sense since the invasion has yet to occur. But this is an emblematic image to which we will return in the final credit sequence, so in this shot, Zanuck is sacrificing realism for a consistent, imagistic frame. The message printed over this image tells us that this is "Occupied France" during the fifth year of the war. As the music stops, we hear French BBC messages for the resistance (in this and all foreign language scenes, the characters speak their own languages, and subtitles appear below). The music shifts to German drums, and we see a montage of scenes from the German occupation, concluding with one in which Rommel (Werner Hinz) addresses his commanders while all stand on the bluffs above a beach. He delivers the statement from which Ryan selected the title, arguing that the first day of the invasion will be "the longest day." As soon as Rommel repeats the words for emphasis, the *Fifth Symphony*'s opening returns powerfully, with the full orchestra, and we see the title on screen over the image of the beach. After this scene, however, we have entered into the dramatic time frame of the film, which places us on June 5.

The film's opening sequence itself not only establishes tone and provides exposition but also offers a key to the film's overall emblematic structure. Throughout the film, as we move from sequence to sequence, scene to scene, what we witness are not so much moments of actual, documented events (though some indeed are) as much as emblematic vignettes that allow the small scene and group of people to stand briefly for the whole of the day's action. The use of iconic actors, a feature that tends to make any film feel less realistic, heightens the symbolic and emblematic quality of the scenes. Thus, we are seeing two films at once. On the surface, we view a docudrama, based on actual historical events and people and filmed in black and white to connect it with the realism of newsreels and combat footage. At the same time, we also view a highly symbolic, almost ritualistic film, an episodic morality play drawn from the experience of the war. This "second film" also justifies the black-and-white format because that style links it with so many earlier World War II films and their well-established conventions.

At this second level, the emblematic features of the film take over, and we recognize that each scene, or each pattern of scenes with a specific set of characters and circumstances, tries to convey some particular emotion or to teach some specific lesson. British Major John Howard (Richard Todd) teaches us stoic obedience as he and his small band of airborne troops "hold until relieved" at the bridge they have captured. German fighter ace, Colonel Josef "Pips" Priller (Heinz Reincke) demonstrates how reckless boldness can save his and his wingman's lives when they are the only two German planes attacking the beachhead. We witness the tragic workings of fate when a planeload of American paratroopers accidentally drops into the square of Sainte-Mère-Église, right on top of the German machine guns that slaughter them. We learn of the unpredictability of serving a tyrant, when Hitler's tantrum prevents the release of the reserve panzer divisions to Von Rundstedt (Paul Hartmann). Brigadier General Theodore Roosevelt Jr. (Henry Fonda) demonstrates the qualities of quiet courage and decisiveness when he has to adapt attack plans because his division has landed on the wrong part of the beach. Late in the film, we see an encounter between RAF Flight Officer David Campbell (Richard Burton), who has been shot down and injured, and lost American paratrooper Dutch Schultz. They meet by the body of the German whom Campbell killed with his pistol, and we witness how, for the individuals involved, the "Great Crusade" is largely an experience of ironic confusion. "He's dead. I'm crippled. You're lost. Do you suppose it's always like that—I mean war," says Campbell with sad irony. These two characters' immediate experiences of the war have consisted chiefly of fearful uncertainty, mixed with sudden terror and violence. A contrasting closing comment comes from Brigadier General Cota when, after Omaha Beach has been secured, he waves down a passing jeep, pulls out a new cigar, and wearily says, "O.K. Run me up the hill, son." Both Campbell and Cota have made an elegiac comment on the passing of the day, but Campbell's was characteristically British and poetic, a neatly structured triadic expression. Cota's characteristically American understatement belies the look on his face, a look suggesting the weight of what he has seen that day. The line tells us basically that we know the cost, and now it's time to go on.

This massive film thus proceeds, episode by episode, as an emblematic drama of small incidents that move us to feel specific emotions and/or instruct us in how war reveals basic features of human nature and experience. Emblem literature is a traditional form usually associated with the Renaissance; and emblem books combined illustrations with short poems to convey an emotion or teach a lesson in a memorable way. Ultimately, *The Longest Day* works much as did the old emblem books. The film's history of D-Day breaks down into a set of interwoven mini-dramas, each of which influences us emotionally and intellectually, leading us to feel, and then allowing our feelings to motivate us to contemplate the events of that day in relation to our own lives. The individual scenes have a strong emblematic quality, with image and dialogue jointly constructing the emblem. The lessons are straightforward but often tinged with irony and pathos. *The Longest Day* is therefore far more a symbolic film than a realistic one, allowing us to experience the events of the day through a series of symbolic encounters. Emblematic in approach and choral in structure, *The Longest Day* thus becomes a ceremonial and ritualistic film celebrating the mainstream American narrative of World War II. Using factual content and a realistic visual style, it nonetheless presents a highly mythic rendering of D-Day, which then itself becomes the prevailing metaphor for the American experience in the European Theater, and for the whole of World War II.[18]

A Narrative Too Far and the Master Commander

Throughout the decade following *The Longest Day*, many filmmakers tried to duplicate its success by producing similar epic World War II films.[19] Elaborate, on-location epics had already defined Hollywood's concept of big success, regardless of subject matter, and so throughout the 1960s and even into the 1970s, studios produced a number of such films. A few were successful, but most were critical and commercial failures, including many about World War II. *The Longest Day* had capitalized on the commonplaces established during twenty years of World War II films while also attempting to surpass its predecessors and stand as the consummate epic of the war. Yet few of Zanuck's imitators could repeat this achievement. Moreover, *The Longest Day* not only ushered in this period of imitation, but it also began closing the era when Hollywood's traditional World War II films had their greatest influence and box-office appeal—roughly from the late

1940s through the mid-1960s. Television began competing even more intensely with Hollywood war films, offering World War II series and thus diffusing the audience for new war films. The best of these series was *Combat!* (1962–1967), developed in part by war veteran Robert Pirosh. Others included *The Gallant Men* (1962–1963) and *12 O'Clock High* (1964–1967). In addition, World War II films from the 1940s and 1950s made frequent appearances on television, in both local and network programming. As a result, Americans increasingly chose to stay home and watch the small screen rather than view the latest war epic at the movie theater.

Still, for over a decade, filmmakers kept trying to match Zanuck's success. In 1964, Andrew Marton, director of the American unit for *The Longest Day*, brought out a badly adapted version of James Jones' Guadalcanal novel *The Thin Red Line*. Otto Preminger made the awkward Navy epic *In Harm's Way* (1965). Ken Annakin, director of the *The Longest Day*'s British unit, was far less successful when directing *The Battle of the Bulge* (1965). Both *Anzio* (1968) and *The Bridge at Remagen* (1969) also employed some epic structural elements with moderate success, but they represented the war in more ambivalent, even negative ways (see chapter seven). Of course, 1969 also brought *The Battle of Britain*, one of the most accomplished and successful of the post–*Longest Day* epics, but this was essentially an English film. *Tora! Tora! Tora!* came out the next year. It accurately depicts America's intelligence failures prior to the Pearl Harbor attack, but even its stunning final attack sequence cannot compensate for the slowness of the film's first three quarters. Less accurate and more disappointing was *Midway* (1976), memorable for little more than initiating "sense-around" sound technology. *A Bridge Too Far* (1977) much more effectively depicted the Allies' failed airborne attempt to outflank the Siegfried Line in September 1944. Also based on a Cornelius Ryan book, this film appropriately ended the epic cycle as it had begun, with an adaptation of Ryan's work. *A Bridge Too Far*, however, is the exception to the rule concerning this period's epic war films. Even by 1965 it had become evident that Zanuck's achievement had been unusual, if not unique, and that subsequent efforts at the World War II epic were usually going "a narrative too far."

★ ★ ★

Patton (1970) was the most successful war epic from the period following *The Longest Day*, and significantly, it offers an entirely different focus. While the D-Day film covers one battle during only two days, *Patton* follows the experiences of General George S. Patton Jr. throughout more than two years of war—early 1943 through late 1945—and whereas Zanuck's film tells the story of "many men," *Patton* concentrates on its flamboyant title character. Though not the last World War II epic of its time, *Patton* largely closes out the period inaugurated by Zanuck because, by emphasizing one heroic figure, it returns the epic to its aristocratic roots. *The Longest Day* and most of its imitations try to construct a democratizing narrative of World War II, with victory achieved only through the teamwork and sacrifices of many. In contrast, *Patton* celebrates the single man who stands across the battlefield like a colossus. From the film of "many men" and their collective efforts, we move to the film of the one "great man" whose leadership makes all the difference in times of crisis.

    Patton achieves its epic quality by focusing on one of America's most influential but controversial World War II generals. Producer Frank McCarthy and director Frank Schaffner, along with screenwriters Francis Ford Coppola and Edmund H. North, concentrate on Patton's mercurial, rebellious nature while also giving free reign to his expressive personality. Drawing on multiple accounts, including General Omar Bradley's memoir *A Soldier's Story* (1951) and Ladislas Farago's *Patton: Ordeal and Triumph* (1963), the filmmakers had ample background material. From these sources, they crafted a story in which Patton is the aristocratic, brilliant, and egocentric artist of warfare, who contrasts with the workmanlike professionalism of Omar Bradley (Karl Malden), known as the "G.I. General." The film uses this contrastive characterization to highlight Patton's eccentricities. Actually, though the historical Patton was indeed quite the showman, the real Bradley was no closer to the G.I.s who fought for him than were most of his fellow generals. Still, Bradley was an extraordinarily bright and gifted leader—more as a campaign organizer than as an operational field commander. He contributed significantly to the Allied victory while still demonstrating concern for the average fighting man. In many ways, Bradley was fairly typical of America's high-level commanders, of the same mold as Eisenhower and Marshall, with whom he shared respect and friendship.[20] Patton was the one who stood out among American generals in Europe, a fact that he gloried in. Thus the colorful figure of Patton in the film, while an artistic construct, still does reasonable justice to the historical original.

    While McCarthy, Schaffner, and North also saw Patton as a rebel, Coppola probably added to that characterization a particular pattern of rebelliousness. In this and other films, Coppola constructs romantic rebels who are living tragically in a time that has passed them by. Characters such as Don Vito Corleone in *The Godfather* (1972) and Colonel Walter Kurtz in *Apocalypse Now* (1979) exhibit qualities similar to those found in Coppola's Patton. These characters are all essentially warrior heroes, their standards defined by a heroic and mythic past—perhaps one that existed nowhere but in a literary and artistic imagination. As values change over time, the institutions served by such figures become far more pragmatic, leaving no place for romantic heroes. In a sense, these warrior characters act as if they really *were* heroes out of epics. They are men trapped in their own cultural fictions of what it means to be a "great man," but they live in a time when the "great man" approach to history has significantly eroded. They are bound to fail in the long run, but their brilliance and passion still carry them far. Like protagonists of Greek tragedies, they are necessarily over-reachers whose ambitions tempt fate. In a sense, they are not unlike Coppola himself, a brilliant maverick who often risks too much and goes too far. Thus, Coppola's work explores the epic as genre and the loss of the epic vision in a modern world. *Patton* deals with the futile attempt to maintain that vision in the face of all the onslaughts of modernity, and as such, it is as much about art as about war and warriors—at least as far as Coppola is concerned.

Both historically and as represented on film, Patton is also a traditional "amateur"—not in the pejorative sense, but harkening back to the term's original meaning: an individual who pursues his or her passion out of love, not because of professional necessity. Amateurs are self-defining, self-motivated, and often self-taught, and they are frequently at odds with the structures of modern, bureaucratic institutions, such as the U.S. Army in World War II. Professionals, in contrast, are dedicated to the institutional structures that define the values of their work. Despite his graduation from the military academy and his lifelong service in the U.S. Army, much of what Patton knew of war and history he learned on his own initiative, not at West Point. Amateurism is also distinctly antimodern, characteristic instead of aristocratic societies, and Patton was uncompromisingly aristocratic. He came from a relatively wealthy Virginia family, and in at least one instance, during the lean years between the wars, he used his private funds to purchase spare parts for his unit's tanks.[21] At a crucial moment in the film, Bradley confronts Patton and says, "There's one big difference between you and me, George. I do this job because I have been trained to do it. You do it because you love it." It is a love that Patton does not deny. His military service was a labor of love, and directing a battle was his art. Thus, the film focuses on and celebrates qualities displayed in the man himself: that he wished to be a heroic warrior of epic proportions, not a managerial general. Say what one will about Patton, he was never the "very model of a modern major general."

Of course, no construction of Patton's character could have succeeded without the right actor in the role, and George C. Scott gave the performance of a lifetime, seeing in the natural expressiveness of Patton an actor's dream character, but also identifying with the rebel nature of this haughty outsider. What many Americans now think of Patton is inevitably shaped by Scott's characterization, and at times the mythic representation may have replaced history. Given Patton's own penchant for self-mythologizing, however, this may be appropriate. In one telling scene during the Battle of the Bulge, Patton declares to his staff, "if we are not victorious, let no man come back alive." After the other staff officers have left in stunned silence, his aide, Lieutenant Colonel Codman (Paul Stevens), says, "You know, General, sometimes the men don't know when you're acting." Patton coolly replies, "It's not important for them to know; it's only important for me to know." For Scott, this is the most revealing moment of the film, since Patton is seen as the consummate actor, who by his own role-playing propels whole armies across Europe. Here the naturally titanic ambitions of an actor meld with those of the character he plays, creating one of the most powerful figures in the history of American cinema. Ultimately, the film portrays Patton as tragic, relieved of his command after the war and lost without the war to challenge his powers. Scott himself never again had such a commanding role, despite his relatively young age (he was only forty-three when playing Patton). Hollywood seemed to pass by the actor much as the Army had done the general.[22]

Of all the scenes in *Patton*, perhaps the most memorable is his speech before an enormous flag. The film opens with this scene, which plays even before the credits. Those credits subsequently role over a series of shots showing the devastation resulting from the American defeat at the Battle of the Kasserine Pass. We see partially naked American corpses by their burnt-out tanks, their bodies being stripped and looted by Bedouin tribesmen. Such imagery is distinctly negative and anti-war, especially given the assumptions of American audiences in 1970 when the Vietnam War was daily shown in graphic detail on the evening news. In contrast, the precredit scene occurs outside of any time or place, in a kind of cinematic eternity from which the title character can address us with godlike authority. In this scene, viewers have been "drafted" by the film, since we are put in the position of being Patton's troops, the collective group of soldiers he had commanded in one or another situation throughout the war. We view it as if from seats in an auditorium, where what seems the world's largest American flag hangs behind the stage, a flag so large that it dwarfs even the commanding presence of Patton. We are literally called to attention, and kept there by the bugle call, as Patton walks up to the stage from behind, on steps out of our sight, thus making him seem to rise into our field of vision like a mysterious apparition. He stands in the center, salutes, and holds the salute as the bugle plays through its full call. All the while, the camera focuses on separate areas of his body, from medals, to starred helmet, to steely eyes. Once the bugle falls silent, and we are allowed to be "at ease," he begins the famous speech recalled by so many viewers, containing lines like, "…no bastard ever won a war by dying for his country. He won it by making the *other* dumb bastard *die* for his country." Scott delivers his speech in the gruff, gravel tones that gave him such presence in many roles. The scene incarnates the qualities of the imperial leader, right down to the highly decorated, regal-looking uniform. He looks less like a soldier in the U.S. Army than a figure of his own creation, literally "an army of one." While Patton addresses the audience of supposed soldiers, and his remarks concentrate on them, even lauding them as "wonderful guys," all our attention is on the general as he struts, strides, and intones across the stage, in a language that moves with ease from formality to profanity and back again.

This speech, of course, never existed; rather, it comes from a compilation of remarks Patton supposedly uttered at different times and places. This is a kind of rhetorical reverse-engineering. Whereas it is a commonplace rhetorical tradition to use brief quotations from famous speeches and texts, just the opposite happens here. Patton's statements, often quoted in Farago's text, are stitched together to create a seamless whole, a speech that characterizes the man, his character in the film, and the story the film is about to portray. Like a prologue speech in a Shakespearian play, this one functions as a commentary on the drama we are about to witness, an opening frame of reference through which viewers can interpret the film. If one imagines the film without the opening speech, audiences would first witness the ghastly sights of the American corpses at Kasserine, suggesting an antiwar message. Without the timeless quality of the opening, we would begin with very downbeat imagery and prepare to see only a film that condemns the horror of war. As is, we see the aftermath of battle only after having met the mythic hero, and thus we view the horror as something from which the hero will rescue us.

Of course, we are meant to measure this scene against the film's end, which is not exactly a matching frame, but which carries Patton's voiceover as he walks into the distance. Now reduced to a mere titular command, the general is walking his dog up a hillside in Germany. In the distance, almost too emphatically, we see a windmill, making an overt visual connection with Don Quixote. As we view his departing image, we hear Patton speak of the triumphs held for Roman conquerors, and how in the chariot with the victorious general rode a slave who held the laurels above the hero's head and whispered in the great man's ear, "All glory is fleeting." This elegiac closing leads us to assume that the mythic hero is gone, not only from the stage and film but also from the life of the modern world against which he struggled. The film urges us to feel no small sadness at his passing, for supposedly in losing such heroes, we have lost the commanding presences that gave us all a sense of potential heroism.

★   ★   ★

Those who released *Patton* in 1970 may have thought they were elegizing a figure truly extinct in a modern culture, where bureaucrats and technocrats were now in charge. Yet they may have misunderstood how modernity had also become useful to men of grand ambition during the twentieth century, some quite sinister, despite their sense of grandeur. *Patton* came out as the Vietnam War was boiling with controversy, continuing to spur nationwide antiwar protests. How counterintuitive to construct such an autocratic warrior for an America increasingly suspicious of such figures. It was obviously a film looking to the past, and yet it was prescient as well, for the figure of Patton touched a cord in the American psyche. Even as Vietnam divided us, many Americans longed all the more for a strong leader. Richard Nixon sought to portray himself as one such figure, but the role did not suit him, and the next two presidents did not even attempt it. In 1980, however, Ronald Reagan managed to win overwhelmingly by projecting, in a different register, the ethos evoked throughout *Patton*—a leader who is uncompromising, confident, and powerfully in charge. But where Patton's demeanor had been aristocratic, Reagan expressed power through an affable, folksy persona. In either case, many Americans welcomed the figure of a strong man to lead and protect them, also allowing them to ignore difficult policy questions and ambiguous moral problems. So regardless of its makers' intentions, *Patton* revealed the nation's underlying desire for an imperial figure in American politics, a desire that many Americans would then satisfy in their unqualified support for Reagan.

Ultimately, comparing *The Longest Day* with *Patton* can help us understand changes in American cultural and political life during the 1960s, as well as the general trends from midcentury to the present. From the 1930s through World War II, our cultural values generally reflected the concerns of ordinary people—the collective identity of what, however simplistically, Carl Sandburg had evoked with the title *The People, Yes*.[23] After the war, fears of communism began to supersede such democratic optimism. While the 1960s brought a temporary return to New Deal–style liberalism in domestic social policies, by that decade's end, a more conservative and authoritarian vision began asserting itself, supported by those who feared domestic social change even more than they feared the specter of international communism. The Nixon White House openly inaugurated a process of "imperialization" in national politics that has been growing, on-and-off, for several decades.[24] While *Patton* shows the general with his warts, it is ultimately most effective at conveying his mastery as both the icon and the manipulator of power—an authoritarian figure perhaps unique in American cinema. Whereas *The Longest Day* emphasizes sweeping shots of hundreds of men at such places as Omaha Beach, *Patton* shows the man alone, magisterial and supreme, directing the battle. Whatever the filmmakers' conscious intentions, *Patton*'s iconography is distinctly imperial, autocratic, and even, at times, fascistic.

Thus, by 1970 a portion of the American cultural imagination could openly accept our story of World War II as the story of a great leader, in contrast to the story of the many who fought under his orders. This was a major divide, after which the war could be seen as something other than the collective struggle of all people to be free—once a central theme of OWI during the war. Rather, the war was now also seen as the achievement of American empire during what Henry Luce had called "The American Century."[25] While this theme had been evident all along, it came to the fore most powerfully in the imagery and characterization of *Patton*. Although some Americans found this representation disturbing, many celebrated the film's portrayal of Patton, recognizing in that imperial visage something they wished to emulate and follow.

For decades after the war, both liberal and conservative communities had shared a common narrative of World War II as a "good war." The mainstream American war narrative justified our fighting as part of a universal struggle for freedom and justice, regardless of our economic self-interest. Although our actual motives for fighting had been mixed, and our human rights record continued to be uneven and often openly hypocritical, we had still recognized the threat of fascism and had fought the war to defeat it and all its oppression and injustice. In our national narrative of World War II, we acknowledged the terrible cost, but we also honored those who had fought, largely because we believed our victory had achieved something that would eventually lead to a better world. Underlying this common narrative, however, was a deep if unacknowledged division between different communities of belief regarding the war's legacy: those who, in the tradition of Henry Wallace, saw the legacy as a call to continue a global struggle for human rights, and those who, in the tradition of Henry Luce, saw it as a call to maintain and extend American hegemony in the world. Cold War politics blurred the differences between these two interpretive communities, since both competed in asserting their anticommunism, from different sets of motives. Thus the common "Good-War" narrative persisted into the 1960s, leading both groups to suppress the darker side of the war, and all the ways in which, at times, we had acted no better than those whom we had fought, even imitating their vices in order to achieve the final victory.[26] By the late 1960s, however, political contention over the Vietnam War drove to the surface the underlying divisions between these opposing views of our World War II experience. As a result, the consensus "Good-War" narrative gradually broke down, with human rights advocates now adopting a more ambivalent and critical interpretation of the war, and national power advocates more openly asserting our right to international hegemony by virtue of our military victory and continuing military strength.

Therefore, America's master narrative of the war, long shared by competing ideologies, broke down in the late 1960s as the Vietnam War revealed itself to be a military, political, and moral failure. As the old narrative of World War II collapsed, a minority view emerged, for a time, as a new way of understanding our past—a "conscientious objection" to our conventional, accepted pattern of representing World War II. Yet this "new" perspective, like so many other things in our culture, was not new at all, and had actually been with us throughout the war and the postwar period. Some Americans saw value in a post-Vietnam reappraisal of our World War II narratives. Others rejected any counter-statement as unpatriotic, and in the conflict and chaos left by Vietnam and the 1960s, their hopes focused on the new imperial character, the neo-mythic leader manifest so fully in the figure of Ronald Reagan.

Since then, the history of how we have retold the story of World War II has been itself a conflict, one that persists to this day. Before we can understand that conflict, however, we must first examine the works that, from the war's end through the 1960s, voiced opposition to the mainstream narrative.

CHAPTER SEVEN

Conscientious Objection

"The First Dead Man. . . ."

"The first dead man on Omaha Beach must be a sailor"—so says Admiral William Jessup (Melvyn Douglas) in *The Americanization of Emily*, a 1964 war satire written by Paddy Chayefsky and directed by Arthur Hiller.[1] The plot builds from this bizarre claim, as well as from Jessup's demand that his personal staff film the landings to record that first death. Just prior to D-Day, Jessup has come to London to publicize the U.S. Navy's role in the invasion, and despite his apparent outrageousness, the film still treats him sympathetically. Dedicated to his service, he concentrates on highlighting the Navy's role in the war because the Navy must struggle with the Army and Air Force for future congressional appropriations. Under normal circumstances, he behaves reasonably, demonstrating genuine concern for those under his command. Now, however, grieving over the loss of his wife, the aging Jessup overworks to the point of psychological collapse, and his "high concept" cinema formulation emerges just as extreme fatigue propels him into a manic state.

Jessup utters his outlandish pronouncement while bursting unannounced into the hotel bedroom of his aide, Lieutenant Commander Charles "Charlie" Madison (James Garner), just as Charlie is being passionately embraced by his beautiful English motor-pool driver, Emily Barham (Julie Andrews). Standing in the doorway, the admiral is completely oblivious to Charlie's situation. After Jessup leaves, Emily inquires, "Does he often say things like that?" Here Andrews' delivery echoes her "Mary Poppins" character from earlier that same year. For American audiences of the time, it does seem as if Mary

Poppins is climbing into bed with Bret Maverick (Garner's popular television role) when both are accosted by a mad admiral in his night-shirt. Clearly, we are "not in Kansas anymore"—or at least, we are no longer in America's mainstream narrative of World War II. Instead, we are viewing the D-Day invasion from an absurdist perspective, where winning the interservice fight for appropriations is just as important as winning the actual war. Yet, this "mock-epic" film comes merely two years after *The Longest Day*. What had changed? For one thing, the October 1962 Cuban Missile Crisis had greatly amplified Americans' fear of nuclear war.[2] Perhaps even more emotionally wrenching had been the 1963 assassination of President Kennedy. In the wake of such frightening events, major films such as Sidney Lumet's *Fail-Safe* and Stanley Kubrick's *Dr. Strangelove* (both from 1964) openly questioned our national defense policies. Yet World War II material itself still seemed relatively sacrosanct in early 1960s Hollywood, so the Hiller/Chayefsky film was an innovative project that signaled possible changes in how future films might represent that war.[3]

The Americanization of Emily uses a standard formula for wartime romantic melodrama. A charming, self-centered American officer comes to England on special duty and is assigned a beautiful British war widow as his motor-pool driver. She resists his initial advances, show-ing a cool exterior to shield her passionately romantic nature. Despite their differences, they still fall deeply in love. Obstacles arise, however, when he proposes marriage, and they break up angrily just before he leaves for a dangerous mission. When he is presumed dead, she is devas-tated, but fate proves less than cruel. He returns, limping but unbowed, and she runs to his arms. Fade out and roll credits.

This familiar plot replays many films, including *A Yank in the RAF* (1941), to which Hiller and Chayefsky make some obvious allusions (see chapter one). Charlie Madison, however, is not a daring pilot but a pro-ficient "dog robber," an admiral's aide whose responsibilities encom-pass everything from public relations to high-level pandering. While Jessup's colleagues plan the Normandy landings, Charlie ensures that these senior officers live the good life. He himself takes an "antiwar" stance, professing to be a "devout coward." Although working for an admiral who promotes war keeps Charlie safely away from battle, he still attacks any glorification of war. When Emily voices her contempt for rear-echelon Americans who show no respect for England's war-time sacrifices, Charlie counters that the war has resulted from cen-turies of European greed and stupidity.[4] Beneath this surface anger, however, both share an obvious attraction, with Emily's heightened because, unlike other men she has known, Charlie will not get himself killed. Jessup complicates matters, however, by insisting that Charlie personally film U.S. Navy demolition teams clearing beach obstacles on D-Day. A baffled Charlie turns to Lieutenant Commander Paul "Bus" Cummings (James Coburn), the admiral's chief of staff, who assures him that the admiral will soon forget about the project. Meanwhile, Charlie enjoys his blossoming romance with Emily, eventually proposing marriage. However, when Jessup suffers an acute psychotic episode, Bus develops a sudden fervor to complete the film, ordering both the enraged Charlie and himself to join the invasion. To his relief, Charlie discovers that mistaken travel arrangements will bring them to Portsmouth only after the invasion fleet has sailed, a fact he does not share with Bus. Yet Charlie's delight at missing the invasion alienates Emily, leading to their angry breakup just before his departure. When severe weather postpones the assault, Bus has a second chance to haul a crestfallen, intoxicated Charlie aboard an LST. The next morning, as they approach shore with the first wave, their landing craft is hit, sending both men into the water. Charlie runs away from the beach, but Bus chases him back by shooting at and slightly wounding him. As Charlie runs forward, dodging bullets and shells, an explosion comes too close and leaves his apparently lifeless body lying on the sand.

Captured by a photographer, Charlie's apparent heroism makes front-page news across America. This does little to console Emily, who has finally realized how much she loved Charlie the honest coward. Jessup, quickly recovered from his depression, prepares to return to Washington, hoping to use Charlie's new image as a wedge in congressional hearings. He is chastened, however, to learn that Charlie died making a film conceived during Jessup's recent manic episode. Just before the scheduled departure, word comes that Charlie has returned, wounded but safe.[5] Charlie and Emily reunite, but when Bus appears with a plan to make Charlie a national hero, Charlie angrily declares that he will reveal the truth about the incident even if he ends up in a military prison. Now Emily must argue against "principle" and for the pragmatic basics of their life together. Using Charlie's own maxims of "devout cowardice," she shows him that his "noble" self-sacrifice would also condemn her to virtual widowhood again. Charlie finally agrees to act like a traditional hero so he might stay with Emily.

Ironically, having come to the satirical cutting edge, Hiller and Chayefsky cannot cut deeply. Their antiwar satire is undermined by a desire for a traditional romantic ending and by the fundamental inconsistencies of Charlie's character.[6] Charlie himself refuses to glorify war, but to preserve his personal safety, he still works faithfully for an admiral dedicated to publicizing the Navy's glorious wartime sacrifices. Interestingly, Charlie's refusal to sacrifice his life for any abstract cause links his fictional, satiric character with many real American soldiers, who often did not really want to fight until someone was trying to kill *them*. Many veterans who returned, limping in body or mind, also shared Charlie's subsequent desire to expose the military "snafus" that had wasted precious lives. Like Charlie, most ultimately relented, choosing instead to marry a woman who had waited and to begin a new life far from the horrors of war. From Charlie's perspective, as long as he and his loved ones remain safe, the rest of the world must look out for itself. To maintain this safety, he willingly serves those who perpetuate war. Thus, Charlie cements a bargain not unlike the one temporarily struck by Yossarian in *Catch-22*—to escape combat by agreeing to say "nice things" about those running the war.

In another sense, Charlie's pragmatic self-interest reflects some common but unacknowledged American attitudes toward the war. Although many American fighting men made heroic sacrifices in battle, and even more soldiered on stoically through numerous other hardships, only about a third of the 17 million in the military saw any combat in the war, and far fewer did most of the actual fighting. On the home front, many other Americans benefited from wartime economic growth, ultimately proclaiming the war to be "good." Like Charlie, some of those forced into danger returned wounded and angry, but most survivors saw no point in bucking the system. Instead, they focused on rebuilding their lives. They also accepted a mainstream narrative of the war that masked war's true cost, a narrative also used to support Cold War militarization. Despite its inconsistencies, *The Americanization of Emily* illustrates such self-interest in the service of myth, while also satirizing the mainstream cinematic representations of the "Good-War" narrative. Therefore, it shared in demythologizing that narrative and constructing a contrasting one. Starting as early as 1948, a number of American novels had begun this process, and even prior to *The Americanization of Emily*, so had several films, though no major film had yet been so openly satirical. Like this film, few of these works are unalloyed artistic successes. Together, however, they voiced a "conscientious objection" to America's mainstream World War II narrative, and to the Cold War policies it had come to represent.

War and Neo-Naturalistic Fiction: Mailer and Jones

Norman Mailer's *The Naked and the Dead* (1948) and James Jones' *The Thin Red Line* (1962) concentrate heavily on World War II infantry combat, reflecting both writers' personal memories of fighting in the Pacific theater. Their grim experiences led Mailer and Jones to represent a negative and generally unpopular counternarrative to America's mainstream story of the "Good War."[7] Though published fourteen years apart, both works are also linked because, in style and in substance, they draw on the traditions of literary naturalism—focusing on the physical limitations, psychological weaknesses, and social disorder experienced by the characters.[8] These novels represent a life governed largely by random chance, a naturalist assumption also consistent with the combat experiences of most veterans. Traumatic and debilitating, modern combat evokes a pessimistic determinism like that expressed during the earlier period of naturalism. Of course, although naturalism originally focused on the social consequences of organizing people for mass production in a mechanized culture, World War II neonaturalism examines a similar oppressive regimentation in the service of mass destruction.[9] Thus, in Mailer and Jones, naturalism has progressed from gritty urban life to grizzly combat death.

Both writers portray the dehumanizing experience of army life, where soldiers live and die inside the bellies of great twin beasts: the military organization and the war. The two novels reveal the squalid existence of the ordinary dogfaces who constitute a combatant "underclass," but depicted here with none of the humor or pathos found in the work of an Ernie Pyle or a Bill Mauldin. Instead, as revealed by Mailer and Jones, army life is humiliating and degrading, with each soldier subjugated to the arbitrary dictates of power manifest throughout the organization and exploited by every petty tyrant, from corporals to generals. The downtrodden G.I.s respond to their superiors with sheepish obedience and truculent passive-aggressiveness, while also turning on one another with violent hatred. Any possible nobility decays in the stinking holds of transports carrying men across the ocean, and it disintegrates in the muddy fields or fetid jungles where they must fight.

Language itself becomes one register through which Mailer and Jones reveal the terror and frustration of soldiers, for through language they respond to the mindless drudgery of the military life and the cruel unpredictability of combat. Central to the soldiers' language is the f-word. Having moved from civilian to army discourse, soldiers find that "f——" in all its forms—noun, verb, adjective—has been issued to them as standard equipment, and their freedom to use the word separates them from the restraints of bourgeois civilian conversation. Though wartime civilians were hardly innocent of this language, it was rarely *represented* as normal in everyday life because it was banned from regular fiction, drama, film, and broadcasting. Because the term so proliferates in military life, a neonaturalist representation of war demands its use, yet in 1948, censors would have prevented Mailer from publishing a novel using the word. A compromise allowed Mailer to use the equally communicative dialect spelling "fug."[10] Jones faced fewer limitations in 1962; benefiting from landmark censorship cases decided during the previous decade, he could be more direct. In each case, the writer manages to convey the authentic quality of what might be called "squad-speak."[11] Despite its initial shock value, the f-word carries far less power than we might assume. It seems a cry of freedom from social restraint as well as a word of sexual power. Yet these qualities exist only on the semantic surface since the Army cancels individuality and eliminates most freedoms. Thus, "f——" becomes the sigh of exhausted powerlessness, a mere grunt in the face of systematic oppression and overwhelming fate. What power it has is redirected as an expression of the fear and anger of combat, where "f——ing" is also killing. This ultimately connects the sexualized violence of combat with violent male sexual expression in earlier peacetime relationships.[12]

Although Mailer and Jones represent the futility and dehumanization of army life in general, their views of combat amplify these qualities. Combat turns out to be a debased consummation of all prior training, as sordid in its way as everyday army life is squalid. Fighting in a modern total war is dehumanizing because of its massive regimentation, yet it is also isolating for the individuals and small groups who feel lost in the chaos of battle and disconnected from their personal lives and from the military's organizational structure. Many soldiers kill, and many also die, and the killing and dying run the range from depersonalized shelling to the sudden, intimate encounter of two enemies with trench knives. Life at the front plunges soldiers into a badly managed slaughterhouse, with blood and body parts scattered everywhere. The result is a continuous condition of disgust and fear.

This endemic fear afflicts troops like a disease, producing both chronic psychic pain and episodes of acute agony. Soldiers fear not only death or injury but also losing control and humiliating themselves. As represented by Mailer and Jones, such humiliation leaves each man more vulnerable to the arbitrary authority of superiors and to the violent anger of comrades. In these two novels, many soldiers fight neither from unit pride nor from mutual loyalty, but from fear of commander and comrade alike. Some, such as Mailer's Sergeant Croft, also fight out of a sense of violence distilled from deep frustration. Others, such as Jones' Sergeant Welsh, are motivated by an unnamable, psychic pain that spawns destruction. For most, the constant fear ultimately produces a near psychotic state that leads troops to fight even more aggressively from pent-up frustration and anger, often leading to horrific acts of violence in the wake of combat, such as torture and murder of prisoners and mutilation of corpses. To experience combat in this context is to be completely unmanned, to lose all power, and to be seized by alternating forces of paralyzing fear or maniacally violent anger. Thus, as represented by Mailer and Jones, fighting becomes both a flight from and an expression of fear, a fundamentally naturalistic condition.

★   ★   ★

With *The Naked and the Dead*, Norman Mailer sought to establish himself as the first major novelist of the World War II generation. He was also positioning himself in relationship to existing traditions of modern American fiction, specifically seeking Hemingway's mantle as America's preeminent war writer. Ironically, neither writer had had extensive combat experience. Hemingway himself had never been a combat soldier, serving only in the Red Cross for merely a few months near the end of World War I. In addition, he had spent only a few weeks at the front before being wounded.[13] Although Mailer served three years in the Army, he still saw relatively little fighting. Drafted in February 1944, he did not enter a combat zone until January 1945, in the Philippines.[14] Serving there with the 112th Cavalry Regiment, he performed various noncombat duties before volunteering for the regiment's intelligence and reconnaissance (I&R) platoon, thus gaining some limited combat experience.[15] Mailer closed out his army career as a cook. He was not a hardened combat veteran, and generally, he did not pretend to be. Prior to being drafted, Mailer had felt that he would have to go to war to achieve the major literary reputation he so desired.[16] Following Hemingway's logic, he viewed combat as a fundamental challenge against which he could measure both himself and his art, a baseline experience for his career as a writer. Unlike Hemingway, however, Mailer also wanted to use the war as a site from which to explore the national psyche and its political manifestations.

The Naked and the Dead depicts combat mostly in the context of one long patrol, but the novel as a whole examines the psychology of power so evident in all aspects of army life. It specifically tells the story of an American invasion of a fictional Pacific island, Anopopei. Commanding the assault force is the politically ambitious Major General Cummings, a career army officer who also has a highly refined sense of how to observe and manipulate people. The novel represents Cummings as having repressed homosexual desires that resurface in his lust for power over men. His "will to power," however, goes beyond an expression of sublimated sexual urges. Essentially a crypto-fascist, Cummings sees wartime command as the basis for future political power. Paralleling Cummings is Sergeant Croft, the capable but sadistic leader of the I&R platoon at division headquarters. Whereas Cummings' fascism is cerebral, Croft's is direct and physical. Yet Croft is also a clever manipulator of people. Caught between these two men is Lieutenant Hearn, an intelligent but ineffectual liberal serving as the general's aide. Sometimes Cummings uses the intellectual Hearn as a sounding board for his own ideology, but as the young officer shows resistance, the general begins playing subtle power games. Their growing friction ends with Hearn assigned to lead the I&R platoon, whose dead lieutenant had never been replaced. Naturally, Croft bristles at his own loss of authority, and his growing resentment will prove deadly for Hearn. Mailer constructs the other members of the I&R platoon as a collection of psychological grotesques, representing America's regional, ethnic, and socioeconomic differences and conflicts. Their idiosyncratic stories become variations on the same power struggles that propel the novel's central conflicts, suggesting how those struggles also involve every element of the American population.

When American forces are halted before a formidable defensive position on the island, Cummings sends Hearn and the I&R platoon on an extended patrol to find a passage over Mt. Anaka so that the enemy can be outflanked. The general then leaves the island to secure further naval support. During his brief absence, however, forward American units discover gaps in the enemy lines, allowing the otherwise lackluster Major Dalleson to organize an attack. Despite Dalleson's awkward management, the attack still breaks through and defeats the enemy, so fate cheats Cummings out of his chance to appear as an architect of victory. Meanwhile, the I&R patrol has struggled to find a way up the mountain. After they are ambushed once, Hearn considers turning back, but he has now realized that, just like Croft and Cummings, he has begun to enjoy the feeling of power. He wants to prove he can complete the mission, and so he orders the men to go on. But the jealous Croft sets up Hearn, allowing the lieutenant to be killed in a second ambush. Croft then takes over, intimidating the men so they will continue up the mountain. He almost reaches his goal, only to be defeated when he knocks over a hornets' nest whose residents drive off the already exhausted patrol. As it had with Cummings, fate defeats Croft in his attempt to control his men and to conquer the mountain. The men retreat back down the mountain only to learn that all their efforts had been unnecessary—the campaign was already over.

This novel's greatest power grows from Mailer's ability to communicate the subtle features of characters' relationships and states of mind. He also reveals the connection between physical experience and mental state, especially during the long patrol. Few writers have represented so effectively the excruciating pain and fatigue endured by men in combat. Throughout, Mailer also demonstrates his wide knowledge of earlier modern American fiction, trying to situate himself as both its heir and its new leading voice. He reveals a range of stylistic and cultural influences, most obviously from the literary naturalists and Hemingway. Many readers have noted that his extended flashbacks, each labeled "The Time Machine," allow him to give insights into characters, while the "Chorus" sections provide a dialogic commentary on group experience. Both of these experimental narrative interruptions show the structural influence of John Dos Passos, but their narrative content is a different matter.

Although a few of the men come from New York and the Northeast, Mailer's home turf, most are from Midwest, the South, and the West, areas with which he was relatively unfamiliar, despite some brief youthful travels. Army service had brought Mailer into contact with men from across the country, and yet the "Time Machine" segments give detailed narratives of the men's lives in their original, regional settings, often with a level of specificity that the writer was unlikely to acquire merely by sharing time with his army comrades. Where then did Mailer acquire his range of portraits from American regions? Most likely from literary precedents—from Midwestern and Southern writers among the first generation of American modernists. In particular, we can see the shadowy outlines of Sherwood Anderson, since almost every one of these detailed characters conforms to Anderson's concept of the grotesque as explained in *Winesburg, Ohio* (1919).[17] Also evident are influences of Sinclair Lewis' social and political satires of the Midwest, along with downbeat representations of Southern rural poverty and desperation, such as those found in Erskine Caldwell.

Through these complex imitations, Mailer demonstrates his broad knowledge of modern American fiction while simultaneously establishing himself as a writer who has earned a place in its tradition. Furthermore, Mailer attempts to situate his massive war novel in relationship to a wide range of demographic groups who collectively stand for the nation as a whole. His political analysis of American culture can thus represent the entirety of the American people and not be isolated as the attitudes of a "typical East Coast intellectual." Since he did not yet have the extensive experience from which to develop these regional portraits, he most likely drew them on the basis of his literary predecessors. Mailer therefore presents a portfolio of academic character studies—portraits *by* the artist as a young man. Even though these efforts reveal great skill and extensive reading, they often betray some lack of authenticity. It is a testament to Mailer's literary talent that he comes reasonably close to pulling off this deception.

Hemingway critiqued *The Naked and the Dead* as "poor cheese pretentiously wrapped," and while the remarks reveal Hemingway's own jealousy, there is still some truth in the analysis.[18] Mailer attempts to reverse Hemingway's well-known "iceberg" theory of fiction—that writers must know far more than they reveal in the story. In contrast, Mailer puts every possible ounce of knowledge and experience into a single mammoth undertaking. While the earlier writer had tried to pare down his fiction by leaving much unsaid, Mailer wants to push all into the foreground. Rather than an iceberg, we have a vast ice sheet, impressive in its own way, but not towering. Unsurprisingly, *The Naked and the Dead* shows a gifted writer's youthful failings. A more mature novelist might have condensed the material, concentrating the alternating stories of the command level (Cummings) and the tactical level (Croft), with the gradual moral tragedy of Hearn linking both. If handled with greater subtlety, the warning against America's own homegrown fascism would also have had more impact. Ironically, even in this political message, Mailer owes a partial debt to Hemingway. In an introduction to a collection called *Men at War* (1942), Hemingway acknowledges that the war must be won, but he warns, "We must win it never forgetting what we are fighting for, in order that while we are fighting Fascism we do not slip into the ideas and ideals of Fascism."[19] In many respects, *The Naked and the Dead* is an elaborately orchestrated fantasia on the brief political theme articulated earlier by Hemingway and a number of others.

The Naked and the Dead, although a fundamentally important work of fiction about the war, is not a masterwork. It is too derivative, both stylistically and culturally. It may be a work *by* a young genius, but it itself is not a work *of* genius. Mailer tries so hard to demonstrate his literary credentials, in part so that he might more powerfully deliver his political message, that he forgets that a novel's principal authority comes from the authenticity of the characters and story. Even so, this novel contains some of the most effective representations of combat ever written. In addition, coming during a period of growing American paranoia about left-wing politics, Mailer's unabashed criticism of America's mainstream war narrative, and of America's accelerating movement to the political right, was an act of moral courage by a young, unknown writer. More than any artistic accomplishment, the very fact of writing and publishing this novel stands as a wholly different and far more important achievement—a personal act of political bravery.

★   ★   ★

From Here to Eternity (1951), portraying an unprepared Army stumbling into war at Pearl Harbor, established James Jones as both a successful novelist and a critic of the mainstream narrative of the war. *The Thin Red Line* (1962) continues this critique by showing the men of an infantry unit, "C-for-Charlie" Company, undergoing the stresses of combat on Guadalcanal. The intelligent but self-conscious Captain Stein commands the company. A former lawyer, he takes his responsibilities seriously but is sometimes indecisive. He also senses that some men regard him skeptically because he is Jewish. Despite his own and others' discomfort with his leadership, Stein stands up to authority to support his men, at one point refusing Colonel Tall's direct order to continue a disastrous attack. In contrast, the company top sergeant, Welsh, is tough and sometimes quite nasty, but thoroughly confident and professional. Although showing some cynical delight in the psychological discomfort of others, Welsh does not manipulate the men to achieve greater power, unlike Mailer's Sergeant Croft. To maintain his composure, Welsh drinks heavily, yet he keeps the company going, and he is the unit's best tactician.

Additional important characters include Private Witt, an independent Kentuckian always spoiling for a fight. Witt acts like a free agent, doing only what suits him. When frustrated with Charlie Company, he leaves to join a different unit; but when he misses the company, he returns. Yet he is also an instinctively good soldier, one of the best in the group. Another highly competent soldier is Private Bell. A lieutenant in the engineers before the war, he had resigned his commission to remain with his beloved wife. Now Bell has been drafted back into the Army, and the wife, about whom he constantly daydreams, eventually sends him the classic "Dear John" letter. Almost in a compensatory fashion, the Army offers him an officer's field commission for his effectiveness in combat. Somewhat less effective is the always frightened Corporal Fife, forward company clerk. Because he is probably based on Jones himself, who had served in a similar position, Fife's reactions to combat most likely reflect those of the novelist.[20] More than any one individual, however, the novel's true protagonist may be the collective entity known as Charlie Company. Whereas Mailer's I&R platoon seems a disparate collection of grotesque characters who never bond together, Jones' Charlie Company develops its own identity, inspiring a grudging loyalty from many of the men.

The company lands on Guadalcanal during the latter stages of the campaign, as the Army and Marine Corps units begin the fight to push the remaining Japanese off the island.[21] The company's attempt to capture a set of grassy ridges forms the heart of the book, illustrating in great detail the experiences of men in combat. Wishing to impress the high-ranking officers, Colonel Tall orders Charlie Company to make a quick frontal assault on the heavily defended slopes, but Stein, fearing heavy casualties, asks for a reconnaissance around one of the flanks. When Tall refuses, Stein carefully plans the difficult assault, but two inexperienced platoon leaders grow reckless and make a charge instead of following the original plan. Both are killed, and their platoons are widely scattered and pinned down. Jones spends considerable time showing how these isolated groups of men manage to survive and make their way back to the line of departure. When Tall orders the stalled attack to go forward again, Stein refuses. In the meantime, however, a few men have found a concealed path up the ridge. On the next day Captain Gaff, battalion executive officer, leads a small patrol to capture the main bunker complex. Charlie Company and the rest of the battalion then continue advancing and capture a Japanese bivouac. This last action becomes an orgy of killing, as pent-up fear and rage propel the men through the Japanese encampment, shooting whomever they find. Despite Charlie Company's success on the second day, Tall still relieves Stein of command and sends him home. Shortly after this, the company is taken off the line, but they do return to combat during the closing days of the campaign.

As the novel ends, the company is leaving the island. Most of the original officers have been killed or relieved, some former privates are now sergeants, and Bell is once more a lieutenant. Fife has been relieved of duty for medical reasons, having accidentally aggravated an old ankle injury that makes walking difficult. Welsh, who sought release in drink, finally finds emotional numbness at the close of battle—though he still keeps his two canteens filled with gin. A number of men have been killed or wounded, though fewer than one might have thought in such intense fighting. In another sense, however, all the men are casualties, scarred by the violent death they have both witnessed and inflicted. They share the secrets of the bizarre excitement of combat that becomes almost sexual at times, and they are bound by these secrets in ways they could not even begin to express. They are both awakened and numbed at the same time, indifferent to consequences and yet alive to circumstances.

Indeed, the men of Charlie Company have "evolved" into soldiers; as Jones would explain in his later book *WWII*, the "EVOLUTION OF THE SOLDIER" [Jones' capitalization] occurs as men grow experienced in combat and realize they must consider themselves already dead.[22] Once released from anticipation and hope, the men feel much more alive in every moment of experience, and each day takes on a poignant savor it had never had before. The men of Charlie Company have proceeded through this evolution, achieving their true condition as soldiers. In doing so, they have crossed the "thin red line" of the title, a phrase derived allegedly from two epigraphs cited at the book's opening. The first comes from Kipling, who writes of the "thin red line of 'eroes" who fight "when the drums begin to roll." The other is supposedly an "old middlewestern saying" that "There's only a thin red line between the sane and the mad." Charlie Company, now a "thin red line of heroes," has crossed that other line, becoming witnesses to and participants in the orgiastic madness of battle.

The Thin Red Line is thus Jones' neonaturalistic portrayal of the psychology of men in combat, exploring various aspects of male identity, role-playing, interpersonal conflict, isolation, and affection. The novel examines what isolates men, keeping each locked in an individual psychic prison, but it also explores what opens them up and joins them together. For example, the free-spirited Witt keeps returning to Charlie Company because he loves it and the men, but he also grows violently angry with a number of his comrades, especially Welsh. The latter's bitter cynicism, however, isolates him not only from Witt but also from the company of men in general. Jones also pushes his exploration of male relationships to include homosexuality. Fife and Private Bead engage in a brief series of homosexual encounters that grow more from boredom than from desire, while the newly promoted Sergeant Doll develops genuine homoerotic desires for one of his men. Whereas Mailer links homosexuality with a perverse desire to exercise power over other men,

Jones portrays it as just one more aspect of male relationships. In their "evolution," Jones' soldiers grow to appreciate what pleasures they find, regardless of social norms and mores of civilian life.

Jones' emphasis on extreme emotional experience sometimes leads readers to lose sight of *The Thin Red Line*'s rather dark sociopolitical satire. Like Mark Twain's *The War Prayer*, this novel shows open contempt for the easy platitudes voiced about war by those who remain safely in civilian life. As the dedication notes:

> This book is cheerfully dedicated to those greatest and most heroic of all human endeavors, WAR and WARFARE; may they never cease to give us the pleasure, excitement and adrenal stimulation that we need, or provide us with the heroes, the presidents and leaders, the monuments and museums which we erect to them in the name of PEACE.[23]

Anger seethes through these satiric comments, but not all of the satire is so obviously bitter. Names of characters also take on some satiric, symbolic meaning. Officers such as Tall and Band prove to be officious and annoying, while Witt, of course, shows instinctive wisdom in combat. The high-pitched tone of Corporal Fife's terror resonates in the sound of his name, just as Doll's concern with how others perceive him is suggested by his. There is, however, little systematic consistency to the naming symbolism, making it seem offhand. It is as if Jones actually wants these and other aspects of his style to appear careless, and that his naturalistic method in this novel is actually a conscious rejection of style.[24]

The satire within the narrative itself is more muted, surfacing in brief epiphanies that reveal the larger social and political forces at work behind the war. One compelling incident comes shortly after the company has made an unopposed landing on a beach already in American hands. Fife watches as enemy planes subsequently attack the transports anchored offshore. American fighter aircraft rise in defense from the airfield, and Fife begins to realize that all the elements of what he sees fit into a larger economic whole. He recognizes the fighting as merely a "regular business venture" of machines fighting one another and "that there were men in these expensive machines" meant little.[25] The whole socioeconomic significance of modern war becomes momentarily clear to Fife in a terrifying way as he sees all too well a new version of "why we fight":

> The very idea itself, and what it implied, struck a cold blade of terror into Fife's essentially defenseless vitals, a terror both of

unimportance, his unimportance, and of powerlessness: his powerlessness.... He did not mind dying in a war, a real war,—at least
he didn't think he did—but he did not want to die in a regulated
business venture.[26]

Before the novel's action begins, Welsh had apparently reached a similar realization that he repeatedly expresses by saying, "Property. All
for Property." Through these and other characters, Jones thus raises
political issues similar to those examined by Mailer, but he does so
less overtly, without lengthy philosophical dialogues on the nature of
power. Jones wants to appear unaffected in both his style and his ideas,
as if such reflections are mere throw-away revelations and not part of
a larger pattern, so he seems far less systematic in expressing an ideology than does Mailer. Instead, Jones suggests that the oppressive social
conditions revealed in war, and thus common in society, cannot be
changed but must still be represented honestly.

Here we find a naturalistic fatalism consistent with the "EVOLUTION
OF THE SOLDIER." The mess sergeant, Storm, comes to a succinct realization of this while preparing a special meal that he knows will not even
reach his own company. While still continuing to do his work, he thinks,
"Modern war. You couldn't even *pretend* it was human."[27] Certainly this
view runs counter to America's mainstream narrative of the war, a narrative that did more than "pretend," asserting directly that a modern war
could be not only "human" but also "good." Despite often devastating
wartime experiences, many veterans acquiesced to that mainstream narrative, and in 1962, few were ready to contest it with the intensity demonstrated by Jones, an irony that he acknowledges openly at the novel's
end: "One day one of their number would write a book about all this, but
none of them would believe it, because none of them would remember
it that way."[28] Having "evolved" in combat, these men would gradually
"de-evolve" to civilian life again, deeply burying their memories of battle. While the mainstream narrative still held sway, Jones remained merely
a voice crying in the wilderness, a successful but oddball writer of hyperbolic novels. It would take another war before veterans felt free to share
their traumatic combat experiences in a new literature of memoir.

Cold Facts of the Military-Industrial Complex

When President Eisenhower, in his 1961 farewell speech, warned
Americans against the "military-industrial complex"—the increasingly

integrated relationship between both public and private segments of the defense establishment—he was also unintentionally preparing the public for Joseph Heller's *Catch-22*, which came out later that year. Like many Americans, both president and novelist realized that the nuclear arms race and the escalating conflicts across the globe could not continue unchecked. Still, few Americans showed the courage and wisdom to confront that madness. Both Republicans and Democrats feared being labeled "soft on communism," so more bombs, missiles, and other armaments continued to roll out of defense plants. America also acclimated itself to the Cold War by reconstructing World War II, in print and on screen, in ways that confirmed both our national values and the absolute necessity of military preparedness. To take our minds off the arms race, many could simultaneously indulge in uninhibited consumerism during a period of unparalleled economic expansion. Although incoming bombers or missiles could be just over the horizon, we could still, quite literally, shop until we dropped.

This is the cultural universe that Heller explores in his darkly comic *Catch-22*. A veteran of World War II, Heller had completed sixty missions as a bombardier on a B-25.[29] After the war he finished his education, taught college English, and worked in advertising. Based on his experience of World War II itself and the subsequent Cold War era, he was thus well equipped to critique the military-industrial complex at the heart of 1950s America. His vehicle would be a complex novel that defied narrative conventions by using a circular or spiraling structure, returning repeatedly to one instance of horrific, meaningless death. Just as the mainstream American story of World War II was being used to support our Cold War policies and culture, Heller uses his World War II narrative to critique them. Indeed, *Catch-22* satirizes not only the defense establishment but also the whole economic enterprise to which it was inextricably linked and that had made war into what James Jones calls a "regulated business venture."[30] Heller brings this concept to its absurd fulfillment when his arch-villain, Lieutenant Milo Minderbinder, contracts his bomber group to the Luftwaffe, forcing the American pilots to attack their own base. Although Mailer had warned that America might fall under the control of crypto-fascists, Heller was the first to depict the Nazis as just one more client in our endless quest for profit and power.

In "The Death of the Ball Turret Gunner," poet Randall Jarrell uses merely five lines to construct an indelible image of combat death in the air war. In *Catch-22*, Heller uses several hundred pages to narrate variations on the same theme—the death of Snowden, waist gunner in the same bomber as the novel's main character, Captain Yossarian. The novel returns repeatedly to Yossarian's witnessing of Snowden's death because Heller uses this traumatic incident to represent war's horror in its most concrete, intimate, bodily form. Distant from but directly tied to such deaths are the absurd men and organizational structures controlling both Yossarian's bomber group and the whole war effort. The combined construct includes both civilians and servicemen, both private and public entities, with all rooted in the life-denying principles of "Catch-22."

"Catch-22" is mentioned first during Yossarian's interview with the group's physician, Doc Daneeka. Yossarian wants to be relieved of flying missions because he has already flown the number of missions originally specified for a tour of duty. Commanding officers, however, keep raising that number before anyone can leave. Yossarian seeks a way out. Doc explains that, if Yossarian wants to stop flying missions, he need only be declared mentally unfit, but there is a "catch": one must ask to be declared mentally unfit, and since the request itself demonstrates a healthy desire to stay alive, all such requests are denied because the act of asking is proof of sanity. The circular logic of "Catch-22" is flawless in its absurdity.

The novel continues with this *reductio ad absurdum* satire on all aspects of military life, the war, and the American economic system, revealing the continuity between the events of World War II and the political and economic constructs of the Cold War. Lieutenant Minderbinder turns out to be the great Machiavellian manipulator of the narrative, yet he remains oblivious to the consequences of his behavior because he truly believes in the righteousness of his fundamental economic principles. As group supply officer, Milo is the ultimate "supply-side" economist, using the group's matériel and supplies as merchandise for his black-market trading company known as M&M Enterprises. With these resources, he wheels and deals to make a profit for his corporation at the expense of his fellow soldiers. Milo rationalizes that each member of the group has received a "share" in the corporation, and thus they have lost nothing—even though they cannot trade or sell the shares, nor have they had any say in the transaction. He also justifies his behavior with the basic American mantra that "it is good for business." The war's raison d'être, from Milo's perspective, is to advance the interests of private enterprise. Since the military exists to protect private enterprise, using military supplies for Milo's corporation can be justified as supporting the war effort. Such rationalizations parallel the same tautological structure as "Catch-22," and indeed, Milo's whole "corporation" is merely a more comprehensive manifestation of that fundamental formula.

In contrast to such abstractions, Yossarian lives in a world of concrete, bodily experience. He focuses on everyday realities, preferring comfort over discomfort, pleasure over pain, and life over death. In a world of dehumanized killing, Yossarian wants to be both productive and reproductive. His sexual energy, while expressed in a regrettably sexist fashion by Heller, is represented as life-affirming in a world that otherwise worships death of the body in war and death of the soul in commerce. To his comrades, Yossarian therefore often appears mad, but he is frequently reduced to mad gestures because of his absurd circumstances. At Snowden's funeral, for example, he sits naked in a tree because his only remaining uniform was ruined by the blood and gore from when he had tried to bandage the gunner's wounds. His fellow airmen constantly criticize Yossarian's absurd behavior, yet he always turns the tables on them, revealing even greater absurdity in their rationalizations for both killing and dying. Obviously, Yossarian is a soldier who refuses to consider himself "already dead"—he will not "go gently" into the nightmare of death in combat.

Innocent as he may seem, Yossarian is still implicated in the practices of death that he seeks to escape. Heller reveals this in several ways, but most poignantly in the character of the Roman woman with whom Yossarian has a brief affair. Even while engaging in sex, she refuses to uncover a back scarred from a bombing raid, and her scar delivers its own silent indictment of Yossarian the bombardier. Nately's Whore also judges Yossarian, holding him responsible for Nately's combat death even though he has merely delivered the message. The military often euphemizes bombing as "delivery," so delivering the message of death to Nately's Whore becomes the emotional equivalent of a bombing mission. Yossarian has become desensitized to both the results of his actions as a bombardier and the emotional effects of the message he carries. Yossarian is surprised when Nately's Whore misdirects her hyperbolic grief and fury at him, but whether or not he acknowledges the fact, he has still become a representative of the culture of death. Indeed, Yossarian is personally responsible for having become a killer and for having put his own life at risk because he volunteered, as did all members of American combat aircrews during World War II. Although those who did not volunteer might have been assigned to the infantry or other combat units, many men willingly sought combat duty in the Air Force because it seemed exciting to those still ignorant of the details.

In the novel's opening, Heller suggests the destruction in which Yossarian has been a participant through the metaphorical act of censoring letters. As an officer, Yossarian is ordered to censor the men's mail, but to relieve his boredom, he begins to censor the addresses as well: "He began attacking the names and addresses on the envelopes, obliterating whole homes and streets, annihilating entire metropolises with careless flicks of his wrist as though he were God."[31] This ironic description of extreme censoring also reflects Yossarian's role as bombardier. It is a bombardier's job to "obliterate" homes and "annihilate" cities with careless "flicks of his wrist" as he toggles the switch that drops the bombs. Yossarian has become accustomed to these "flicks of the wrist" both as bombardier and as censor. The letters that go nowhere, like the dead letters of the title character in Melville's "Bartleby the Scrivener," testify to Yossarian's other destructive actions.

The Snowden incident, however, personalizes death for Yossarian— his own potential death, the deaths of comrades, and the countless deaths of innocent victims of war. Snowden's death is so important that the narrative cycles through it multiple times before revealing it, in its full horror, near the novel's end.[32] During one mission, Yossarian hears a call on the plane's intercom to "help him," and replies "help who?" "Help the bombardier." "I am the bombardier, I'm o.k." he answers. "Then help him, help him." Crawling back into the plane's shrapnel-torn midsection, Yossarian finds Snowden lying on the floor, with a serious leg wound. "I'm cold" is the refrain that Snowden speaks throughout the incident. Though disturbed by what he sees, Yossarian displays self-control as he bandages the leg and reassures Snowden that he will be o.k. But Snowden continues the refrain, and Yossarian senses something wrong as the gunner motions with his chin to a different wound that Yossarian had not detected. Opening up the man's flak suit, Yossarian looks on as Snowden's insides begin to slide out through an enormous hole beneath his ribs. A piece of shrapnel had torn all the way through, eviscerating the young gunner. Yossarian vomits in disgust, while Snowden, echoing his chilly name, keeps repeating "I'm cold." Yossarian grows cold as well now, mechanically repeating, "There, there," "There, there."

Snowden's horrific death is a concrete manifestation of the death culture to which Yossarian has belonged all along. Heller wants us to realize that, in Cold War America, we also participate in a culture of mass death merely by paying our taxes. As part of the system, we are dying and cold, like Snowden and like the Cold War. We are cold because we have become insensitive to the death machinery within which we work, be it military or economic. We are cold as well because, escaping into a mindless consumerism that masks the military-industrial complex, we implicitly accept this Faustian bargain even in the simple transactions of daily life. This is the horror that Yossarian reads in the entrails of the young gunner, a horror for himself in that moment as well as for all of us in the future.

Having seen "the great death" writ small in the torn body of Snowden, Yossarian is driven even more wildly to escape, though he has yet to acknowledge fully his responsibility as part of this system of death. In fact, to escape he finally acquiesces to the system, accepting an offer from the group's commanders, Colonels Cathcart and Korn. They will relieve him of combat duty and send him home if he agrees to say "nice things" about them to the American public. In other words, he must support the system, continuing to be an instrument of death through representation if not through direct action. Shortly after accepting this Faustian bargain, Yossarian is duly punished—stabbed by Nately's Whore. He survives and so receives another opportunity to choose. But his options seem limited until he learns that Orr, whom he thought dead, had purposely ditched his plane and rowed to Sweden. Inspired, Yossarian decides that he will stow away on a flight to Rome and then try to make it to Sweden himself. He is now running toward life. As he begins his run, his supporters, Major Danby and Chaplain Tappman encourage him, but tell him that he will have to "jump." "I'll jump," Yossarian replies. Absurdly, Danby shouts "Jump," and Yossarian obeys. As a result, Nately's Whore misses when she tries to stab him again. By following that one final order on his way back to life, Yossarian manages to save himself. Because the order itself is absurd, it runs contrary to the system. Yossarian survives, both physically and morally, by following this absurd but life-affirming order.

Catch-22 depicts war as an extremely violent Wonderland that we refuse to acknowledge in our everyday lives, and it propels readers into a mad universe run by the military-industrial equivalents of the Queen of Hearts. Of course it is difficult to conclude such an absurdist satire without a deus ex machina or narrative escape clause for the protagonist. Having effectively and bitterly satirized the mores of the antebellum South in *Huckleberry Finn*, Mark Twain allowed Huck "to light out for the Territory." Heller offers Yossarian a similar rescue, and the bombardier's heading for Sweden is the narrative equivalent of Huck's heading for the territories. Of course, the novelist offers no easy escape for the readers, whom he forces to recognize, and urges to counteract, the universal madness of "Catch-22."

Counterstatements on Screen

From the late 1940s through the mid-1960s, Hollywood's World War II films helped establish and then reinforce the "Good-War" narrative that dominated America's historical understanding of the conflict for over two decades. Given the anti-communist fervor in McCarthy-era Hollywood, and the need for military cooperation, filmmakers represented the war in ways that supported America's military and its Cold War policies. When making films based on literary works even marginally critical of the military, such as *From Here to Eternity* (1953) and *The Caine Mutiny* (1954), directors and producers had to offer significant concessions both to studio executives and to the Pentagon.[33] Filming Mailer's more openly critical novel *The Naked and the Dead* demanded so much Bowdlerization that the author washed his hands of the project long before its release in 1958.[34] Although war veterans themselves recognized that Hollywood routinely oversimplified the complex experience of combat, often for ideological reasons, few cared to object. Most wanted merely to return to regular civilian lives, as they had earned the right to do, and those with intensely traumatic combat memories wanted desperately to forget such horrors. Furthermore, few combat veterans were major filmmakers, and those in Hollywood who wished to represent the war in more realistic or critical ways faced potentially career-ending accusations of being unpatriotic or pro-communist. Thus, throughout the early Cold War years, Hollywood actively supported the growing "military-industrial complex."[35]

By the mid-1950s, however, the atmosphere slowly began to change. Edward R. Murrow and others finally confronted the belligerent Wisconsin senator, and mounting criticism led to Joseph McCarthy's censure by the Senate. With the arms race accelerating, critics of nuclear policy saw their ideas supported more broadly in "ban-the-bomb" rallies. In addition, our failure to secure a permanent peace treaty on the Korean peninsula made both Republicans and Democrats more critical of defense policy. Filmmakers, always dependent on conservative studios and investors, discovered that even they had more liberty in offering criticism. Despite these changes, however, Robert Aldrich's *Attack* (1956) was exceptional for its highly negative portrayal of American infantry officers during World War II. Based on Norman Brooks' play *The Fragile Fox*, the film highlights problems with National Guard units mobilized for World War II. In some, old-boy networks still influenced the selection of officers, regardless of competence. While the Army weeded out most poor leaders before sending Guard divisions into action, some incompetent officers remained, discovered only when they performed poorly in combat.[36]

Attack dramatizes what happens when officers are more concerned about home-state politics than about command responsibilities and are thus willing to tolerate incompetent but politically influential subordinates. Set in Europe during late 1944, the film focuses on Fox Company and its commander, Captain Cooney (Eddie Albert). Unstable and cowardly, Cooney fails to give needed support when sending his men into action, angering his best platoon leader, Lieutenant Joe Costa (Jack Palance). Complaints to the battalion commander, Lieutenant Colonel Bartlett (Lee Marvin), achieve little because Bartlett wants to curry favor with Cooney's father, a powerful politician back home. Bartlett redeploys the company to a quiet area of the front, but this sector soon becomes the focus of an unexpected German attack. Costa threatens to kill Cooney if he fails the men again, but when Costa's platoon is decimated, the lieutenant dies before he can fulfill the pledge. One of the men kills Cooney when the commander wants to surrender the company to the Germans, and the other survivors shoot into the corpse so as to share the responsibility. Bartlett tries to cover up the incident and make a hero of the dead captain, but one remaining officer vows to reveal the truth.

Attack is a provocative film, and its contempt for the officer corps anticipates a similar attitude in a later Aldrich film *The Dirty Dozen* (1967). Despite its ambitious critique of Hollywood's mainstream view of the war, *Attack* is still a disappointing production. The film's strongest segments come in the more stagelike scenes that dramatize conflicts among characters, whereas the action sequences seem unconvincing, clearly suffering from both a low budget and a lack of military cooperation. Yet the flaws run even deeper. Still inexperienced as a director, Aldrich lacks adequate control. He frequently pushes the film from dramatic intensity into hyperbole. Moreover, he fails to elicit effective performances from the cast, so at the climactic moments, the acting becomes both inconsistent and exaggerated. Although still noteworthy, *Attack* ultimately disappoints just when it most needs to be convincing.[37]

Cornel Wilde's *Beach Red* (1967) is another important but deeply flawed antiwar film about World War II. Released at a time of increasing public dissatisfaction with the Vietnam War, *Beach Red* grew from a truly innovative concept. While depicting the dehumanizing brutality of combat on a Pacific island, it makes extensive use of flashbacks and imaginative mental sequences to reveal the inner workings of the characters (similar to what Mailer does in *The Naked and the Dead*). The film also reflects the loosening of Hollywood production codes, showing unusually horrific images of combat—a marine standing on the beach in shock, his arm severed near the shoulder, and the smoldering bodies of dead Japanese who have been incinerated by a flamethrower. More importantly, *Beach Red* consistently represents both Americans and Japanese as human beings who should resist being turned into insensitive killing machines. It is therefore unusually evenhanded in its portrayal of both sides, one of the first American war films to offer a genuinely sympathetic portrayal of the Japanese.[38]

Unfortunately, despite its innovative concept, *Beach Red* remains a failed effort in every other respect: the writing is awkward and forced; the acting alternates between wooden and exaggerated; and the directing is confused and uninspired. Indeed, the film is an encyclopedia of the worst clichés of 1960s filmmaking. Particularly bad are the still-photo montages that serve as passages of memory or imagination, so poorly executed that they quickly become self-parodic. In 1967 some critics praised the film, perhaps reacting more to Wilde's antiwar stance than to the film's actual aesthetic qualities.[39] Yet sympathy with a film's politics, liberal or conservative, is an insufficient basis for critical analysis, just as the desire to make an important film does not necessarily result in artistic success. Despite the excellent underlying concept, *Beach Red* is a barely mitigated artistic disaster. As a historical artifact, however, it does effectively illustrate Hollywood's break with the "Good-War" narrative.

As the Vietnam War intensified, other films like *Beach Red* began to question more openly the "Good-War" narrative and its implicit support for Cold War. These would include "anti-epics," such as *Anzio* (1968) and *The Bridge at Remagen* (1969), each depicting a major battle while being highly critical of the military establishment. Other films, such as *Kelly's Heroes* (1970) and *Catch-22* (1970), parody and/or satirize traditional war films and the values they support. In addition, consistent with the new problem-drama Westerns and crime films, a more cynically violent subgenre of war film emerged, best represented by Aldrich's *The Dirty Dozen.*

All such counterstatement films reveal the cultural impact of the Vietnam War, reflecting many Americans' growing dissatisfaction with the "Good-War" narrative and Cold War ideology. While never questioning America's justification for fighting in World War II, these films interrogate the mainstream narrative of World War II that, for two decades, had been used to justify Cold War policy. They also explore the sometimes mixed motives and moral lapses in how we had fought World War II. Counterstatement films attempt to draw further lessons from the experience of war, lessons we had yet to learn before becoming mired in Vietnam. Far from unpatriotic, these filmmakers believed that Americans must thoroughly examine the war's history before we could truly achieve the peace for which so many men had already died. Even then, these films remained controversial, disliked by those committed to a simplistic view of the war and also subject to intense criticism from right-wing politicians and journalists.

★   ★   ★

By 1970, the "Good-War" narrative had begun to collapse, along with the national consensus that united both liberals and conservatives in support of what might ultimately be called "The Good-War Project." This "Project" interpreted World War II as a triumph of American values, while also considering that war to be an analogue for the emergent Cold War. In the tradition of Henry Wallace during the war, Cold War–era liberals continued to view World War II as one major phase in an ongoing effort to bring greater freedom and dignity throughout the world. During the Cold War, the effort demanded fighting communism as we had once fought fascism, but liberals hoped that this fight could be pursued while maintaining respect for human rights and self-determination. In the tradition of Henry Luce, Cold War conservatives viewed World War II as the first stage in an ongoing deployment of American power to assert the dominance of our political and economic values in direct opposition to the spread of communism. They argued that our increasingly imperial foreign policy was justified as "democratization," even if our democratizing was often a veiled form of colonizing. Whether liberating or imperial in their motives, however, those who crafted "The Good-War Project" generally shared the following beliefs:

1. Americans can be confident of their power only if they properly fund the military;
2. Americans can maintain economic growth and still project worldwide military power;
3. Americans face a communist menace in the Cold War that was merely another ideological danger, as fascism had been during the 1930s and 1940s; therefore, communism could not be appeased and must be opposed vigorously or World War III could take us by surprise with a nuclear Pearl Harbor;

4. Americans are committed to freedom, and despite any temporary
limitations on that freedom domestically, or restraints put on the
freedom of other nations, we were fighting the Cold War to create greater economic and political freedom for all people.

As constructed during the postwar period, our mainstream narrative of
World War II was an attempt to support these principles, but the disappointing experience of Vietnam changed all that, undermining the
principles and the informal coalition supporting them. By 1970, liberals
were questioning the imperial underpinnings of our Cold War policies while still acknowledging the oppressive nature of Soviet rule. In
contrast, conservatives more openly embraced that imperial role with
less shame, as people such as Henry Kissinger brought Realpolitik out
of the closet. It was now acceptable to claim American interests rather
than worldwide liberation as the principal goal of our foreign policies.

The Vietnam experience thus altered not only America's political
consensus about the Cold War but also repositioned World War II in
our evolving national narrative. As literature and film representing
the often negative experience of Vietnam commanded greater attention, representations of World War II moved more to the cultural margins. Indeed, during more than two decades following the end of the
Vietnam War, very few films or literary works emerged representing
World War II. Though the "Good-War" narrative persisted and was
still used for rhetorical effect in Cold War policy debates (especially by
some conservative groups), that narrative no longer served to represent
a national consensus about war in general. From the late 1970s into the
1990s, the battle for national opinion about Cold War policy was influenced increasingly by books and films about Vietnam or about hypothetical Cold War scenarios. It would be the imaginations and opinions
of men such as Oliver Stone and John Milius, Tim O'Brien and Tom
Clancy, that would compete to shape our national consciousness.

Of course representation of World War II did not cease, but as that
war became far less central to national policy debates, its representation
opened up to a wider variety of voices and views. A range of historians,
both liberal and conservative, reexplored the causes and effects of the
war, while numerous combat veterans, silent for decades, began to give
voice to their experiences in memoirs or in oral history collections.
What had once been viewed as counterstatements of minority opinion
could carry greater weight in representations of World War II, now
that such representations were no longer central to supporting national
policy. Thus, for twenty years following the Vietnam War, America's

narrative of World War II was no longer dominated by bestselling novels and major motion pictures. Instead, the continuing construction
of that narrative was taken on by historians and by combat veterans
themselves, leading to a new and much more complex pattern of representation still with us today.

CHAPTER EIGHT

Now It Can Be Told: Reopening Old Wounds

Ghost Stories

His face is familiar, his voice reassuring. It is Dana Andrews, who played an American serviceman in several wartime films, but now he plays Fred Derry, a decorated war hero, in a film about returning to civilian life. The war is over, but late in the film, we see Fred once more in a B-17 even though he and the plane have long been mustered out. Having survived combat, Fred came home only to lose both his marriage and his old job. He has also fallen in love with Peggy (Teresa Wright), but their love seems hopeless because her parents disapprove. Now, hoping for a new start, he has come to the local airfield for a flight out of town, his air force veteran status apparently still earning him a ride on military transport. While waiting, he has seen the old bombers standing beside the field. So essential a year or two before, these planes now wait to be scrapped. Having climbed into one and taken his old position in the nose, Fred finds the war returning. The audience hears his memory of engines throbbing, voices calling over intercoms, flack exploding, and radio calls for friends to bail out of burning planes. Yet we see only the pained expression on Andrews' face. Suddenly, a new voice shakes him from his reverie—an angry scrap contractor stands outside, telling him to leave. But having faced his demons, Fred can now face the future. The former bombardier climbs from the plane but then persuades the contractor to hire him. Fred Derry finally leaves the war and its ghosts behind him.

The film is William Wyler's *The Best Years of Our Lives* (1946), whose closing sequence depicts the wedding of Fred's friend, disabled veteran Homer Parrish (Harold Russell), who had lost both arms but is still marrying his childhood sweetheart. At the wedding, Fred reunites with Peggy, and we know that the couple will have their chance at happiness, and that veterans really *can* go home again. Such was the dream—returning veterans, however traumatized, moving beyond the war and into a new life. Most did so, but many also lived a double life. Behind daily routines, the war might come back in hidden, unexpected ways—dreams or waking nightmares of which men rarely spoke. Silently, many veterans continued to live among ghosts.

★　★　★

For twenty-five years after World War II, the "Good-War" narrative held sway, supporting Cold War military policies; however, as the Vietnam War revealed the folly of that oversimplified view, more complex alternatives began to emerge. Likewise, a quarter-century cycle of war films, almost always supporting the military, had also come to an end. Generally, Americans still believed in the ideals for which we had fought World War II, but many also began reexamining the connection between our proclaimed values and our actual policies. These Americans were not unpatriotic, many being combat veterans, but they still felt obliged to reconsider the cherished assumptions of Cold War ideology and the historical narratives, many about World War II, in which those assumptions were rooted.

With respect to the Vietnam War, neither government nor media could successfully construct a triumphalist narrative as they had previously done for World War II. By the 1970s, those in power actually struggled to distance themselves from the political disasters in Southeast Asia. Vietnam veterans, however, still had to deal with their traumatic experiences. Like all men returning from battle, they felt contradictory impulses both to repress and to confront that trauma. Having faced combat just as their fathers had in World War II, they found no celebration upon their return. In response, they offered their own personal stories, and these rapidly gained prominence in the absence of any dominant national narrative.

In 1945, World War II veterans came home with similar conflicted feelings, but while the preconstructed victory narrative celebrated their achievements, it left them little room for expressing themselves candidly. Postwar America largely ignored the psychological trauma of these veterans, assuming that the Fred Derrys should get back on their feet quickly and not grieve over the past. In addition, veterans themselves usually accepted a traditional model of male behavior, holding that men who spoke openly of their personal suffering were self-indulgent or cowardly. Silence was the norm, and those who broke the silence found few listeners. As James Jones explained:

> .... most men didn't talk about it. It was not that they didn't want to talk about it, it was that when they did, nobody understood it.... there was no common ground for communication in it.[1]

Historian Rick Atkinson has noted that, throughout World War II, "roughly one million soldiers would be hospitalized for 'neuro-psychiatric' symptoms...."[2] While U.S. Army and Navy physicians regularly treated psychological casualties, psychiatry had achieved only a limited understanding of combat-related trauma. Only after decades of further study, and with the efforts of many Vietnam veterans, did psychiatry finally identify "Post-Traumatic Stress Disorder" (PTSD) as a serious condition suffered by many combat veterans.[3] A lifetime of behavioral problems, including substance abuse and depression, can be rooted in earlier combat trauma—something that few Americans could understand or acknowledge during the immediate postwar period.

Surprisingly, some Hollywood films did explore the struggles of traumatized veterans, *The Best Years of Our Lives* being the most widely known example. Other films followed. *Home of the Brave* (1949), with a Carl Foreman script based on the Arthur Laurents' play, confronts both post-traumatic survivor guilt and racism.[4] *The Men* (1950), produced by Stanley Kramer and directed by Fred Zinnemann, depicts the psychological adjustment process of paralyzed veterans. Somewhat less directly, Nunnally Johnson's melodramatic *The Man in the Gray Flannel Suit* (1956), based on Sloan Wilson's novel, reveals how war memories continue to haunt a veteran as he confronts the postwar stresses of family life and business in the 1950s. Except for *The Best Years of Our Lives*, however, such films were not overly popular, despite their generally optimistic endings.[5] Some novels by World War II veterans more openly acknowledged the long-term effects of psychological wounds (see chapter seven), while poetry, by veterans like Randall Jarrell, Louis Simpson, and Howard Nemerov, provided especially bleak visions of the war. Nemerov's "Redeployment," for example, depicts a deeply traumatized veteran who now hears "the dust falling between the walls."[6] Memoirs of combat trauma, however, were notably absent in the decades following World War II, and those few who wrote nonfiction "trauma narratives" found it difficult to interest publishers.

At this point, I must briefly address issues deriving from the current critical discussion of autobiographical trauma narratives. Some literary theorists have argued that the highly controlled structure of traditional autobiography reflects dominant, often male, cultural assumptions about the construction of identity through narrative. They also claim that writers who are culturally marginalized—because of gender, race, ethnicity, or other identity factors—construct an alternative form of autobiography that interrogates those assumptions. Much has also been written about "trauma narrative," often drawing on various psychoanalytic theories applied to individuals, groups, or whole cultures. My study, however, is a rhetorical analysis of our long history of representing World War II in literature and film, leaving little room to discuss these other theoretical issues in any great detail.

I can, however, briefly explain my approach to reading and interpreting the kinds of autobiographical trauma narratives (trauma memoirs) that have been written by combat veterans. In general, it *is* important to understand the differences between traditional forms of autobiography ("life-writing") that are dominated by a hegemonic narrative structure, and those forms where narrative patterns are more open-ended and fragmented, allowing for reflective passages that examine and interrogate the very act of representation. For convenience, I refer to this second form of life-writing as "memoir," in order to distinguish it from more traditional autobiography. Despite its narrative content, this latter form of life-writing is more exploratory or "essayistic."

The term "essay" originally meant "to attempt," and essays are attempts to reveal the internal mental processes of the writer.[7] The essay is always a kind of meta-writing, foregrounding the writer's efforts to construct meaning from fragmentary experience, so the true essay resists easy closure, always preserving some sense of the "incompleteness" associated with a "work-in-progress." Like much modern lyric poetry, the essay can provide insight into a moment of experience, exposing the richness and complexity of that moment, but often leaving the interpretive reader with as many questions as answers about the nature of the experience and about its relationship to any larger pattern of events. Unlike most poets, however, the essayist goes on to write passages that interrogate and respond to his or her own representations of events, making the form both psychologically complex and formally dialogic—texts in conversation with themselves, bringing a writer's internal dialogue into the foreground. In poetry, ambiguity often arises from what the writer chooses to leave out, but in the essay, ambiguity usually grows from what questions the writer raises about his or her own ability to represent remembered events. A number of strains of modern autobiography are essentially essayistic in form, choosing to represent a person's life not as a narrative whole but rather as a process of experience and reflection that is necessarily more open-ended. In trauma memoirs specifically, the qualities of incompleteness and ambiguity derive from the writer's effort to piece together the fragmented memories of traumatic experience. Although some writers still represent personal trauma in a traditional unified narrative, many choose a more essayistic form, a complex of fragmented narratives linked by ongoing personal reflections that reveal the struggle for order in the midst of disorder. In analyzing combat trauma memoirs, I focus on the writer's specific experience, rather than on cultural identity, and I examine the corresponding narrative strategies and compositional processes, rather than applying psychological theories of trauma itself. In addition, I read such memoirs as examples of essayistic writing, and thus as texts whose very lack of closure calls readers to attend to the psychological "dissonance" brought on by the horrific experiences of combat in modern warfare.

Vietnam veterans frequently constructed trauma narratives of their combat experience, and by the 1970s, many Americans had begun to acknowledge openly that soldiers could be wounded in mind as well as in body. By confronting their losses, telling their stories, and beginning to grieve, Vietnam veterans constructed a memoir literature about their war that revealed in concrete detail what it means to fight, kill, and die in modern combat. Trauma memoirs, such as Tim O'Brien's *If I Die in a Combat Zone* (1973), Ron Kovic's *Born on the Fourth of July* (1976), and Philip Caputo's *A Rumor of War* (1977), were published to critical praise and commercial success. Likewise, oral histories such as Al Santoli's *Everything We Had* (1981) added the painful recollections of an even wider range of average soldiers.[8] In the aggregate, narratives exploring the personal aftermath of combat exerted a major influence on America's understanding of the Vietnam War. Moreover, because veterans themselves developed this trauma literature, quickly establishing it in the national consciousness, it could not easily be erased by any institutionally sanctioned counternarrative.[9] Therefore, the Vietnam generation, though deprived of victory, nonetheless won the battle to tell their personal stories.

As trauma memoirs of Vietnam grew more influential, however, an awakening also occurred among World War II veterans. They seemed to recognize in the Vietnam memoir literature a powerful reflection of their own struggles some thirty years earlier. They had once assumed that such stories could not be told, but now they discovered a new opportunity. In the years following Vietnam, a memoir literature about World War II finally began to emerge as this older generation of veterans seemed inspired by the stories from a younger one. Traumatic memories, long hidden like the souvenirs in veterans' dusty footlockers, were finally brought out in the open, beginning a new stage in the representation of World War II.

Pictures at an Exhibition

Among the first World War II veterans to contribute to the emerging genre of veterans' trauma memoir was James Jones. While still at work on *Whistle* (1978), final novel of his war trilogy, Jones was asked by the art director of *Yank*, Art Weithas, to write text to accompany a volume of World War II visual art.[10] The collection would include works by both military and commercial artists, many of which had never been published.[11] Jones agreed to help, and the resulting volume, titled merely *WWII*, presents many compelling images, some shocking for their graphic detail, others moving for their portrayal of ordinary G.I. life. Jones' parallel text provides a relatively standard history of the war, told from the view of the "average anonymous soldier, or pilot, or naval gunnery rating" who did the actual fighting and dying.[12] Throughout, however, he interrupts his narrative to tell his personal story of the war and to describe, with unflinching honesty, how total war transforms the men who fight.

Much of Jones' memoir comes in the book's first half, from Pearl Harbor through the Guadalcanal campaign. His account of Guadalcanal reveals obvious sources for his 1962 novel *The Thin Red Line* (see chapter seven). In *WWII* Jones describes several personal experiences that closely parallel the novel, suggesting that the writer used himself as the model for the fictional "Corporal Fife."[13] Although the novel closes as fighting ends on Guadalcanal, *WWII* continues Jones' personal narrative of the war years. For most of 1943, he went through surgery and rehabilitation, spending the remainder of the war on light duty at Fort Campbell.[14] Although less exciting, this segment explores the experience of wounded soldiers recovering on the home front.

Jones' personal narrative passages cease halfway through the book while his history and commentary continue, giving the text a disjointed feel. Such structural inconsistency may result from carelessness, or perhaps Jones may be intentionally reminding us that, while war narratives end, war and its lasting effects always resist closure. He openly claims that World War II history has been sanitized and that few combat artists dared to go beyond conventional representations. Thus, he looks especially for unusual works that reveal more than the commonplace, perhaps even against that artist's will. He specifically comments on how the "Good-War" pattern of representation contrasts with Vietnam veterans' "bad-war" experience.[15] Jones, however, makes no such distinction between "good" and "bad" wars because he views modern combat as overwhelmingly destructive in any war. Yet he also admits that many World War II veterans eventually accepted the "Good-War" perspective because they necessarily tried to forget the painful aspects of their past. For writers and artists, veterans or not, this makes telling the story of the war extremely difficult. As Jones notes, "perhaps the hardest thing is to try to recreate it as it really was."[16]

Along with his informal history, Jones offers his own interpretation of events in a language designed both to engage and alienate readers.[17] At times, he interweaves commentary with narration—as in his critiques of General MacArthur and British Field Marshal Montgomery. At other points, he suspends narration, inserting short essays about humor, war art, and historiography. He also discusses the war's end, the Holocaust/Shoah, the cultural changes wrought by the war, the intensity of the final Pacific battles, and the controversy over the atomic bomb. He argues in favor of America's having used that weapon while acknowledging the bomb's horror (he finds the fire-bombing of Tokyo even more horrific). Unapologetic for his acceptance of the bomb's massive violence, Jones views it as a necessary end to the even greater violence of the war as a whole. Throughout the volume, he writes frankly as a combat veteran who has already accepted death—his own and everyone else's.

Jones hopes that his candor does justice to the best art that he and Weithas selected for the volume. The most compelling works are technically simple and stylistically straightforward, such as drawings by Kerr Eby, who captures moments of both action and waiting with the same visual intensity. His charcoal portrait of a marine sniper hiding in the jungle reveals the complex emotions of men in combat, while his sketches of the Tarawa beachhead convey the carnage of battle even more directly than photographs.[18] Yet one of his most moving drawings shows not combat but life off the line.[19] A soldier or marine stands, bending at the waist and leaning on his rifle. With his pants dropped, he is naked from the waist to the knees, revealing a hideous dark infection or rash covering his bare buttocks. A buddy squats behind the man and applies ointment. Here, we see the world that Jones finds so difficult to represent, a world beyond any ordinary social norms. We also see the intimacy and love that many of the veterans reveal in their memoirs.

In a similar vein, U.S. Army Sergeant Howard Brodie also concentrates on ordinary infantrymen, using charcoal and pencil to represent the "rough edges" of war that Jones finds missing in many other artists. With an eye for capturing the right posture and expression, Brodie provides just enough detail to suggest authenticity. Jones became familiar with Brodie's early Guadalcanal drawings when they were published in *Yank* in 1943.[20] Even then, Jones felt that Brodie "had permanently captured on paper the filth and misery and fatigue we had lived through."[21] Transferred to Europe, Brodie continued to draw the rough life of infantrymen. As with Eby, one of Brodie's most compelling drawings shows the care that soldiers sometimes give one another.[22] Two men kneel behind a pile of sandbags, the first one collapsing against the other, with his face clearly in anguish. The second man's face remains partially hidden, but we still see his patient expression. The traumatized man clutches at the other, while the calm one sooths his comrade as one would a terrified child. Both bodies are twisted into a corkscrew pattern that captures all the explosive tension of the moment. With a few powerful charcoal lines, Brodie thus reveals the trauma and love shared by men in combat.

Jones also includes several paintings by *Life* artist Tom Lea, claiming that landing with the marines at Peleliu compelled Lea to break with convention, as revealed in his painting *The Price*.[23] It depicts a man just after shrapnel has torn through his left side, leaving half his body a bloody, unrecognizable mess. Jones interprets this painting as expressionistic, recording "in one swiftly done canvas a distillation of all the death and horror he [Lea] had seen...."[24] Lea himself took a different view. In *Peleliu Landing* (1945), in which an early sketch for the painting first appeared, the artist claims that he was trying to represent realistically an actual wounded marine at Peleliu: "His face was half bloody pulp and the mangled shreds of what was left of an arm hung down like a stick...."[25] It is ironic that combat veteran Jones sees Lea's realism as "surreal," yet both interpretations may be accurate because the reality of combat is often convincingly surreal.

Using both the visual art and his own writing, Jones focuses *WWII* on one basic theme, "THE EVOLUTION OF A SOLDIER"—how America's young men "evolved" into the combat soldiers who fought the war.[26] Drawing on his own and others' experiences, he depicts this evolution with humorous, poignant, and horrific anecdotes, complementing the visual artists' illustrations of the same process. Ultimately, this evolution leads a soldier to accept the fact that he is already dead, and "Only then can he function as he ought to function, under fire."[27] Jones comments on the various stages of this evolution, as well as on its unexpected outcomes—an unusual ability to live in the present and to appreciate each small pleasure that life might offer. He also acknowledges the numbness that allows men to make the "maximum effort," then go even further, though he illustrates the cost as well. At the end, Jones discusses the profound readjustment problems of many World War II veterans. Wives and families could not comprehend why the returning "victorious" soldier now slept with a bayonet under his pillow or sometimes awoke screaming in the middle of the night. The horrific images in the collection begin to reveal the distance between the actual experience of veterans and the sanitized imagery of war provided by the government, the news media, and Hollywood. Thus, families had little to help them comprehend the true mental state of men who had endured battles like those at Peleliu. True readjustment was difficult, sometimes impossible, for both veterans and their families. "There is no telling what the divorce rate was then, in the early year or two," Jones notes, "Certainly a lot higher than was ever admitted."[28]

Yet Jones concedes that most soldiers did slowly complete the process of "de-evolution," so much so that they no longer remembered the war's full horror. For some veterans, however, the ghosts stayed with them, deep in their psyches. In the wake of Vietnam and Watergate, Jones expresses a longing for the lost brotherhood, the lost intimacy that had once led terrified men to care so deeply for one another. *WWII* is Jones' elegy for a ghostly figure, the lost G.I.—he is a dead man buried half a world away, yet he is also a survivor who lost something of his soul in the war. With the passage of time, that survivor lost something else, also precious, by his return to "normal" civilian life. Jones comments on his generation, not as "the greatest" but as men who would always look back to the war experience and try to understand how those chaotic years had shaped them: "None of them would ever really get over it."[29]

"Darkness Visible"—The Long Road Back to Sugar Loaf Hill

In representing the trauma of combat, writers struggle to convey the shock and disorientation experienced by ordinary human beings confronted with the extraordinary violence of the modern battlefield. Because of their inherent creative freedom, novelists can transform such experience into narratives that directly challenge the reader's imagination, somewhat paralleling how war itself challenges the soldier's mind. Arguably, the first rational quality to deteriorate under extreme stress is the orderly sense of time, and novelists who represent the effects of trauma often distort temporal order. Writers of traditional autobiography, however, have less recourse to such distortion because their genre usually depends on temporal organization to achieve both authenticity and accessibility. As events follow one another in nonfiction narratives, we readily accept the pattern of experience as realistic, and such temporal order also maintains our sense of rationality, even for the often irrational conditions of combat.

Writers may abandon these norms, however, when writing a trauma memoir that confronts readers with the psychological devastation experienced in war. Such memoirs represent not only the physical pain of extreme suffering and the psychic pain of profound loss but also the insidious pain of deteriorating rationality. By exploring these very issues, William Manchester's memoir *Goodbye, Darkness* (1979) achieves the intensity and imaginative power of the best fiction. Manchester was already an accomplished historian when he finally confronted his own wartime ghosts by writing a personalized history of the Pacific war. While serving as a U.S. Marine sergeant during the three-month Okinawa campaign, he experienced the full range of war's horror—killing an enemy soldier at close range, struggling through the endless days and nights of terror, and seeing his own men die one by one. His combat ended when he himself was severely wounded, resulting in physical and psychic scars that remained with him all his life.

Sergeant Manchester led an Intelligence and Reconnaissance section in a battalion headquarters of the 29th Marine Regiment. Along with communications and mapping work, this twenty-man unit conducted dangerous intelligence patrols and shared in regular infantry tasks, such as perimeter defense. Yet Manchester describes his unit as a collection of oddballs unlike the usual marines:

> Most of us were military misfits, college students who had enlisted in a fever of patriotism and been rejected as officer candidates because, for various reasons, we either despised the OCS system openly or did not conform to the established concept of how officers should look, speak, and act.[30]

Proud of their nonconformity, they referred to themselves as "the bandits" or "The Raggedy Ass Marines," but despite their oddities, these young "misfits" fought as hard and bravely as other marines.[31] Manchester clearly saw himself in this misfit mold, yet he was also a good soldier and leader though he acknowledges this only indirectly. He possessed excellent vision and was a superb shot—a fact that saved his life on more than one occasion. He claims to have acted mostly out of fear for his own life and for the lives of his men, but such tactical caution makes good sense in combat. Having been wounded and evacuated, however, Manchester went AWOL from the hospital to rejoin his unit. Freed from any obligation to return, he still went back to be with his men. He neither sentimentalizes these actions nor hides his own emotional ambivalence about them. Yet he sacrificed his personal welfare to share the risks his men would face, demonstrating that soldiers fight not only to save themselves but also to keep faith with their comrades.

In constructing his memoir, Manchester employs an unusually complex narrative structure. He interweaves two contrasting main narratives: the first, a linear history of the Pacific war; the second, a fragmented account of his personal experiences in World War II. The former narrative, like many war histories, provides a sense of consistency and order, but interrupting and interrogating that history are passages of personal narrative—brilliant, chaotic accounts of training and combat. Mingled among the combat episodes are vignettes that explore Manchester's relationships with the marines in his unit, revealing the diverse personalities of the nineteen young men under his command. Few survived the battle. Most troubling, however, are passages reconstructing the hallucinations that Manchester experienced in moments of extreme excitement or shock, either during combat itself or immediately before or after. These nightmarish visions dramatically reveal the psychological disorientation that can occur during prolonged, intense fighting.

Complicating the dual narratives of history and memoir is the contemporary story, some thirty years after the war, of a middle-aged man trying to confront the demons of his past. From the late 1960s on, Manchester had been haunted by the ghost of himself as a young soldier. This relentless figure of a young marine sergeant appears in the aging man's dreams, demanding with his silent gaze an explanation for why postwar America had failed to sustain the ideals for which the men had sacrificed so much. Set at Sugar Loaf Hill, site of some of Okinawa's fiercest battles, these dreams drive the public historian to become a personal narrator. They also lead him on a research trip to the sites of major Pacific battles, allowing him to piece together both a personal memoir and a historical record of the fighting throughout that theater. During the trip, Manchester spends days visiting battlefields, sometimes interviewing island residents or combat veterans. At nights, however, he himself is visited repeatedly by his own angry ghost. From these dual processes—probing the facts of the war while also plumbing the depths of his own psyche—the writer constructs both a straightforward history and a fragmented memoir. Balancing these two past narratives, the contemporary story reveals the writing process itself, along with the writer's growing recognition of old loss and ongoing grief. Manchester weaves all these threads into one complex trauma narrative that climaxes with his return to Okinawa—there one final dream returns him to Sugar Loaf Hill to find the young sergeant forever gone. Awaking in tears, Manchester can finally acknowledge the loss of youth, the loss of self, and the loss of myriad friends.

★   ★   ★

Among the first American World War II memoirs to confront fully the awful personal costs of that war, *Goodbye, Darkness* clearly breaks with a narrative tradition.[32] It also achieves a stylistic breakthrough by interweaving history with personal narrative in a new and challenging fashion. Manchester's representation of each battle, from Pearl Harbor through the war's end, is usually interrupted by a brief narrative passage from the author's fighting on Okinawa. The interruptions cause the entire narrative pattern to grow more disorienting because, even though his personal experience of combat was only at Okinawa, he disperses its narration throughout his otherwise linear history of the whole Pacific War. In addition, he selects these personal incidents based on their random connection to the historical event being discussed, so they do not appear chronologically. Shifts in narration are thus abrupt and disturbing, just like Manchester's own experiences when visiting the old battlefields as he suddenly and involuntarily recalls incidents from similar terrain or a similar type of engagement at Okinawa. Both history and personal narrative collide violently in these moments, jarring writer and reader alike, while making us doubt any narrative's power to represent an orderly progress through time. Like Vonnegut's fictional Billy Pilgrim in *Slaughterhouse Five*, Manchester as "character" in his own narrative moves back and forth through time in a nonlinear fashion, making it difficult to follow any of the narrative threads and demanding frequent rereading of passages.[33] Only at the book's end can readers comprehend the order hidden in the fragments, but until then, the text repeatedly forces them into a state of confusion like that experienced by the traumatized veteran himself. Thus, Manchester has written not merely a personal narrative of his own trauma but also a complicated text that immerses readers in the psychological consequences of that trauma. By doing so, he allows the fragmentary nature of personal trauma narrative to deconstruct the self-assured rationality of traditional history and autobiography, especially in relation to war.

Manchester's account of violent combat is also unusually vivid, but we find precedents in World War I writers, who were among the first to confront the extreme brutality of modern war. A new poetics of death and dying grew from writers such as Wilfred Owen, as in his unforgettable depiction of a man suffering the fatal effects of poison gas in "Dulce et Decorum Est" (1918).[34] Ernest Hemingway achieved similar graphic qualities in prose when describing the aftermath of shelling:

> [you] find your legs are gone above the knee... or maybe just a foot gone and watch the white bone sticking through your puttee... or be blown to hell a dozen ways without sweetness or fittingness....[35]

A more imagistic passage in *A Farewell to Arms* (1929) describes being caught in the explosion of a trench mortar shell:

> ...there was a flash, as when a blast-furnace door is swung open, and a roar that started white and went red and on and on in a rushing wind. I tried to breathe but my breath would not come and I felt myself rush bodily out of myself....[36]

Manchester shares a similar experience when a shell hits the courtyard of the Okinawan hillside tomb where he and his men are encamped:

> It [the shell] landed in the exact center of the courtyard. Rip's body absorbed most of the shock. It disintegrated, and his flesh, blood, brains, and intestines encompassed me.... My back and left side were pierced by chunks of shrapnel and fragments of Rip's bones. I also suffered brain injury. Apparently I rose, staggered out of the courtyard, and collapsed. For four hours I was left for dead.[37]

Although Hemingway's passage is powerful, Manchester's phrasing is so direct that the material reality of the event seems to split into fragments and assault the reader with verbal shrapnel. Also embedded in the passage is another fragment, far more shocking for its simple statement. Manchester acknowledges being "pierced" both by shrapnel *and* by "fragments of Rip's bones." Earlier in the book, recalling his hospitalization, the writer explains how the doctor examining his x-rays had been surprised to see a piece of someone else's shin bone embedded in Manchester's body.[38] Here Manchester illustrates the grotesquely symbolic facts of his combat experience—being condemned for life to carry in his body the bone fragment of a dead friend, thus becoming a macabre, walking reliquary.

While direct in describing violence, Manchester employs a more imagistic style when reconstructing his battlefield hallucinations, the most disturbing of which is an apparition he calls the "Whore of Death."[39] Assigned to lead an attack with a squad from a different unit, Manchester trips over a wire and falls into a hole just as a shell burst kills the others. After dark he tries to leave the hole but then discovers that he is crawling through the mangled bodies of the dead marines. He returns to the hole in a state of shock and survivor guilt.[40] Passing out, he wakes later that night, and in the light of the flares exploding overhead, he glimpses a female figure. At first she seems desirable, "dressed like the girls I remembered at Smith and Mount Holyoke."[41] But a closer flare reveals her "deathly white [skin]...covered with running sores."[42] Despite her repulsiveness, the illusory succubus beckons him, arousing his sexual desire in a way that Manchester attributes to the emotional shock of having been so close to death. He knows she is the "Whore of Death," and yet he still craves her. But then he shrinks back, a shell bursts close by, and she disappears in its flash.

Obviously, Manchester is recalling, perhaps amplifying in retrospect, a trauma-induced psychotic incident. Yet his hallucination cuts to the depth of the young soldier's emotional life where his imagination draws together the excitement of danger, the fear of death, and the sexual energy that asserts itself as a contrary force to the destruction surrounding him. From all this emotional intensity, his imagination synthesizes an illusion that reflects the combined power of sexual desire and the passion for destruction experienced by many soldiers in the fury of combat. James Jones recognized the same perverse connection. In *The Thin Red Line*, as Private Bell crawls back from a dangerous patrol, he realizes, "...that his volunteering, his climb out into the trough that first time, even his participation in the failed assault, all were—in some

way he could not fully understand—sexual."[43] Bell goes on to gener-
alize this revelation:

> Could it be that *all* war was basically sexual? Not just in psych
> theory, but in fact, actually and emotionally? A sort of sexual per-
> version? Or a complex of sexual perversions?[44]

While somewhat acceptable in fiction, such revelations had never been
the stuff of World War II history or personal narrative. In a radical
departure from earlier war memoirs, Manchester's experience with the
"Whore of Death" is rendered with Daliesque precision and Bosch-like
grotesquerie, recalling Francis Ford Coppola's *Apocalypse Now* (1979).
Indeed, the perverse synthesis of death and desire is more suggestive
of Vietnam than of World War II. With the revelations from Vietnam
trauma narratives, along with the absurdist fiction of Heller and the
psychological twists of Jones, Manchester had obvious precedents for
representing, at long last, the truth of his own World War II experience.
He demonstrates that World War II combat could be as perverse and
surreal as anything experienced in Vietnam, but our culture had never
been willing to admit those qualities as historical or autobiographical facts. In *Goodbye, Darkness*, Manchester is finally able to reveal
just how psychologically disorienting combat had been for soldiers in
World War II.

For all the shock of such passages, however, it is still Manchester's
depiction of time that most powerfully illustrates the effects of trauma.
As noted earlier, trauma memoirs often fragment accustomed linear
narration, creating interruptions, suspensions, and disturbances that
not only convey the mental state of a traumatized individual but also
question rationality itself. Oddly, despite the graphic violence revealed
in the writing of World War I veterans, their combat narratives generally maintain a sense of temporal order. After World War I, a number of
modernist writers, but not usually those writing directly about the war,
experimented with the representation of time. In contrast, post–World
War II war fiction often alters the representation of time to reflect the
disorientation experienced by combat veterans. In *The Naked and the
Dead*, Mailer's "Time Machine" passages take us into characters' earlier
life experiences, building on more conventional flashback techniques.
Heller's *Catch-22* uses a number of temporal loops as the novel returns
repeatedly to Yossarian's traumatic memory of Snowden's death. More
dramatically, Vonnegut's *Slaughterhouse-Five* blends science fiction with
war literature, abruptly moving its protagonist, Billy Pilgrim, back and

forth through time and space. Subsequently, Vietnam fiction became even more experimental, as in Tim O'Brien's *Going after Cacciato* (1978), which combines both real and imagined storylines to reveal the disturbed mind of protagonist Paul Berlin, who often seems unable to distinguish fact from fiction.

Yet nonfiction about war had rarely attempted such dramatic dislocations of time as found in *Goodbye, Darkness.* Manchester disturbs traditional narrative history with his unstable personal narrative, not only to convey the depth of his own wounding but also to wound, in some small but parallel fashion, the psyche of the reader. This complex text reveals that time, or at least our personal sense of time, resists control and refuses to be channeled. Instead, it overflows and floods our consciousness with the awareness of past and present intermingled. Our traditional sense of history and narrative is injured by this book as it represents the writer's own incurable injuries from times of war and death, terror and trauma. Seeking to exorcize his demons, Manchester has revealed the full range of his trauma. By the book's conclusion, he has achieved some sense of release if not complete closure. In the process, however, he confronts us with an extraordinarily broken pattern of experience and memory as we witness his effort to assemble meaning from the pieces. Thus, the past haunts the reader, just as it haunts the writer, in the full array of scattered fragments. Manchester continues to carry painful fragments in both his body and his mind, but we readers cannot leave the book without also carrying some of those fragments with us, at least in our imaginations.

The Rising Chorus

Beginning in the 1980s, a growing number of memoirs, oral histories, and "interview-based histories" began revealing the traumatic memories of World War II combat veterans.[45] Continuing into the present, this rising chorus has provided new insight into the war, and it has helped Americans recognize that, despite traditional sanitized representations, war is always deeply traumatic, whether it ends in victory, defeat, or stalemate. World War II was no exception. To this new cultural narrative, journalist Studs Terkel contributed his massive oral history *"The Good War"* (1984), putting the title in quotation marks to highlight its irony.[46] Calling this a "memory book," Terkel offers accounts from people on all sides, including many American veterans. Although perspectives vary, all who witnessed the war's violence attest to its horror and devastation. Most Americans featured in the book accept the war as having been an unfortunate necessity, but a few see all wars, including World War II, as a waste. Likewise, some have transcended their traumatic memories while others still carry the war with them.

The richness of *"The Good War"* comes from this variety of viewpoints, illustrating the complexity of wartime experience. The first recollection comes from John Garcia who, like many, had ambivalent reactions to combat. Garcia had witnessed the Pearl Harbor attack and then served in the infantry throughout the Pacific. By the Okinawa campaign, however, he was drinking over a fifth of whiskey a day just to get through all the killing. He felt the worst about the death of innocent civilians. One night he shot at a figure moving through his unit's perimeter, discovering the next morning that he had killed a woman and her infant. Now he admits, "That still bothers me, that hounds me."[47]

Friends Robert Rasmus and Richard Prendergast met when training with the 106th Infantry Division (Vonnegut's division). Rasmus, however, became seriously ill and ultimately had to join a different unit. Prendergast continued with the 106th, becoming a POW during the Battle of the Bulge and witnessing, as did Vonnegut, the Dresden fire-bombing. Neither man seems unduly scarred by the violence he witnessed, though Prendergast speaks little of Dresden. He does tell how, after Russians had liberated his POW camp, he traveled back to American lines with some friends. Staying in an abandoned house one night, he was awakened by a noise and almost fired his pistol before discovering that the housebreaker was a small boy seeking "Mein teddy bear."[48]

Despite such painful moments, Rasmus and Prendergast acknowledge the war's necessity while admitting that they grew insensitive to all the death they had seen. Subsequently, both viewed problems in civilian life to be, in Rasmus' words, "...minor compared to having to do a river crossing under fire."[49] They also express satisfaction at having participated in momentous events. Says Prendergast, "...in spite of the really bad times, it was certainly the most exciting experience of my life."[50] This echoes James Jones' view that men of his generation would spend the rest of their lives looking backward. Finally, Rasmus and Prendergast most fondly recall their brotherhood with fellow soldiers. Rasmus notes that "The reason you storm the beaches is not patriotism or bravery. It's that sense of not wanting to fail your buddies."[51] This intimacy bound men into close-knit units that seemed like families, where mutual trust helped many survive combat, but where that same closeness also made losses more painful.

In contrast, close friendship caused Joe Hanley to suffer loss and survivor guilt. His best friend Kevin was killed when both men were caught in an artillery barrage. Although Kevin had a wife and child, Joe had no family, so Kevin's death seemed completely unfair. After the war, Joe contacted Kevin's widow to pay his respects, and they gradually developed a friendship that led to marriage. Still, despite an otherwise happy relationship, the couple continues to feel guilty. Joe carries other scars as well—a habit of heavy drinking and a strange death wish that expresses itself in a desire for dangerous jobs. His conclusions also fly in the face of the traditional "Good-War" narrative: "No wars can be just. During combat, I would say to myself, this whole damn thing isn't worth one ounce of American blood or anybody's blood."[52] Despite some unusual circumstances, Hanley's experience is consistent with that of many other veterans whose traumatic memories continued to haunt them.

Terkel's book is also unusually inclusive, allowing those from marginalized groups to tell their stories. One is Charles A. Gates, an African American who reveals the struggle of serving in a highly segregated army. Despite the difficulties, Gates rose to command a company in the all-black 761st Tank Battalion in Patton's Third Army. Stories such as his challenge the mainstream narrative of the war that had rarely acknowledged the contributions of African Americans. Timuel Black, another African American, witnessed the liberation of Nazi concentration camps, leaving him to wonder if, given America's troubled racial history, a similar tragedy might someday befall African Americans. Despite such fearful, bitter feelings, when he saw the Statue of Liberty on his return, he still felt "Glad to be home, proud of my country, as irregular as it is. Determined that it could be better."[53] Stories like these finally call attention to the hypocrisy of an America that fought against fascist racism abroad while still accepting a different form of racism at home, even in the Army itself. Although Gates and Black transcend bitterness, stories like theirs effectively interrogate the mainstream "white" history of World War II.

The aggregate effect of so many different voices blended together makes *"The Good War"* a truly "polyphonic" work, balancing many diverse memories to offer readers a more complex understanding.[54] The fragmented but compelling narrative that emerges can question, by its very diversity, the traditional history of the "Good War." Many accounts seem elegiac, reflecting sadly on the war's pain and loss. Others speak of reshaping postwar lives, finding a new strength along with that persistent sadness. Most also reveal how the nation changed because of the war. Like Manchester, these veterans contrast the home they had fought for with one they actually found upon their return. Proud to have helped defeat the Axis, most saw the war as a horribly destructive necessity. Veteran and cartoonist Bill Mauldin expresses these complex reactions: "I didn't feel we had accomplished anything positive. We had destroyed something negative: Hitler."[55] Despite Mauldin's ambivalence, he still acknowledges the unique importance of having fought that war: "It's the only war I can think of that I would have volunteered for."[56] Rear Admiral Gene Larocque, a veteran who continued his Navy career, is even more critical, calling war "just a miserable, ugly business."[57] Echoing President Eisenhower's critique of the "military-industrial complex," Larocque goes further:

> World War Two has warped our view of how we look at things today. We see things in terms of that war, which in a sense was a good war. But the twisted memory of it encourages the men of my generation to be willing, almost eager, to use military force anywhere in the world.[58]

Larocque's testimony reveals much about the complex views of World War II veterans. Despite differences in background and experience, almost all demonstrate a deep love of country. A surprising number, however, also express skepticism about America's postwar militarism. By the 1980s, many could speak openly of the war's horrific destruction, critiquing the simplistic "Good-War" narrative that had so long dominated our nation's understanding of the war. During the war, they discovered in themselves and in their comrades much that was quite good; however, having been in combat, most found war itself, and the glorification of war in retrospect, to be anything but good. They conclude that there is no such thing as a genuinely "good" war, merely a necessary one. Moreover, they recognize that, if we draw the wrong lessons from war, and if we perpetuate an inaccurate or incomplete narrative of war, we serve only to encourage its continuance. In *"The Good War"* Terkel gives veterans and others a new place to express their views, to reconstruct what is indeed good in their experience, and to distinguish that goodness from the destructive evil that *is* war.

★   ★   ★

It is impossible to mention all the World War II combat memoirs published since Manchester's book, but we can briefly examine several significant examples: Eugene Sledge's *With the Old Breed: At Peleliu and*

Okinawa (1981); Raymond Gantter's *Roll Me Over: An Infantryman's World War II* (1997); Roscoe Blunt's *Foot Soldier: A Combat Infantryman's War in Europe* (1994/2001); and Robert Kotlowitz's *Before Their Time: A Memoir* (1997). All four reflect broader trends in the World War II memoirs published after 1980, providing striking insights into traumatic combat experience.[59] Like many who wrote war memoirs, this group had more education than the average soldier, and after the war, they also pursued careers dependent on writing, such as journalism, radio, or college teaching.[60] Yet all were enlisted men, with only Gantter reluctantly becoming a junior officer near war's end, so these memoirs clearly represent the experiences of frontline soldiers. Sledge, Gantter, and Blunt had all begun recording their experiences during the war, and the latter two completed full-length memoirs just afterward, though these remained unpublished for decades. Given their graphic depictions of war's squalor, filth, and death, it is not surprising that such works were deemed unacceptable during the immediate postwar period.

★   ★   ★

Eugene Sledge's *With the Old Breed* (1981) came first, covering his service with the marines during the last year of the war.[61] Like Manchester's memoir, *With the Old Breed* also reveals a veteran's traumatic wartime experiences, but unlike Manchester, Sledge constructs a straightforward narrative to represent the savage fighting on Peleliu and Okinawa.[62] Having become a biologist after the war, he also brings a scientist's eye for significant detail to a narrative whose simple surface belies its careful construction. Yet recognizing Sledge's self-conscious effort diminishes neither his candor nor his accuracy. Moreover, Sledge's book is not only clear but also relentless, concentrating almost exclusively on combat episodes, forcing readers to confront the intensity of fighting as it dragged on during both bloody campaigns. His comrades, many "Old Breed" prewar marines, had begun fighting long before Sledge joined them in summer 1944. During the subsequent months, however, all shared some of the war's most intense combat. The worst experience was being shelled, when soldiers could only wait out the earthquake of explosions and the blizzard of shrapnel. As Sledge notes, "I learned a new sensation: utter and absolute helplessness."[63] Sledges claims that what frequently helped men overcome their individual fears was the desire not to let down their friends. Yet witnessing the death of those friends left a "wild desperate feeling of anger, frustration and pity" that became "the bitterest essence of war."[64]

Physical environment exacerbated this combat stress with deprivation and misery. On tropical Peleliu, marines suffered debilitating heat
and humidity, while at Okinawa, in more temperate latitudes, they
fought alternately in dust or in rain and mud. Similar to World War I
battlefields, Okinawa's muddy hillsides held thousands of half-decayed
corpses from both sides, and one slip into that mud left men covered
with disgusting maggots that had fattened themselves on the dead. In
these circumstances, little remains of the idealistic impulses or easy
slogans that bring young men into recruiting offices. Truth may be the
first casualty of war, but bravado and jingoism also die quickly in combat, reduced to silence or ironic absurdity. Like a number of memoir
writers, Sledge also identifies what really motivates men to continue
fighting under such pressure: they fight to stay alive and to keep their
comrades alive. He not only confirms the trust he had shared with
his fellow marines but also reveals the terrible trauma that all had suffered, whether killed, wounded, or like Sledge himself, a technically
"unscarred" survivor.

★   ★   ★

Unlike the teenaged Sledge, Raymond Gantter was thirty in 1944,
with a wife and two children, when he turned down his third defer-
ment and joined the army. Assigned to the veteran 1st Infantry Division
as a replacement, he endured the usual period of adjustment, but the
college-educated Gantter was also the "old-man" of his unit and initially felt cut off from fellow soldiers. Combat eventually dissolved
those barriers, and as he fought with the division from November 1944
until the war's end, he also rose from private to platoon sergeant. When
finally promoted to second lieutenant, however, he still identified with
enlisted men and not with fellow officers, whom he often found arro-
gant and selfish. Gantter grew accustomed to combat, but during occasional rest periods, he kept a cryptic diary in which he could reflect on
his experience and confront his fears: "I started to write because I was
scared."[65] He acknowledges pride at having led men successfully, but
he notes that what seems heroic at a distance can be basic necessity in
combat. Having seen too many men die, often unnecessarily, Gantter
resents uncaring civilians who find the war profitable, but he reserves
his greatest wrath for incompetent officers who cause such deaths.
Brutally honest, however, he also admits that his own mistakes sometimes caused needless casualties. Later, in occupied Germany, Gantter
witnessed the consequences of Nazi rule, confirming his decision to

fight, but even so, he remains ambivalent about the war and highly critical of the U.S. Army.

Stylistically, *Roll Me Over* demonstrates neither Manchester's sophistication nor Sledge's clarity. Instead, the patchwork quality openly reflects how Gantter stitched together his memoir from a combination of journal notes and letters sent to his wife. Yet the uneven structure makes more emphatic the equally uneven qualities of an infantryman's life. Unlike a consistent narrative, the life of a combat soldier includes long periods of discomfort and boredom, made more troubling by constant fear. Also, although combat episodes may be brief, their intensity distorts the rational sense of time and causality. Manchester brilliantly captures this disorientation with his complex narrative structure, and Sledge obscures it, emphasizing instead the graphic physical detail of the battlefield. In contrast, Gantter shows us the "rough-cut" of the soldier's experience, complete with its many inconsistencies. He describes combat episodes in a spare, clear style, but intersperses them with other passages of reflection and commentary. Throughout, we see the writer's mind at work, interpreting his experience. Even though the resulting text is sometimes hard to follow, it also provides a deeper revelation of how an intellectual man reacted to the trauma of the war in Europe.

Clearly, Gantter never accepted the "Good-War" narrative, and after the war, he grew even more critical of how Cold War politics perverted the meaning of sacrifices made in World War II. The aggregate effects of all he witnessed during the war, along with postwar political hypocrisy at home, left Gantter deeply angry. He is the thinking man who grieves at the cost accrued from others' lack of thought, and so his trauma is as much intellectual as emotional. His closing commentary about the Cold War era remains relevant today: "once again America dithers in a soprano hysteria of suspicions and denials, charges and countercharges.... We know how to fight; we don't know how to make peace."[66] Gantter's intellect allows him to understand the cost of men's folly, leaving him even more deeply hurt by that awareness. His experience recalls a line from T. S. Eliot: "after such knowledge, what forgiveness?"[67]

★ ★ ★

Foot Soldier reveals Roscoe (Roy) Blunt as a highly emotional young man, the youngest in his unit, whose extreme behavior distinguished him from the average G.I. Indeed, he actively courted danger, volunteering for a mine clearance unit. Like others in his small unit, Blunt worked as a loner, farmed out to various rifle squads in an infantry company. He shared combat duties while also defusing mines, but he never grew close to the men with whom he fought, remaining isolated and fearful. Almost as a psychological compensation, he became obsessed with taking unnecessary risks, actually "hunting" and killing individual enemy soldiers so that he might take a souvenir "death trophy" from their bodies. While knowing that his behavior increased his chance of death, he grew increasingly addicted to its emotional rush. It was as if Blunt had to channel all the fear and tension of combat into specific, dangerous acts, whether those were his assigned tasks of defusing mines and killing enemy soldiers, or his particular passion for collecting a special "trophy" from those he killed.

Foot Soldier honestly explores these ironic contradictions in a young soldier's complex psychology. Along with his more dangerous obsessions, Blunt was also a jazz enthusiast. When not in combat, he played drums whenever he could, often with sections of divisional or visiting bands, and he even earned a bandsman's classification at the war's end. Yet while music provided an occasional creative outlet for Blunt, combat offered a more frequent and destructive focus, even during episodes of traumatic shock. Once, when an explosion had blown him out of his foxhole, an obviously "shell-shocked" Blunt ran around in the open, "...yelling 'Come and get me, you bastards. I'll kill you all.'"[68] Another time, a violently angry Blunt tried to kick the head off a badly mutilated enemy corpse. While many soldiers behave strangely when in shock, his hyperbolic reactions made him unusual, and his choices reflected an unstable psychology. Like the mines he defused, or the jazz drums with which he diverted himself, Blunt was explosive, a "ticking time-bomb" personality. Remarkably, however, he ultimately admits and makes no excuse for these impulses. In the preface, a much older Blunt acknowledges how the war changed him: "if these psychological, emotional scars have not healed in more than half a century, they are never going to."[69] Despite extreme behavior, Blunt still shares with many veterans an acceptance of the past. He identifies a persistent "sadness" derived from the war, "...part of the emotional price so many of us are still paying for our combat experience."[70] Yet like many, he also claims to be "...increasingly proud" of what the G.I.s contributed to America's history.[71] Blunt is both mournful and proud, but such contradictory emotions reflect the experience of many combat veterans. The war was their great adventure that mutated into their great horror; though its scarred survivors forever suffer the pain of loss, they continue to experience understandable pride in their endurance and self-sacrifice.

⋆   ⋆   ⋆

Grief and anger, rather than pride, are central to Robert Kotlowitz's *Before Their Time*. An intelligent, young draftee, Kotlowitz was originally selected for the Army's Advanced Specialized Training Program.[72] After the program was largely disbanded, he was transferred to infantry training and then to combat in Europe, where he witnessed the tragic consequences of decisions made by careless or poorly trained officers. Though he became a successful writer after the war, it still took Kotlowitz fifty years before he could write of his traumatic wartime experience. Once started, however, he composed a powerful memoir whose deceptively simple style amplifies its tragic climax.[73]

Kotlowitz frames his main narrative between segments of a post-combat assignment, when he was guarding personal equipment left behind by men going into battle. The central story is told in flashback, beginning with his training and building to one catastrophic day of combat. A somber tone foreshadows the tragedy as does a vignette about men who drowned during a practice river-crossing back home. Throughout, Kotlowitz carefully portrays the men in his unit, helping readers share in their awkward but intense comradeship. When they are finally at the front, the inexperienced company commander sent Kotlowitz's platoon into action without prior reconnaissance, and they walked right into an ambush from three sides. Machine guns ripped through the ranks, and as survivors hugged the open ground for cover, mortars rained down further injury and death. For many hours afterward, German snipers also fired at any movement on the slope, forcing Kotlowitz to play dead for so long that he wondered if he were dead. Long after dark, medics rescued him and two other survivors, the only ones left from a forty-man platoon.

In the last quarter of this memoir, Kotlowitz examines the tragedy and his own reactions to it. Having suffered greater trauma than the other memoirists discussed here, he often sounds more like the survivor of a terrorist attack than a soldier suffering from combat exhaustion. He describes his therapy sessions with an Army psychologist as well as after-action interviews with an Army historian documenting the attack. The therapy passages reveal his complex emotions of pain and guilt while his dialogue with the historian shows the insensitivity of the military and of "history" itself, neither of which took much note of this "minor action." Kotlowitz continues the narrative to the starting point of the opening frame when he was guarding equipment. Ordered to move duffle bags, he discovered those of his dead comrades. These long objects, physically similar to body bags, symbolized the dead men themselves, and when he heard the sounds of rats hiding in the bags, he was overcome. Even the supposed "rest area" has allowed him no rest.

Kotlowitz's psychological wounds remained open until 1995, when he visited another survivor, Bern Keaton. Spending a whole day together, they openly discussed what neither had dared to speak of for years. Then, having finally unburdened themselves of the past, the two men shared dinner with the Keaton family, and in this atmosphere of warmth and laughter, Kotlowitz found the courage to write his story. At this late date, his old wounds finally began to heal.

★   ★   ★

As noted here, combat inspired in some veterans a powerful need to write—first, to control their fear and pain, and later, to achieve insight into their experiences and share that insight with others. Also, these writers attempt to reconstruct a fragmented past in order to acknowledge, and so begin to heal, their deep psychic wounds. As in all trauma narrative, this is a process of grieving, and while returning veterans grieved in many ways, the attempt to write was often the most self-conscious step in the process. As reconstructions of psychic fragmentation, trauma memoirs are far more fragmented texts than are other forms of autobiography. They make little pretense of seamlessness, though they struggle to maintain some coherence. Pieced together from bits of memory and scraps of notepaper, these works reflect the profound psychological costs of combat in modern war. They also reveal a sometimes uneven compositional process as passages of reflection interrupt or suspend the straightforward narration, leaving fissures that show how traumatic experience resists easy narrative closure. They do not conform to any monolithic structure, and their very incompleteness questions our ability to achieve the kind of control over the past usually sought by traditional autobiography and history. Indeed, the trauma memoir attempts to reconcile with the past rather than to control it, achieving not so much closure as a "separate peace" for the writer. Conversely, trauma memoirs subject readers to unusual disorientation, forcing us to share in, and even to share responsibility for, a world of pain and violence few of us have ever confronted.

Coda: Elegy for the Lost Company

Once again, the face is familiar, but now it is 1973, and the face belongs to Jack Lemmon, playing Harry Stoner in *Save the Tiger*. Standing on the dunes above a vacant Southern California beach, Harry relives painful memories of fighting in Italy thirty years earlier. Financial and personal stresses have brought on these midlife, post-traumatic flashbacks, as Harry, co-owner of a cash-strapped women's casual wear company, must gain new financing or face bankruptcy. Unable to secure bank loans, his only other sources of money are seeking a dangerously predatory loan from the mob or perpetrating fraud by having one of his plants burned down for the insurance money. Isolated from family and friends, Harry seems unable to share his burdens, living increasingly in an idealized memory of his youth, before the war had changed everything.

Save the Tiger focuses on little more than a day in Harry's life, but it is a day of crises. Addressing the assembled buyers at an all-important fashion show, he almost breaks down as he sees, instead of the actual audience, the faces of the long-dead members of his old infantry company. Nearly in shock, Harry is led from the stage before he can spoil the event, but even when the show succeeds in gaining orders, there is still no money to finance production. That night, with his wife and daughter away, he wanders through Los Angeles, eventually picking up a free-spirited young woman whose kindness calms him. He opens up and talks of his youth and his twin passions, jazz and baseball. After spending the night with her, at a beach house where she is housesitting, he once more faces his ghosts as he stands above the beach at dawn. With the camera circling him and his face a tragic mask, we hear his memory of the desperate fighting in which he lost so many men. In the background the crashing waves provide the only accompaniment.

Harry returns to his daily life, finally agreeing to have one of his factories "torched" at a time that it is completely unoccupied—no casualties. Thus, he secures the money to keep the company going, but the personal cost is high, permanently severing his connection with the ideals for which so many died. The film neither justifies nor condemns these unethical actions, allowing us merely to observe Harry's inner struggle and his almost existential acceptance of fate. Implicitly, however, this film exposes the ragged ends of the unraveling "Good-War" narrative, revealing the ongoing costs of a trauma that allows no real closure. The final scene shows Harry watching young boys play baseball, but his choices have now separated him forever from the youthful innocence their game represents. Unlike Fred Derry in *The Best Years of Our Lives*, Harry has moved from traumatic recollection to resignation rather than hope. He is the old soldier still, with wounds hidden and unhealed, whose memory allows him only a partial and separate peace.

CHAPTER NINE

The Once and Future War

Golden Anniversaries

From 1989 through 1995, Americans marked the fiftieth anniversaries of the events of World War II, leading many to reconsider how that war has shaped our national identity. The previous decade, however, had already brought many new publications about the war, including new memoirs and oral histories that questioned and complicated the "Good-War" narrative (see chapter eight). At the same time, conservative historians attempted to revise but preserve that traditional narrative, in part to support the Reagan administration's increasingly aggressive approach to the Cold War. When the Soviet Union and Warsaw Pact ultimately collapsed, American conservatives claimed this as their victory, under Reagan's leadership, often ignoring other more complex causes, such as the influence of the reform-minded Mikhail Gorbachev and the long-term effects of the Soviet war in Afghanistan. In 1991 our country also fought successfully to oust the invading Iraqis from Kuwait. America seemed proud once more of its military strength, and the public memory of our failures in Vietnam had begun to recede, especially for a new, post-Vietnam generation. Thus, a simple victory narrative of the Cold War and the prospect of a "New American Century" were built on the recovered foundation of the "Good-War" narrative of World War II, largely ignoring the complexities and moral ambiguities of both.

From 1980 through 1992, Hollywood made many films about the military, ranging from Vietnam critiques such as Oliver Stone's *Platoon* (1986), to Cold War thrillers such as *The Hunt for Red October* (1997), based on Tom Clancy's novel. Yet only a few films dealt with World

War II combat, among them Samuel Fuller's *The Big Red One* (1980) and a feature-length, fictional version of *The Memphis Belle* (1990). Sprawling television miniseries, such as *The Winds of War* (1983) and *War and Remembrance* (1988), based on Herman Wouk novels, were more like epic soap operas using World War II as a backdrop. In contrast, *A Midnight Clear* (1992), a highly symbolic, antiwar film directed by Keith Gordon, confronted the traumatic nature of World War II combat in ways comparable to film critiques of Vietnam. These, however, were exceptions in a period when a *Variety* headline actually claimed "WWII DEAD AS GENRE."[1] Indeed, from the 1970s through most of the 1990s, World War II was largely absent from American movie screens. Instead, the struggle to represent the war was continued by historians and memoirists.

Hell or Glory, Fussell or Ambrose

During the past two decades, two writers have exemplified America's reconsiderations of World War II: Paul Fussell and Stephen Ambrose. Although only two among many, each writer has articulated a distinctive understanding of the war around which numerous other books and films can be clustered. Such influence may surprise us since both men were career academics and neither originally intended to focus intensively on World War II. Fussell, a World War II veteran, was a scholar of eighteenth-century English literature, and Ambrose, a historian, focused more on biography than on military history. At midpoint in their careers, neither would have seemed likely to shape our national discussions of World War II.

As a second lieutenant in the U.S. Army, Fussell led an infantry platoon during the campaigns in northwest Europe. After several months in combat, he found it increasingly difficult to control his fear and stress. Standing out in his memory is March 15, 1945, when a superior officer threatened him with a court-martial after seeing Fussell lag behind as his platoon advanced.[2] Later, while the platoon took shelter in a bunker, Fussell forced himself to stay outside to continue observing; two of his sergeants stayed with him. When a shell burst nearby, it killed the other two and severely wounded Fussell, and subsequently he has held himself responsible for risking their lives needlessly. Whether this self-criticism is justified, the event crystallized for Fussell the full range of his wartime experiences, leading him eventually to critique and deconstruct the traditional "Good-War" narrative.

Ambrose, in contrast, was a child during the war. In the epilogue to *Citizen Soldiers* (1997), he recounts growing up in postwar Wisconsin, where veterans completing their college education would play ball with the young Ambrose and also take him deer-hunting. Their personalities and experiences had a lasting influence on the future historian. Few can argue with Ambrose's respect for such men, but he also tends to politicize veterans' experience, and the representation of the war itself, to justify postwar American culture and our Cold War policies. In short, Ambrose revives the "Good-War" narrative in a new context and with a new tone, but with a similar set of political objectives to those of the 1950s.

★   ★   ★

As a historian, Stephen Ambrose was drawn to study World War II most intensively through his work on his Eisenhower biography and with the Eisenhower Center. Depending largely on interviews and primary sources, Ambrose is really more a compiler than a narrator. As he notes in *Citizen Soldiers*: "I make my living by reading other people's mail, listening to their stories, reading their memoirs."[3] Though a competent writer, Ambrose has an unremarkable style, the power of his work coming from the words of veterans themselves, whether quoted directly or summarized. Though he conducted only some of the interviews himself, this direct contact with veterans still significantly influenced his perspective. More importantly, he also sifted through mountains of material to find those stories that best illustrated his understanding of the American G.I. Having already completed extensive research on Eisenhower, Ambrose naturally concentrated his World War II histories on the European theater. During the 1980s, he began working on a major book about the Normandy invasion, apparently seeking the mantle of Cornelius Ryan, long the authoritative popular voice on the subject. This D-Day research led to close relationships with veterans of the 101st Airborne Division, and from these contacts, Ambrose compiled *Band of Brothers* (1992), a specific history of one airborne company. His comprehensive book about the Normandy invasion, *D-Day, June 6, 1944*, came out two years later, in time for the fiftieth anniversary of the invasion. This book, along with the subsequent *Citizen Soldiers*, established Ambrose as America's preeminent popular historian of World War II.

Unlike military historians, Ambrose spends little time analyzing broad strategy. Instead, he allows veterans' own recollections to shape the narrative even if that makes the narration somewhat episodic. While Ambrose provides the overall historical scaffolding, his books actually unfold as very personal stories, revealing directly the emotions of men who did the fighting. Though he corrects inconsistencies in these accounts, he usually does not pass judgment on issues in dispute. Rather than weakening his books, these ambiguities energize the narratives, giving them a polyphonic quality. Indeed, Ambrose successfully integrates these disparate stories into an understandable pattern of individuals responding to events, giving readers a sense of personal contact with the men who actually fought the war. Obviously, other writers have used similar approaches, including Cornelius Ryan in *The Longest Day*. Yet Ryan always emphasized the larger narrative, never focusing on any one person for too long. In contrast, Ambrose is a biographer at heart, allowing his subjects to supply the principal narrative structure, thus allowing readers to understand the subjects in greater depth. Ambrose also treats his subjects in a generally positive light, highlighting the struggles, sacrifices, and triumphs of the American G.I. in Europe, but he does not overly glorify the G.I.s' exploits because that would violate the often unpretentious tone in which these men tell their own stories.

While many historians were publishing important books on World War II during the 1990s, it was Ambrose who rode that war's "golden anniversary" years to the greatest popular success. By 1997, he had become a kind of one-man show, his Eisenhower Center generating the research on which he based books, articles, and prefaces.[4] As a historical biographer of American G.I.s, Ambrose made the war personal once more to a broad spectrum of American readers, eventually reaching an even wider audience through his film collaborations with Steven Spielberg (*Saving Private Ryan*, 1998, and the *Band of Brothers* miniseries, 2001). In the aggregate, Ambrose's work has helped enrich the traditional World War II narrative.

As he praised the ordinary American G.I., Ambrose also tried to defend the American military against critiques from historians such as Max Hastings. In *Overlord* (1984) and later works, Hastings asserts that the American soldier in Europe performed badly, receiving poor leadership from junior officers. He generally claims that overwhelming technological and logistical support were the reasons for the Allied victory over the Nazis rather than the quality of soldiers. *Citizen Soldiers*, while not confronting Hastings directly, establishes a thorough argument for the effectiveness of American soldiers in Europe in 1944–1945. Combining documentary evidence with extensive interviews, Ambrose successfully counters the Hastings school of thought.

But this defense was only part of Ambrose's project. Although these histories foreground veterans' experiences, Ambrose's conservative political views still surface, especially in introductory or concluding sections. He is prominent among historians who have reconstructed a more conservative reading of America's war experiences, and by concentrating on the European theater, he has avoided such controversial issues as the atomic bomb. In addition, Ambrose sought to enhance the reputation of Eisenhower as one of the great American presidents. This effort grows from his overriding desire to reconsider all twentieth-century American history in a more conservative light. While Eisenhower was an accomplished military leader, his presidency was uneven at best, with a number of significant foreign policy failures. Even Eisenhower himself would probably have been troubled by the level of "Ike-olatry" practiced in retrospect by Ambrose and others. In addition, this enthusiastic support for Eisenhower would be more understandable had not Ambrose also chosen to disparage the leadership of FDR and other more liberal figures. It is clear that Ambrose wants to place Eisenhower atop the pantheon of America's twentieth-century leaders, in part so that he can displace others. Unfortunately, such political partisanship diminishes the overall worthiness of his efforts as a historian. It is one thing to praise the G.I. or to laud Eisenhower, but Ambrose builds on the effect of such praise to further his overall political agenda: to represent Eisenhower as the initial leader of America's gradual move from the New Deal to the New American Century. Thus, he subtly connects the more moderate but iconic figure of Eisenhower with the neoconservative right, making the neoconservatives seem less extreme. In doing so, Ambrose necessarily leaves equally praiseworthy men, such as George C. Marshall and Franklin D. Roosevelt, open to scorn. He also implies, without adequate evidence, that the majority of the World War II veterans have long shared his particular political views. That seems an inappropriate use of the G.I. legacy with which Ambrose wished to be entrusted.

★   ★   ★

Although not enjoying the popularity of Ambrose, Paul Fussell has still established himself as an influential cultural historian and a leading critic of the "Good-War" narrative, even though it took him decades before he could confront the subject. After the war, Fussell earned

a doctorate in English and began teaching eighteenth-century literature in college. This seems an escape from the memories of combat, but Fussell also claims that wartime experience drew him to the
ironic tone of eighteenth-century literature. In mid-career, however,
he shifted from traditional literary analysis to a broader interpretation
of cultural issues. Influenced perhaps by theoretical changes in literary studies, he developed a scholarly approach somewhat paralleling
Cultural Studies, but without the overt theoretical emphases or explicit
ideological frameworks associated with most academic work in this
area.[5] Examining not only works of literature but also a range of cultural behaviors, representations, and attitudes, Fussell began pursuing
an ongoing critical, cultural history. Also, based on his New Critical
training, he still focuses on the ambiguous feature of irony. Making use
of extensive source material, from letters and diaries to poetry and fiction, Fussell seeks out cultural fissures and fault lines. He explores these
to discover inconsistencies between institutionally sanctioned representations of history and the thorny details of common life that constitute
an in-depth social history.

Some have described Fussell's work as a form of ethnography. If so,
it is largely a text-based ethnography, focusing consistently on textual
representations as the basis for analyzing the differences between superficial, mainstream views and the marginalized voices that question
those views. Even though employing traditional historical and New
Critical analyses, Fussell also studies the kind of "social texts" valued by
more recent theoretical approaches. Fussell, however, distances himself
from overt theoretical discourse in order to make his writing more
accessible. Although some academics may view this as dumbing down,
few scholars regularly achieve the clarity and elegance of Fussell's writing nor do they usually draw on such a wide and detailed knowledge
of primary material. Thus, although readers without extensive background knowledge can understand Fussell's work, it also challenges
all readers to explore the subject matter more deeply. In short, Fussell
achieves the most basic goal of literary analysis—encouraging others
to read more widely and with greater understanding. In addition, in
applying his critical method to our cultural representations of war,
Fussell adds the insight of a participant to an otherwise ironic approach
to cultural history.

Fussell began focusing his critical attention on war in *The Great
War and Modern Memory* (1975), still the essential study of the British
literature of World War I. It also clearly connects Fussell's earlier
eighteenth-century studies with his later work on the cultural history

of modernity. In both cases, he examines many forms of irony and how they reveal the inconsistencies and instabilities of mainstream history. In his collection *The Boy Scout Handbook and Other Observations* (1982), Fussell makes his first real commentary on World War II. The book's closing section, "Versions of the Second World War," sets forth the basic arguments he will develop more fully in *Wartime* (1989). In the final essay, "My War," he directly states his goal of giving World War II "bad press" and confronting readers with the horrible realities of war.[6] He seeks to disillusion America's fatuous public just as he himself had been disillusioned during the war. Combat experience, he claims, has given him both the inclination and the authority to take this stance. Subsequently, he amplifies these arguments in *Wartime*, a groundbreaking work in both representing the war and critiquing other representations of it. Thereafter came his editing of *The Norton Book of Modern War* (1991) and his memoir *Doing Battle* (1996). *The Boys' Crusade* (2003) continues Fussell's ongoing critical project. Throughout these works, Fussell critiques mainstream representations of war as lacking depth, honesty, and completeness. He expresses great frustration with simplistic narratives of World War II, a war that caused so much devastation. While accepting the war's necessity, Fussell finds little glory in it. As many Americans were "celebrating" the war's fiftieth anniversaries, he chose instead to interrogate America's continuing acceptance of the "Good-War" narrative. As he notes in the preface to *Wartime*, "For the past fifty years the Allied war has been sanitized and romanticized almost beyond recognition by the sentimental, the loony patriotic, the ignorant, and the bloodthirsty. I have tried to balance the scales."[7]

To counter dominant perceptions, Fussell highlights often-ignored texts and underreported events, many of which are at once horrific and self-parodic, often generating intensely ironic accounts. Like Ambrose, Fussell also emphasizes the experience of the ordinary soldier, sailor, or airman, but he examines all theaters of the war and explores work not only by Americans but also by the British and other nationalities. Fussell's approach, however, concentrates on texts rather than interviews, and he selects the more literary representations, frequently from poetry. Even when using memoirs, letters, and diaries, Fussell more often cites those by well-known writers, skewing the sample in favor of reflective intellects more likely to question conventional wisdom.[8] Yet Fussell maintains balance throughout his work, reminding us, as Oscar Wilde once noted, that truth is "rarely pure and never simple."

Fussell's work does have its weaknesses, especially an occasional tendency to overstate his case in ways that detract from the persuasiveness of otherwise sound arguments. In "From Light to Heavy Duty" (in *Wartime*), he argues convincingly that the Allies were not mentally prepared for the realities of the war, but he also uses some exaggerated examples. He examines popular representations of fast but vulnerable American jeeps and contrasts them with the power of German tanks, and he criticizes America's sending a million rifles to England in 1940, after the British Army's evacuation from Dunkirk. These instances illustrate, according to Fussell, America's unwillingness to face the facts of the new war. The jeep, however, was not principally a weapons system to confront tanks but a highly efficient transport vehicle. Indeed, the Germans used jeeps whenever they could capture them. Likewise, although sending artillery and tanks to England in 1940 would have been more useful than sending the rifles, our choice did not grow from ignorance. We simply had no tanks or artillery to send at that time, but we did have one or two shiploads of rifles. Sending what aid we could was a diplomatic gesture rather than a strategic effort at rearmament.

Fussell also comments on the debacle suffered by the British and French armies in 1940, quoting one "Briton" who says that the Allied response to the German offensive was to "gape" and exclaim 'What big tanks they've got.' "[9] This statement provides a nice rhetorical flourish, but it is fundamentally inaccurate. What is more, Fussell is informed enough to know it is inaccurate. He and the editors of the paperback edition of *Wartime* follow up a couple of pages later with contrasting pictures of a tiny British "tankette" in 1938 and a mammoth German King Tiger of late 1944, clearly an anachronistic comparison. In actuality, the German panzer divisions of 1940 had smaller, lighter tanks than did the French and British. The Germans just had more tanks and were prepared to use them in a war of maneuver. Indeed, the heavier British tanks almost won the Battle of Arras, being stopped only when German heavy antiaircraft guns were used against them. The Germans won France in 1940 the same way the Allies won it back in 1944, with greater numbers of light and medium tanks, handled with greater operational facility in a dynamic campaign of maneuver. More importantly, both the Germans in 1940 and the Allies in 1944 held air superiority over the battlefields. There was little to stop the Stukas from decimating British and French columns in 1940 just as the Germans could not stop the Allied fighter-bombers in 1944. Yet despite Fussell's rhetorical sleight of hand in such passages, his argument is still basically correct. As the fighting began, the Allies had no conception of what devastation the war would bring. What he fails to acknowledge, however, is that no side could fully appreciate the scope of the war in these early stages.

The Germans themselves took their relatively vulnerable tanks into the Soviet Union in summer 1941, and though they continued winning with superior tactics, they ultimately were stunned when confronted by the new Soviet T-34s. The Soviets taught the Germans to build big tanks though the Soviets themselves suffered hundreds of thousands of casualties before they figured out how to use those tanks, and their whole army, effectively. So all sides were shocked by the ferocity and destructiveness of World War II, and few postwar representations can convey its devastation. This is Fussell's main point, and he is absolutely correct, without the need for the hyperbole.

Tanks and rifles aside, readers can grow frustrated to see a writer as careful as Fussell resorting to the equivalent of rhetorical cheap shots. This unproductive tendency also leaves basically sound arguments open to unjustified criticism, but Fussell seems to care little about this defect, possibly assuming that few readers are likely to know or check the facts. On balance, however, he resorts to such tactics infrequently, and most of his analyses remain rigorous and accurate. In the end, the picture he paints of the Allied war effort is not one of complete incompetence or moral depravity; rather, he demonstrates that the Allies were a collection of flawed, very human soldiers rather than epic heroes in mythic fictions. In contrast, actual soldiers live in the grimy consequences of the follies that occur when a culture becomes captive to such fictions. Fussell's incisive critiques are a necessary counterweight to the excesses of the mainstream narratives that so often fail to acknowledge war's grim realities. Of course, though Fussell claims to be skeptical about "human instincts for reason and virtue," his very effort to shock the American public into recognizing the war's true horror reveals his belief that people can learn from history when it is thorough and honest.[10]

Unlike Ambrose, Fussell does not reveal a specific political agenda in his work. His critique of the "Good-War" narrative marks him as a liberal for many, but his defense of dropping the atomic bomb on Japan (as one who was scheduled to invade there) brought him criticism from liberal historians. Fussell refuses to be pinned down. He can write a full volume on the "boys' crusade," implicitly critiquing the well-known "great crusade" metaphor used by Eisenhower in his address to the troops on D-Day. In the closing pages of *Wartime,* however, he praises Eisenhower for writing that brief acknowledgment, never sent out, of responsibility for an Allied defeat on D-Day if the invasion had failed.[11] Fussell makes much of Eisenhower's changing the note from passive to active voice, thereby taking even greater responsibility for the imagined disaster of a failed D-Day. Perhaps justifiably, Fussell reads nobility in

Eisenhower's brief text and in that editorial choice. What seems missing here is Fussell's usual counter-example. Eisenhower penned no similar note about the terrible intelligence gaff at his headquarters that allowed the Allies to be surprised by the Germans' December 1944 offensive in the Ardennes. That error was ultimately Eisenhower's responsibility, leaving tens of thousands of American casualties in its wake. Yet even the aggressively skeptical Fussell sometimes needs an authority figure to praise, and he selects Eisenhower. It is not that Eisenhower does not deserve commendation; rather, it is Fussell's shift from skepticism to admiration that seems unusual. Ironically, Fussell shapes his praise by quoting Norman Mailer about nobility, but given Mailer's politics in the 1950s, one cannot imagine him supporting Fussell's endorsement of Eisenhower. Despite this brief lapse into apparent sentimentality, Fussell has consistently challenged America's simplistic assumptions about war. In making that challenge to all of us, he has had to confront his own wartime demons. For these brave efforts, Fussell deserves a great deal of praise.

★　★　★

Both Ambrose and Fussell explore the experience of the American G.I. in World War II, but each obviously does so from a different perspective. Countering criticism directed at the combat record of American soldiers in Europe, Ambrose asserts that they actually demonstrated great skill and courage while fighting the war in a particularly American way. Led by the quintessentially American figure of Eisenhower, these self-effacing "crusaders" helped rid Europe of the Nazi menace—Ambrose's variation on the "Good-War" narrative. Fussell, in contrast, attacks the notion that any war can be labeled "good." Like General William Tecumseh Sherman, he finds that all war is indeed "hell," and like Walt Whitman, Fussell argues that "real war" never gets "into the books," much less onto the screen. Insofar as literature even dimly reflects the true war, it still has failed to shape America's mainstream narrative of World War II. Fussell notes quite correctly that America persists in its mythic understanding of the war, established by all media during the war and maintained principally by Hollywood thereafter. Ambrose is also accurate, however, in praising the ordinary American soldier because, despite the folly and SNAFUs, the G.I.s still endured and prevailed. Both Fussell and Ambrose thus provide useful though contrastive perspectives on a complex history.

In his excellent analysis *The Good War's Greatest Hits* (1998), Philip Beidler explores a similar contrast between what he calls the "the Good War" and "the Great SNAFU." Beidler asserts that "the Good War and the Great SNAFU really *were* each other, often in self-parody."[12] He examines both views in light of postmodern theorist Jean Baudrillard's concept of "simulacra"—self-perpetuating representations that become more influential than the events they represent.[13] In one sense, Beidler is correct because both Ambrose's and Fussell's analyses of the war are accurate in their own registers of experience while also seeming contradictory, and because only very few Americans still understand World War II as anything more than a pattern of representation.

Further examining these contradictions on a more practical level, we can note that Ambrose and Fussell employ two distinctive methodologies that reinforce their contrasting views. Although personal experience shapes Fussell's assumptions, he maintains his ironic perspective largely because he examines the war almost exclusively through texts. Conducting few interviews, he confronts no direct counterarguments. Perhaps because of his own painful memories, Fussell can reexamine the war only through such textual mediation. More than direct experience, textuality is the basis for Fussell's ironic stance. Ambrose himself never experienced the war, yet he still engages directly with the veterans through interviews. His empathy is the counterpoint to Fussell's irony. Both writers question the representations of the past, but Ambrose questions people whereas Fussell interrogates texts. The difference may seem merely procedural at first, but it is fundamentally psychological as well. Ambrose can maintain his vision of the "Good War" because he is never distant enough from the interviewees to question them with full skepticism and because he can focus on veterans likely to confirm his assumptions. Fussell can maintain his vigorous skepticism because he directs it at selected texts rather than at fellow veterans who might offer contrary views. Thus, both writers portray the G.I. experience honestly, but each works within the constraints of his individual methodology.

Some readers, however, may still be dissatisfied with this "both-and" response to the problem. Beidler's analysis can be useful, but perhaps it is also too caught up in a postmodern exploration of self-parodic simulacra. There are other voices to be heard: the voices of veterans found in memoirs, oral histories, and other materials.[14] The complex social history constructed by collective narratives of veterans can serve as a basis for interrogating any simply binary constructed from the "Good War"/"Great SNAFU" comparison. As revealed in these primary sources, American G.I.s came from a wide range of socioeconomic backgrounds. They went to war from a sense of duty, but they quickly abjured the commonplace slogans found in popular media. Most fought as best they could under the circumstances, and they kept fighting for many reasons, some too subtle to articulate fully. Acts of apparent heroism, as Raymond Gantter has noted, were sometimes bred of necessity or fear while acts of seeming cowardice might result from shock, stress, or even mere confusion. Heroes were not necessarily liked by their fellow soldiers even if they were respected for their heroic acts. Some men experienced close comradeship while others felt isolated and confused. Many felt both ways at different points in their experience. Still, most agreed that shared terror could bring unexpected intimacy to combat soldiers, binding them in a relationship that cannot be explained fully to others. So many days and nights in combat, so many deaths witnessed, and so many traumas suffered by survivors—all this forms the aggregate experience of the American combat veteran. It is reducible neither to a neat binary nor to a postmodern self-parody. The experience of combat veterans ultimately resists containment by any one narrative structure or theoretical analysis. To appreciate the war's complexities, we must listen as much as possible to the full range of veterans' narratives. The war's narrative is the chorus of all their stories—polyphonic and often cacophonous. This narrative proceeds not merely in the simulacra of popular media but also in all the processes of personal recollection and retelling—a living social history. The war, with its promise of glory and presence of hell, cannot be summed up. It resists closure just as the veterans' memories resist closure. In the end, veterans pick up their fragments of memory, reexamine them, and share them with us. As witnesses, we can testify to what we have been told, but we do not have the authority to contain it fully with any neat labels. Both Ambrose and Fussell would probably have agreed on this point.

Once More onto the Screen: The Battle for History and the Neo–World War II Film

In 1998 journalist Tom Brokaw effectively renamed the World War II demographic with his book *The Greatest Generation*. Like Ambrose, Brokaw had been only a child during the war, but like many Americans his age, along with those of the "baby-boom" generation, he wanted to commemorate World War II.[15] Although Americans coming of age during the 1950s and 1960s had often rebelled against their elders, by the 1990s many had grown to admire those whom they once had questioned. Generational identity and attitudes, however, are never so simple. America's World War II "generation" was really a cluster of generations, some born as early as the century's first decade, and some as late as 1927. Also, about a third of the 18 million called by the Selective Service for World War II were rejected.[16] Thus, millions of the "Greatest Generation" could not even serve. Many others remained in civilian life, but over 17 million, including over 6 million volunteers, did serve during the war.[17] World War II combat veterans, however, did not label themselves as "greatest," and such hyperbole seems inconsistent with their very sobering experiences. Though justly proud of their wartime service, many veterans still remain saddened at having shared in such enormous destruction. Those who endured the worst suffering and showed the greatest courage have often achieved a deep humility that transcends any superficial label.

Of course, broad generational categories often reduce people to a uniform status that belies their diverse experiences.[18] Although Ambrose and Brokaw are justified in praising Americans who struggled through World War II, too much of the "greatest generation" discussion has merely reinforced an oversimplified view of the war that is inconsistent with accounts from actual veterans. Likewise, the title "baby boomer" belies the experience of that younger generation that came of age in the 1960s. Did fighting in Vietnam in 1968 make one less a soldier than doing so in Europe in 1944? Combat veterans from either war do not usually make the distinction. Americans who fought in World War II did their country a great service, but as with any large group caught up in complex events, their motives were often mixed and uncertain. This fact takes away nothing from their courage and sacrifice. What does diminish them is the attempt to contain them within a limited category, and veterans like Fussell justifiably resist being so neatly packaged. Implicitly, however, Brokaw is not only praising the World War II generation but also attaching himself to it and to its achievements while distancing himself from the baby boomers, who must seem less than "great" by comparison. For his part, Ambrose has scoffed at 1950s academic "liberals," who supposedly dominated his graduate education with critiques of Eisenhower-era America. He misinterprets these as critiques of World War II veterans even though many of those critics were themselves veterans (like Fussell). Ironically, Ambrose has gained his reputation by celebrating the individualism of the American soldier. Of all people, he should have realized that those who attacked 1950s conformity were not criticizing the World War II veterans but criticizing the social norms being imposed upon those veterans, as well as upon Americans in general. Furthermore, while Brokaw offers well-crafted portraits of Americans of the war generation, he has also encouraged a return to superficial labeling that undermines the best qualities of those he seeks to praise.

In *Goodbye, Darkness* William Manchester somewhat ironically describes himself and his generation as caricatures—old men "who...carry their wives' pocketbooks around Europe" when on vacation.[19] In his dreams, however, he sees a ghostly vision of the young marine he had been long before, now glaring contemptuously at the aging Manchester because the postwar world had failed to fulfill the promise for which so many had died (see chapter eight). Like many veterans, Manchester feels called to account not by a younger generation but by the memory of his own youth. His example illustrates how the real conflicts over the war's history are not so much intergenerational as intragenerational. America's World War II veterans struggle with painful memories of a war that ended in victory but left the world devastated and still in conflict. Likewise, baby boomers—forever trivialized by the name but often veterans of Vietnam—struggle with their own conflicted experience in both war and peace. Some members of these younger groups (both pre-boomers and boomers) have appropriated the mainstream narrative of World War II, perhaps because it seems so definitive compared to their own ambiguous experience of the 1960s. Thus, the concept of the "Greatest Generation" grows not so much from the World War II generation itself but from subsequent generations seeking comfort in an oversimplified narrative of a past they had never experienced. Ironically, the Vietnam generation's personal accounts of their own horrific combat experiences may have helped World War II veterans finally confront their earlier trauma. Possibly the fathers learned to speak of trauma from their sons even though some sons would still seek closure in stories about their fathers' war. In part, these generation gaps lead to our current, conflicting narratives of World War II.

★   ★   ★

Even as writers such as Brokaw and Ambrose were refocusing national attention on the war, Hollywood was energetically reviving the World War II genre, and Steven Spielberg led the effort with *Saving Private Ryan* (1998).[20] During the early 1990s, the media had already prepared audiences for these new films by paying special attention to World

War II retrospectives, especially with cable television providing multiple venues for documentaries and frequent opportunities to revisit
"classic" war films. In addition, advances in special-effects technologies allowed filmmakers to represent, in painfully graphic detail, the
horrors of modern combat, and the resulting new films, unlike traditional predecessors of the 1950s and early 1960s, were not bound by
the old Production Code. On screen, soldiers no longer simply fell dead
but now experienced all the agonizing forms of wounding, mutilation,
and death suffered on the battlefield—something already apparent in
Vietnam films but not previously associated with Hollywood's representation of World War II. While more realistically portraying war's
carnage, this new style has also encouraged our voyeuristic fascination
with screen violence. As early as 1945, when film critic James Agee was
reviewing combat newsreels from Iwo Jima, he warned audiences that
they might develop an almost pornographic attachment to watching
graphic films of battlefield violence.[21] For good or ill, however, the
neo–World War II film usually immerses viewers in high-resolution
dismemberment and death, affecting audiences in whole new ways.

A master at manipulating an audience through such special effects,
Spielberg is also an effective storyteller, and he draws on all these tal-
ents in making *Saving Private Ryan*. Recalling traditional Hollywood
war films, *Saving Private Ryan* also reflects the growing awareness of just
how traumatic combat had been for World War II soldiers. Influenced
generally by the new histories and memoirs of the war, and particularly
by Ambrose, the director wanted to commemorate the sacrifices of
American G.I.s while also revealing how survivors continued to suffer
trauma from the war. Of course, Spielberg also sought to succeed Daryl
F. Zanuck as the filmmaker who created a D-Day epic for a whole new
generation of viewers. Critics have noted that such egocentric motives
lead to excesses in Spielberg films, and others have argued that the
director's work is generally more style than substance. *Saving Private
Ryan*, however, transcends most of Spielberg's limitations, serving as an
important reintroduction of the World War II film genre.

Structurally, *Saving Private Ryan* is complicated, integrating three
different kinds of films. It has a double-frame structure, with two
separate narrative frames around the central story. The first frame is
an elegiac story of trauma and survivor guilt, depicting an aging veteran's return to the cemetery above Omaha Beach. The old man is
still trying to justify his own survival when so many of his comrades
died. Unfortunately, however, the only ones who could judge are the
dead, whose gravestones form the mute chorus in response to the old

veteran's dilemma. Contained within this frame of trauma narrative is a second frame of epic combat, with one major battle sequence near the film's beginning and another near its end, and though each battle is distinctive, together they frame the central story.

The first combat sequence shows a U.S. Army Ranger company, led by Captain John Miller (Tom Hanks), landing at Omaha Beach and being decimated by the machine gun and mortar fire of the German defenders. Nearly in a state of shock, Miller recovers his composure and leads the surviving men to outflank the German pillboxes. Though the rangers win the engagement, they suffer appalling casualties, and Spielberg reveals the horrific violence of combat, including graphic images of traumatic amputation and evisceration. Even the film's harsher critics have praised this sequence for its startling realism.

Only after this lengthy and painful opening does Spielberg begin the film's central narrative, a small-unit story that is also a quest. After D-Day, Miller's unit is assigned to retrieve a paratrooper, Private James Ryan (Matt Damon), whose three brothers have been killed in action—as the sole survivor of four sons, Ryan must be sent home. This rather unlikely mission still symbolizes the very real reasons that G.I.s did fight—to save each other. Thus, at its core, *Saving Private Ryan* is symbolic narrative about the shared brotherhood of soldiers—the love that motivates men to kill and/or die for one another in war.

As in traditional small-unit films, the patrol's slow progress allows viewers time to grow familiar with the men.[22] Tough, even cynical, they are still loyal to each other, and when one is killed, the audience shares the sense of loss. Yet Miller himself conveys the strongest emotional impact. Outwardly as tough and experienced as his men, he is inwardly near despair when thinking of all the men he has lost during nearly two years of combat. Speaking with his confidant, Sergeant Mike Horvath (Tom Sizemore), Miller rationalizes that, for every man he has lost, more must have been saved, but he remains unconvinced by his own argument. At times Miller's hands shake uncontrollably, and at one point he goes off by himself and breaks down in tears.[23] Obviously, Miller is close to the end. As many combat memoirs attest, an actual officer in this condition would soon become a casualty—killed, wounded, or evacuated with "combat neurosis."

The small-unit story concludes with an intimate sequence in the village where the patrol finds Ryan and his fellow paratroopers. Because the airborne men must stay to defend the town, Ryan elects to stay with them, and so do the rangers. Awaiting the assault, the men tell stories that reveal more of their individual personalities, intensifying the

emotional impact of the deaths we will witness in the subsequent battle. Spielberg here evokes the spirit of John Ford films, where soldiers
quietly show their true camaraderie as they anticipate a fight against
terrible odds.

Spielberg places the second epic battle near the film's closing, as the
rangers and airborne troops fight desperately to defend the town and
its vital bridge. This sequence forces the audience to witness gruesome deaths of several major characters, such as the slow stabbing death
of Private Stanley Mellish (Adam Goldberg). Also during this battle,
Private Timothy Upham (Jeremy Davies), a naive soldier who seems to
speak from his conscience, makes all the mistakes of the poorly trained
rookie he is. Unable to shoot during the battle, he grows so guilt-
ridden and angry that he finally kills a German prisoner after fighting
has ceased (behavior consistent with many historical accounts of simi-
larly inexperienced soldiers). In the classic war film, however, Upham
would have overcome his fears and fought well, perhaps sacrificing
himself in the process (not unlike young Robert Walker in *Bataan*, see
chapter eight). Surprisingly, Spielberg resists this cliché, leaving viewers
with a more complex, disturbing portrait of a neophyte infantryman.
As the sequence nears its end, we witness both the heroic death of
Captain Miller and the appearance of a deus ex machina. In shock from
a nearby shell blast, Miller still tries to blow the bridge, but before he
can do so, a bullet strikes him in the chest. As he lies dying, he keeps
firing his pistol futilely at a tank crossing the bridge. Suddenly the
tank erupts into flame, effectively blocking the bridge and the German
advance. Did Miller actually kill the tank with a lucky bullet? No,
a fighter plane flies over, and viewers realize that a bomb or rocket
hit the vulnerable rear of the tank. Then, after reinforcements come
up and drive back the Germans, a dying Miller tells Ryan to "earn"
the salvation his comrades have brought him. This concludes the final
combat sequence and the second half of the epic battle frame, returning
us to the old veteran whom we now know to be Ryan.

Saving Private Ryan closes with ambiguity rather than assurance. The
old Ryan asks his wife if he has led a good life, but her response does
little good. Standing before the silent gravestones, Ryan finds no salve
for his psychic wounds. He remains a prisoner to the past, never certain that he can justify his survival. The final image is of a waving
flag, which might seem a patriotic cliché, but light shines through this
flag, not on it, bleaching out the color to an image that is white and
pale gray. Is this sanctifying light, giving a ghostly affirmation to the
honored dead? Is it the light of truth that changes the patriotic image

into a kind of shroud? The film does not tell us the answer, concluding instead with a necessary ambiguity that may be its greatest strength.[24]

Many have praised and many others have attacked *Saving Private Ryan* both as a confirmation of the "Greatest Generation" myth and as a rebirth of America's mainstream narrative of the war. Political conservatives have celebrated the film as a justification of their view of American exceptionalism, and liberals have criticized it as an unquestioning acceptance of a right-wing vision of America. These critics also find Spielberg guilty of sentimentalizing World War II to reinforce the "Good-War" narrative. Both these political communities, however, are arguing with each other more than analyzing the film. Although *Saving Private Ryan* has its flaws, including uneven pacing caused by the complex, double-frame structure, it is not an unabashed endorsement of American hegemony. The film portrays war as excessive, violent, confused, and ambiguous, doing justice to accounts from veterans. Though the plot becomes contrived at some points, the overall structure maintains both power and elegance. In directing the film, Spielberg exercises greater control over his own potential excesses, while still displaying his mastery of the medium. Finally, the film honestly explores the psychology of combat soldiers, revealing their traumatic combat experience and the lasting effects of that experience upon its survivors. Despite the critical conflicts surrounding the film, *Saving Private Ryan* has added to, rather than detracted from, our national understanding of the war. Many critics use the film only as a reflection of their own preconceptions, but viewers willing to study the film itself can find it a far richer and more complex work than most of its admirers or detractors will admit.

★   ★   ★

The release of *Saving Private Ryan* in 1998 made it clear that Hollywood had returned to the World War II combat film, but while Spielberg's film was influential, it was merely one of many new films in this reemergent genre. Some, such as *The Great Raid* (2005), based on an actual 1945 rescue of American POWs in the Philippines, resemble traditional World War II films.[25] Although such contemporary films employ a more graphically realistic style, they still emulate the structures and themes of the classic World War II films. Others, such as the HBO project *When Trumpets Fade* (1998), depicting the disastrous 1944 Battle of the Huertgen Forest, deploy graphic realism in an antiwar drama that critiques and interrogates the "Good-War" narrative.

One of the more thought-provoking new films has been Terrence Malick's *The Thin Red Line*, based on the James Jones novel (see chapter seven). Andrew Marton had directed an early film version in 1964, but that film had badly mangled both story and characters. In some ways, however, Malick's film takes even greater liberties with Jones' story, but to better effect, even though the film received a mixed reception from both critics and audiences. Unlike most directors in Hollywood, Malick brings a highly philosophical agenda to each of his films. Throughout his work, he uses cinema to explore the basic philosophical problems that underlie American cultural history, and so his films reflect the literary traditions of the nineteenth-century American philosophical novelists such as Nathanial Hawthorne and Herman Melville.

In making this new version from Jones' novel, Malick blends the neonaturalism of Jones with the dark romanticism found in Melville. Indeed, the opening segment places the main character Private Witt (James Caviezal) in a tropic paradise where he can speculate on good and evil in relation to the "natural" life of the indigenous people. There is no corresponding episode in Jones' novel, but this sequence echoes Melville's South Seas narratives like *Typee* (1846). From Jones, Malick does adopt one key feature—the collective character of the unit, C-Company. Melville constructs similar collective characters in the ships crews in *White-Jacket* (1850) and *Moby-Dick* (1851), which become microcosms of human societies. Witt's foil in the film, as in the book, is Sergeant Welsh (Sean Penn). Whereas Jones shows Witt as a truculent, even bigoted southerner, as well as a consummate soldier, Malick turns him into a Christ figure who sacrifices himself both to save the lives of the company and the soul of Welsh. Welsh, rather than the novel's troubled authority figure, is more like one of Melville's dark antiheroes, seeking comfort for hidden spiritual wounds. Thus, Malick has made a film of Jones' *The Thin Red Line* so that he might tell an inner story that could have come from Melville. Although the director is quite realistic in his tone, and often faithful to the original novel, he still uses it only as a springboard for examining basic questions of good and evil in the context of a group of men bound together in war. At times a startlingly effective war film, Malick's version of *The Thin Red Line* is less about World War II than about the relationship between brotherhood and violence in human nature. As such, it stands apart from other war films, but it does illustrate the potential depth and diversity in the new genre of World War II films.

One of the most ambitious, new World War II films was developed for the small screen: the Tom Hanks-Steven Spielberg collaboration

Band of Brothers, a ten-part mini-series based on the 1992 Stephen Ambrose book (see above). Like the book, the series covers the whole arc of war—from initial training in 1942 through the fall of Germany in 1945—through the focal experiences of one parachute infantry company in the 101st Airborne Division.[26] With ten hours of screen time, Hanks and Spielberg can pace the narrative, allowing for thorough exposition and complex character development. At the same time, by designing each episode as a self-contained mini-drama, with its own director and writer, the filmmakers also achieve a dramatic intensity that grows as the series develops. Because the film portrays actual people and events from Ambrose's book, it carries an unusual level of authenticity. Of course, while keeping faithfully to the facts, Hanks, Spielberg, and their team do exercise some creative freedom in structuring dramatic situations for each episode so they might bring the events to life more vividly. This dramatic license does nothing to undermine the authority of the series, especially because that authority is also supported by on-camera interviews with surviving veterans that introduce each episode. As these aged men speak softly but compellingly of their motives and experiences, they reveal the pain they still suffer as they struggle to speak of the friends they lost and how close they themselves came to dying. In the end, the Hanks-Spielberg *Band of Brothers* so effectively dramatizes the story of Easy Company that the series supplants the book as few films do. For a short history of a specific unit, *Band of Brothers* is a successful book, but as a television mini-series, it is extraordinarily powerful.

Spielberg also had a producer's role in what may be the most extraordinary recent film projects about World War II—Clint Eastwood's excellent pair of films about the Battle of Iwo Jima. The first, *Flags of Our Fathers* (2005), is based on James Bradley's (2000) account of his father's experiences as a U.S. Navy corpsman attached to a Marine Corps unit at Iwo Jima, and as one of the three surviving members of the group that raised the iconic flag on Mt. Suribachi. Paired with this is the equally compelling *Letters from Iwo Jima* (2006), which views the same battle completely from the Japanese perspective.[27] *Letters* is unique in the history of American films about the Pacific war. Whereas Hollywood had sometimes gone beyond mere racist stereotypes in presenting Japanese characters in previous World War II films, they only rarely showed any real sympathy for these characters—Cornell Wilde's *Beach Red* (1967) being a rare if flawed exception (see chapter seven). If influenced by Wilde's film, Eastwood goes far beyond him in achieving his vision, effectively making American audiences identify closely with the Japanese characters by focusing exclusively on their perspective. Never before had American audiences witnessed so intimate and intricate a portrait of the individual Japanese soldier, from the commanding general all the way down to the lowliest private. The film will stand as a benchmark for all that follow.

For the purposes of this study, however, it is *Flags of Our Fathers* that has the greater significance. Bradley writes not only a memoir of his father's service but also an exploration of the effects of the unwanted fame that derived from John "Doc" Bradley's role in raising the flag. It is a touching portrait of a veteran father by a son who struggles to understand the inner suffering that lies beneath public image, and only near the end of Doc's life does he reveal much about his experience. Starting with this powerful material, Eastwood interweaves action and recollection, moving back and forth across multiple time frames. These include the Iwo Jima battle itself, the present day when Doc is growing closer to death, and episodes before and after the battle, during which we learn much about the inner life and struggles of the three flag-raisers who survived to return home: Doc Bradley (Ryan Phillippe), Rene Gagnon, (Jesse Bradford), and Ira Hayes (Adam Beach). Gagnon, never respected by his fellow soldiers, spends his life futilely trying to capitalize on his reputation. Hayes, a Native American, experiences multiple traumas, from the effects of the racism he suffers in the unit, to the more troubling survivor guilt that dogs him for the remainder of his short, unhappy life. Only Bradley returns to what might be considered a normal civilian life, taking up his old job at a mortuary of which he eventually becomes owner. The irony is obvious but not overstated that the former mortician had become a corpsman who attempted to save lives, returning to spend the rest of his life burying the dead. Of course, Doc also buries his memories, but not so deeply that they do not surface in his own disturbing dreams. Only as he nears his death does Doc reveal these memories to his son, James, beginning a process that leads to the book and to the film.

What Eastwood achieves in *Flags of Our Fathers* is a representation of the traumatized psyche, a revelation of the secret ghosts that haunted thousands of veterans after the war—even though those same ghosts often remained invisible to a veteran's family and friends. Interweaving memory and action, the director brings to the screen some of the same complexity found in Manchester's *Goodbye, Darkness* and other trauma memoirs of the war. At the same time, Eastwood also reveals how the very act of representing the war has used and abused these veterans. We see that Gagnon, Hayes, and Bradley were all returned from combat after the battle and redeployed in a massive public relations effort to support war bond sales, often ordered to restage the dramatic moments of the flag-raising. Even after the war ended, they continued to be used as iconic figures at commemoration ceremonies that helped reinforce public support for the military. For Doc Bradley, however, memories of combat and dead friends mix with these absurd public events, and Eastwood employs intricate crosscutting, flashbacks, and flash forwards to demonstrate how Doc has occasionally become almost "unstuck in time," like Vonnegut's Billy Pilgrim. Although some critics have complained that this technique overly complicates the film, one can think of few better ways to illustrate the inner life of the traumatized mind. In both these war films, Eastwood has made powerful statements about the lasting effects and the profound costs of modern war, and in *Flags of Our Fathers*, he has provided unique insight into what many veterans have struggled for years to express.

Collectively, the growing body of new World War II films reflects the increasingly complex patterns of the new cultural history of that war. The films display a wide range of styles and approaches, not to mention a considerable variety of political perspectives. Still, all of these films benefit to some extent from the extensive memoir literature by World War II veterans, a literature that had not existed during earlier periods of World War II filmmaking. New films emerge every year, and it seems apparent that both Hollywood and the American public are willing to continue exploring this subject matter. More importantly, however, than the mere making of films about the war, is the question of how such films will acknowledge and incorporate the painful revelations found in so many of the recent memoirs and oral histories by veterans. If filmmakers do little more than concentrate on dramatic conflict and opportunities for dazzling special-effects, they will merely repackage the old clichés. However, if they listen to the voices of veterans, to the true chorus of "many men," filmmakers have a chance to make an unprecedented contribution to our cultural understanding of the war. Certainly, a number of these recent films give us reason to hope.

Coda—Making the Image of War, Then and Now

We are now engaged in another war that we have called, until quite recently, "the war on terror." Like the Cold War, this new war came without any formal congressional declaration and thus has no easy form of closure. Unlike the Cold War, however, this war has emerged from a singular national tragedy that has the impact of a Pearl Harbor: the terrorist attacks of September 11, 2001. So although we have a specific opening event, we still have only a limited sense of the full potential structure for this war. Ironically, the 9/11 attack occurred mere months before we were to observe the sixtieth anniversary of the attack on Pearl Harbor. This latter-day Pearl Harbor has led to direct military action in Afghanistan and Iraq, and to all the ongoing consequences resulting from our occupations of those countries.

This new war has also come to us at a crossroads in our attempts to understand and represent the dynamic, frightful, and perhaps inspiring past of World War II. The stories of World War II that we have constructed during the past sixty-odd years have shaped much of our mythos and ethos as a nation, as a people. The evolving and shifting forms of narrative, with all their political and personal intricacies, in the aggregate create a modern American consciousness. In these stories we are both an innocent people and a corrupt people; we are a peaceful people drawn by necessity to war and a warlike people seeking opportunities to fight. These stories reveal us as we hope we could be, and also as we fear we might be. We see ourselves as a victorious people who have transcended loss and trauma, conquering as well the temptation to be no better than our enemies. Yet we also see ourselves as a people whose moral losses outweigh our political victories, becoming one of the principal architects of a world ever more likely to seek solutions in the energy of terrible violence.

During the Cold War, the poet Czelaw Milosz accused Americans of being ignorant of war, and he predicted that we could learn the nature of war only when and if our own cities and countryside suffered the ravages that Europe and Asia had experienced in World War II.[28] Whether our representations then and since have led us to knowledge or self-delusion is a question of interpretation. Certainly the events of 9/11 made us more knowledgeable about the horrors of civilian casualties, not unlike those caused by the kind of bombing that has been an American strategic commonplace at many times during the past sixty-odd years. We have yet to discover if the events of 9/11 will be isolated or will become part of an emergent pattern of experiences that will be with us for years to come. Our response to these events is to look for meaning in the available material of our prior stories, to see this attack in terms of Pearl Harbor, and to view our actions now in relation to those taken at the outset of our declarations of war in 1941. In the weeks and months following 9/11, much was said about the nature of American life and the character of the American peo-ple. Flags and other symbols of patriotism, along with a national lan-guage of determination and commitment, emerged as commonplaces that cut across the usual political and social divisions in our land. It remains to be seen whether this was more than the surface structure of our media–dominated social discourse, a mere passing phase and fash-ion, or if it reflects something essential in the character of our coun-try and its people. Our current divisive national politics belies these images of unity, so we cannot be sure if our connections transcend our differences. As this new war proceeded into the second term of President George W. Bush, Americans became increasingly dissatisfied with our military actions in Iraq and Afghanistan, if not with the cen-tral themes of fighting terrorism. Although the election of President Barack Obama has brought new hope of a national political consensus for many Americans, it remains to be seen if our nation can maintain a sense of unity while transcending its equally powerful sense of fear that manifests itself in both our domestic politics and our international rela-tions. Eight years after 9/11, and over six years after invading Iraq, we have yet to construct a clear, consistent, and meaningful explanation of our current wars, except to argue that we continue to respond to our having been attacked.

Ultimately, however, our greatest problem in representing war, any war, is that our literary and cinematic genres depend so heavily on nar-rative and dramatic closure. It is not that these war stories necessarily glorify war. Rather, war stories suggest that war is like a story and so brings closure. Certainly, the traditional representation of World War II led us to believe that war was an effective if regrettably destructive means of seeking closure in international affairs. That assumption led us into Korea and Vietnam, and a renewed fixation on that assumption led us into Iraq as well. Experience, as acknowledged in history and as con-firmed by so many who have been in wars, demonstrates that war brings no closure, even when it may be a necessary and justifiable war. In war's wake come all the ghosts and demons that seemed silent during the shell-ing and gunfire, all the inconsistencies that rob victory of the promise of peace. World War II led to the Cold War, and to all the client wars of that global conflict, from Central America, to Africa, to Asia. With the Cold War over, we found newer conflicts along the old fault lines of cultural and religious difference, conflicts that had seemed quiescent during the decades when competing economic ideologies had framed global affairs. And with each passing year, some place in the world erupts into fighting, and with each day comes a new slaughter of innocents.

Meanwhile, we return to the formative mythos of the war that some have called "good" and that others have called into question. Certainly, our fighting World War II was necessary. The enemy was a genuine threat, and our cause was just, even if all our actions in the name of that cause were not necessarily just in themselves. Ultimately, we won, achieving a unity, a victory, and a subsequent prosperity that seemed to confirm the rightness of what we had attempted. So now, in a troubled time, we return to the images, stories, and metaphors of that great conflict. We display the symbols of national pride and call for renewed vigilance and renewed struggle. But our consciousness as a nation, like our efforts to fight against so vague an enemy as "terror," necessarily remains unfocused. To quote the beleaguered defenders of Wake Island, "the issue is in doubt." Since we do not know precisely "why" we fight or "how" we fight in this new conflict, we crave more intensely the comfort that comes from stories of old victories in more well-defined wars.

Only a long historical view might be able to tell us if our current use of these symbols and stories, resonant with deeper values, represents something positive or destructive in our national character. Even the most honest and self-reflective of us would be unable to step out of time in this moment and answer such a question. It is possible, however, to predict that whatever answers emerge will represent qualities and issues we have seen before. These qualities and issues have been at the heart of our national identity formation for much of the last century, and they continue to drive and be driven by our need to come to terms with the experience of World War II. Speaking of his experience in the American Civil War, Oliver Wendell Holmes once claimed that "in our youths our hearts were touched with fire." Like Holmes, our country might be said to have entered this whole historical process in a youthful condition. In the 1930s, America was neither childlike nor childish in comparison to its current state, but it was in many ways a younger country. Our country, in that period of youth, was touched by the searing fire of World War II, though in ways that were not always clear or self-evident. Certainly, the traumatic experience of combat was the center of that flame, while at a greater distance, the shape of the fire—its light and its warmth—may seem both frightening and desirable in the same moment. We have yet to reconcile fully our distinctive experiences and representations of that war, but our struggle to do so has been a driving force in our national politics and our national consciousness for over sixty years. The imbalances revealed in the history of these representations show us the inconsistencies of our national character, sometimes pointing to the shameful and the painful as we see ourselves living in stark contrast to the values we claim to have fought for. At the same time, the fact that an ongoing, dynamic struggle continues over how to represent our World War II experience suggests that the American people do wish to achieve an honest appreciation of their past.

In achieving that appreciation, we must examine ourselves, as well as others, and in attempting that self-examination, we must honor justly, accuse honestly, judge mercifully, and challenge energetically. As current crises—not merely the recollections of past trials—call us to account for ourselves, call us to understand who we are and what we must do in the face of an emergent history, it is all the more important that we understand our ingrained habits of representation and interpretation of our past. If Joan Didion is correct that "we tell stories in order to live," then perhaps we must examine the history of our storytelling so that we might live honestly, justly, and well. In that spirit, examining how we have told stories of a past war may help us understand how to respond to present wars, as well as how to achieve, at last, a hoped-for and long-delayed peace.

NOTES

Introduction: Faces of the War

1. *The War* was released in September 2007. My book, having been written from 2003 through 2006, could not examine Burns' documentary in detail. Having watched it and found it uniquely valuable, I have endeavored to include it briefly in my revised version.
2. Oliver Wendell Holmes Jr., "Memorial Day," in *The Essential Holmes: Selections from the Letters, Speeches, Judicial Opinions, and Other Writings of Oliver Wendell Holmes, Jr.*, ed. Richard A. Posner (Chicago: University of Chicago Press, 1997), 80–87.

One A War Warning

1. *Reporting World War II: American Journalism 1938–1946*, 1-Volume Paperback Edition (New York: Library of America, 2001), 760–761.
2. Iris Chang, *The Rape of Nanking: The Forgotten Holocaust of World War II* (New York: Basic Books, 1997), 3–7.
3. See Clayton R. Koppes and Gregory D. Black's *Hollywood Goes to War: How Politics, Profits, and Propaganda Shaped World War II Movies* (Berkeley: University of California Press, 1990) for thorough treatment of this period, esp. 17–34.
4. Information in this paragraph concerning the "Short of War" policy comes from Samuel Eliot Morison's *The Two-Ocean War: A Short History of the United States Navy in the Second World War* (Boston: Atlantic-Little, Brown, 1963), 29–30.
5. In this paragraph, factual information about American neutrality and opposition to anti-Nazi films in Hollywood comes from Koppes and Black, 1–16.
6. Until Hitler invaded the Soviet Union in June 1941, many on the American Left were also critical of Hollywood's support for the Allies.
7. In this paragraph, my information on *The March of Time* series comes from Roger Manvell's *Films and the Second World War* (New York: A Delta Book, Dell, 1974), 15–21, 86–92.
8. Once attacked by Nazi Germany, Stalin's Soviet Union would also take on the mantle of a defender of freedom, despite its history of purges and oppression.
9. Koppes and Black, 34.
10. Working for the Institute of International Education during the early 1930s, Murrow helped bring 335 German scholars, persecuted by the Nazis, to American universities. See

Mark Bernstein and Alex Lubertozzi, *World War II on the Air: Edward R. Murrow and the Broadcasts That Riveted a Nation* (Naperville, IL: Sourcebooks-mediaFusion, 2003), 22–23.

11. Throughout this and the subsequent three paragraphs, factual details about the work of Murrow and his correspondents is from Bernstein and Lubertozzi, 94–102. The summaries, analyses, and interpretations of his broadcasts are my own, based on listening to recordings accompanying the Bernstein/Lubertozzi text, as well as on reading the texts of those broadcasts as published in Edward R. Murrow's *This Is London* (New York: Schocken Books, 1989).

12. Murrow, 181.

13. Murrow, 148.

14. Murrow, 144.

15. Murrow, 145–146.

16. Factual information in this paragraph represents general knowledge derived from wide reading about Murrow and his team.

17. President Franklin Roosevelt coined the term "Arsenal of Democracy" in a fireside chat on December 29, 1940. See "Fireside Chat, Dec. 29, 1940" in *A Rendezvous with Destiny: Addresses and Opinions of Franklin Delano Roosevelt*, ed. J. B. S. Hardman, 1944 (Whitefish, MT: Kessinger Publishing Reprint, 2005), 164–173.

18. William L. Bird, Jr. and Harry R. Rubenstein, *Design for Victory: World War II Posters on the American Home Front* (New York: Princeton, 1998), 24.

19. Initiated by a New York philanthropist, the "Bundles for Britain" program collected both funds and homemade garments for the English. See "Give Us the Tools," *Time*, March 3, 1941, 15–16.

20. For more on the "Flying Tigers," see Geoffrey Perret's *Winged Victory: The Army Air Forces in World War II* (New York: Random House, 1993), 63–65, 153–159.

21. Quoted in Joe Morella, Edward Z. Epstein, and John Griggs, *The Films of World War II* (Secaucus, NJ: Citadel Press, 1975), 56.

22. During the 1920s and 1930s, Hollywood generally represented World War I in antiwar films. From 1939 to 1941, however, Hollywood used World War I subject matter to give a prowar message. *The Fighting 69th* (1940) and *Sergeant York* (1941), quasi docudramas, brought back the positive quality of the old song lyric, "the Yanks are coming."

Two   "Why We Fight"

1. Joan Didion, *The White Album* (New York: Simon and Schuster, 1979), 11.

2. Throughout this and the following paragraph, my information on these plans comes from Ronald H. Spector's *Eagle Against the Sun: The American War with Japan* (New York: Vintage Books, 1985), Chapter 2, esp. 55–59.

3. Japan's attack, and our subsequent declaration of war against it, led both Germany and Italy, bound by treaty obligations, to declare war on the United States by December 11, 1941. America immediately reciprocated, bringing us to war with all Axis powers. The FDR administration had assumed that war with any Axis power would lead to war with the others.

4. One cannot help but think, today, of our preemptive strike against Baghdad that began our war in Iraq in March 2003.

5. Samuel Eliot Morison, *The Two-Ocean War: A Short History of the United States Navy in the Second World War* (Boston: Atlantic-Little, Brown, 1963), 51–53, 69–76; Edwin T. Layton, *"And I Was There": Pearl Harbor and Midway—Breaking the Secrets* (New York: William Morrow, 1985), 300–301.

6. Morison, 59.

7. One may study the shaping of national consciousness from a variety of theoretical perspectives. Theorists such as Michel Foucault and Louis Althusser have examined how powerful cultural forces shape concepts of individual identity and group consciousness in mass cultures. Earlier, Jacques Ellul explored the structures of propaganda used by governments and other institutions to create social solidarity or to focus collective fear and anger—integration and agitation propaganda, respectively. These and other approaches are useful, but my interpretive approach examines what I call the "rhetoric of cultural narrative"—how cultures construct persuasive stories that shape our sense of personal identity and social relationships. My approach draws on several theories: Wayne Booth's and James Phelan's concepts of rhetorical narrative; Kenneth Burke's social-rhetorical theory; Mikhail Bakhtin's compelling analyses of social discourses; and Walter J. Ong's study of media and cultural epistemology.

8. All references to the speech are based on the version reprinted in *Reporting World War II: American Journalism 1938–1946*, 1-Volume Paperback Edition (New York: Library of America, 2001), 99–100.

9. John Dower's *War without Mercy: Race and Power in the Pacific War* (New York: Pantheon, 1986), examines in detail the U.S. government's representations of the Japanese as our enemy, including in Roosevelt's speech.

10. See Bernard F. Dick, *The Star-Spangled Screen: The American World War II Film* (Lexington: University Press of Kentucky, 1985), 102.

11. See William L. Bird Jr. and Harry R. Rubenstein's *Design for Victory: World War II Posters on the American Home Front* (New York: Princeton Architectural Press, 1998), 1–9.

12. Clayton R. Koppes and Gregory D. Black's *Hollywood Goes to War: How Politics, Profits, and Propaganda Shaped World War II Movies* (Berkeley: University of California Press, 1990), 58–59.

13. On agitation propaganda, see Jacques Ellul's *Propaganda: The Formation of Men's Attitudes*, trans. Konrad Kellen and Jean Lerner (New York: Alfred A. Knopf, 1965), 70–79.

14. See Dower, 15–32.

15. Roland Marchand, *Advertising the American Dream: Making Way for Modernity, 1920–1940* (Berkeley: University of California Press, 1985), xviii. Ellul's concept of propaganda, articulated in the 1960s, is consistent with what a number of Marxist and material cultural critics generally describe as ideology. According to Ellul, agitation propaganda was a tool for developing governments "to galvanize energies to mobilize the entire nation for war." Integration propaganda, however, is "a propaganda of conformity," in modern, developed mass cultures. Throughout the twentieth century, most governments and cultures have engaged in both kinds of propaganda. Regardless of the terms we use, when we speak of fundamental assumptions about national identity, we speak of cultural epistemology—how we construct our knowledge of who we are as a nation. We are speaking also of the rhetorical processes of constructing that epistemology through all forms of cultural representation. See Ellul, 70–79.

16. "Polyphony" is a concept found in the writings of Russian theorist Mikhail Bakhtin. In Bakhtin's theory, every use of language is potentially shot through with the words of others. He uses this musical metaphor/analogy to talk about those situations in language and discourse where the audience simultaneously experiences several voices or points of view.

17. The two texts are Henry Luce's "The American Century," *Life*, February 17, 1941, and Henry Wallace's 1942 speech "The Century of the Common Man," both of which are referred to in Koppes and Black, 66–67. I am indebted to Koppes and Black for their analysis of these important statements by Luce and Wallace.

18. In postwar films such as *Gentleman's Agreement* and *Crossfire* (both 1947), Hollywood explored the ongoing problem of American anti-Semitism.

19. Complete treatment of this censorship may be found in George H. Roeder Jr.'s *The Censored War: American Visual Experience during World War Two* (New Haven: Yale University Press, 1993).

20. Certainly Ken Burns' documentary *The War* would have been impossible without the extensive film records from both military and civilian sources.
21. Even Ernie Pyle was constrained by censorship. See Paul Fussell's *The Boys' Crusade: The American Infantry in Northwestern Europe, 1944–1945* (New York: Modern Library, 2003), 50.
22. These articles, Ted Nakashima's June 15, 1942, *New Republic* article "Concentration Camp: U.S. Style" and the April 1944 *Fortune* article "Issei, Nisei, Kibei," are reprinted in *Reporting World War II*, 161–163; 421–444.
23. In this paragraph, my information about the wartime filmmaking of Ford and Capra largely comes from Joseph McBride's detailed biographies *Frank Capra: The Catastrophe of Success* (New York: Simon & Schuster, 1992), esp. chap. 16, and McBride's *Searching for John Ford: A Life* (New York: St. Martin's, 2001), esp. chap. 10.
24. Throughout this paragraph, my factual information about Capra's World War II experience comes from McBride, *Catastrophe*, 449–450.
25. In this paragraph, my factual information about Capra's World War II experience comes from McBride, *Catastrophe*, 453–501.
26. The U.S. Army Military History Institute has collected surveys from numerous veterans, demonstrating quite clearly that the *Why We Fight* series did not specifically motivate soldiers to fight.
27. See Charles Wolfe's *Frank Capra: A Guide to References and Resources* (Boston: G. K. Hall, 1987), 139–158, and Capra in his autobiography *Frank Capra: The Name Above the Title* (New York: Macmillan, 1971), 325–367.
28. Wolfe, 140.
29. My factual information in the next two paragraphs comes from Capra's autobiography, 326–343; McBride, *Catastrophe*, 465–468; and Wolfe, 140–142.
30. My factual information in this paragraph comes from Andrew Sinclair, *John Ford: A Life* (New York: Dial Press, 1979), 9–17, 28; and from McBride, *Searching*, 138, 199–205, and 273–277.
31. My factual information in this paragraph comes from Sinclair, 106–112; and from McBride, *Searching*, 199–205, 273–277, and 347–348.
32. Koppes and Black, 54–57.
33. My factual information in the remainder of this paragraph is derived from Chapter 10 of McBride, *Searching*.
34. My factual information about Ford's filming of *The Battle of Midway* comes from McBride, *Searching*, 357–366.
35. My factual information in this paragraph comes from McBride, *Searching*, 353–356, 384–387; and from Sinclair, Chapter 10.
36. In Ford's 1962 film *The Man Who Shot Liberty Valance*, a newspaper editor confronted with a truth that undermines the legend utters the oft-quoted line, "When the legend becomes fact, print the legend."

Three   *How* We Fight: Campaigns of Sacrifice and Service

1. Throughout this paragraph, factual information about the writing and development of *The Twilight Zone* episode "The Quality of Mercy" comes from Marc Scott Zicree's *The Twilight Zone Companion* (Los Angeles: Silman-James Press, 1992), 241–242.
2. Jeanine Basinger's *The World War II Combat Film: Anatomy of a Genre* (New York: Columbia University Press, 1986) provides a useful introduction to a range of World War II films, including a very thorough analysis of several. Unfortunately, her overall concept of genre is a bit too confining, and she limits her definition of the "combat film" to those focusing

almost exclusively on combat. She sometimes misses the point of many important films that effectively represent the experience of actual combat soldiers by showing the full range of that experience (including time in training and on leave), thus revealing the complex psychology of combatants. Still, her contribution to the study of World War II films remains very important.

3. In this paragraph, information about the development of the Alamo Force comes from Lance Q. Zedric's *Silent Warriors of World War II: The Alamo Scouts behind Japanese Lines* (Ventura, CA: Pathfinder Publishing of California, 1995), 33.

4. My factual information about the island's defenses and the battle comes from Ronald H. Spector's *Eagle Against the Sun: The American War with Japan* (New York: Vintage Books, 1985), 101–106. I have also consulted both John Wukovits' *Pacific Alamo: The Battle for Wake Island* (New York: New American Library, Penguin Books, 2003) and Chet Cunningham's *Hell Wouldn't Stop: An Oral History of the Battle of Wake Island* (New York: Carroll & Graf, 2002).

5. Wukovits, 25–27.

6. Wukovits, 61–62. Also note, for those on Wake Island, the Pearl Harbor attack occurred on December 8 because Wake is west of the International Date Line.

7. For a detailed account of the imprisonment of both the military and civilian captives from Wake, see Wukovits, 201–227.

8. Cunningham, 181. Wukovits, 236–237.

9. For the film's release date, see Joseph Morella, Edward Z. Epstein, and John Griggs, *The Films of World War Two* (Secacus, NJ: Citadel Press, 1973), 76.

10. See Jay Hyams, *War Movies* (New York: Gallery-W. H. Smith, 1984), 33–34, 73; Basinger, 55; and Lawrence Suid, *Guts and Glory: The Making of the American Military Image in Film* (Lexington: University Press of Kentucky, 2002), 31–32—all identify this iconic pair and its influence, a fact that I had already recognized from my own reading and viewing.

11. This logic ignores Caton's daughter, seen at the opening to "soften" Caton's tough image.

12. Information about the specifics of the engagement comes from Spector, 102–103. Again, see both Cunningham and Wukovits for detailed accounts.

13. My factual information on the aftermath of the Battle of Wake Island in this section comes from Cunningham, 177.

14. Quoted in Morella, Epstein, and Griggs, 77.

15. Facts about the Bataan campaign used throughout this paragraph come from Spector, 110–119.

16. I do not rely on Basinger's analysis of *Bataan*. She notes structural similarities between *Bataan* and John Ford's *The Lost Patrol* (1934) but overemphasizes *Bataan*'s being derivative because she concentrates on structural rather than cultural or rhetorical patterns. Focusing on the defense of empire, *The Lost Patrol* more likely influenced 1939 films such as *Gunga Din* and *Beau Geste*, rather than *Bataan*, which concentrates on themes of fighting against oppression and for American democratic ideals. Basinger's analysis of the characters, however, is very strong, as is her consideration of how both *The Lost Patrol* and *Bataan* connect to the Western.

17. Dane correctly suspects Todd's true identity, and tension grows between the tough but committed Dane and the equally tough but cynical Todd. Though in charge, Dane is essentially a team player while Todd is always a loner.

18. See Basinger's analysis of Purckett's character, especially in contrast to the "old man," Jake Feingold, 55.

19. The Japanese military engaged in widespread torture and killing of civilians in occupied areas, especially in China. Of course, European powers had subjugated Asia for centuries, joined by the United States from the nineteenth century on.

20. In 1941 and 1942, Hollywood released several films where gangsters redeemed themselves by fighting the Axis, including *All through the Night* and *Lucky Jordan*.

244 *Notes*

21. *Julius Caesar* III.1.273. All Shakespeare citations are from *The Riverside Shakespeare*, Second Edition (New York: Houghton Mifflin, 1997).

22. Films of "the criminal at war" are a specific subgenre, one example being Robert Aldrich's *The Dirty Dozen* (1967).

23. Some serious, postwar writers and filmmakers explored the connection between the psychopathology of criminal violence and combat; examples include John Hersey's *The War Lover* (1959), made into a film in 1962.

24. At Saipan, and later at Okinawa, the Japanese military killed Japanese civilians or ordered those civilians to commit suicide—often telling the civilians that, if captured by Americans, they would be raped and tortured. To American military planners, such events indicated that invading Japan itself would cause significant loss of civilian life, adding some weight to arguments for using the atomic bombs.

25. Pete did not dive "into" the carrier but "at" it, hoping to release his bombs directly above it at low altitude, thus ensuring its destruction, but his as well, in the ensuing explosion. Using a B-25 Mitchell bomber in this fashion is indeed suicidal, so the point remains the same.

26. My information in this paragraph about the final mission and death of Capt. Colin Kelly comes from Gerald Astor's *Crisis in the Pacific* (New York: Dell, 1996), 82–84.

27. My information in this paragraph about Fleming's death comes from Gordon Prange's *Miracle at Midway* (New York: Penguin, 1983), 218–220, 325.

28. Basinger comments on this influence, but as with all her extraordinarily well-researched book, her narrow genre model limits the overall value of her conclusions.

29. *Guadalcanal Diary* also connects with two prewar films, *Sergeant York* (1941) and *The Fighting 69th* (1940), because a religious figure supports those who fight. Sgt. York gains spiritual guidance from his evangelical rural minister, played by Walter Brennan. The fictional Fr. Donnelly perhaps owes more to Pat O'Brien's portrayal of the actual "Fighting Fr. Duffy," regimental chaplain in *The Fighting 69th*.

30. The novel is *Action in the North Atlantic* (New York: E. P. Dutton, 1943). My structural analysis of the film version of *Action in the North Atlantic* is based on my own viewing. Subsequently, I found a similar analysis in Bernard Dick's *The Star-Spangled Screen: The American World War II Film* (Lexington: University Press of Kentucky, 1985), 223–25. He identifies five segments, adapted from the five-part structure of Sergei Eisenstein's *Battleship Potemkin* (1925). I see the conclusion as a coda rather than an integral part.

31. One factor in the script is an unnoticed similarity to an article by journalist Helen Lawrenson, "Damn the Torpedoes," from the July 1942 issue of *Harper's Magazine*, reprinted in *Reporting World War II: American Journalism 1938–1946*, 1-Volume Paperback Edition (New York: Library of America, 2001), 146–152 (also see writer's biographic note, 818). In the film's earlier sequences, some dialogue among the crew closely parallels comments from sailors in Lawrenson's article. It seems that John Howard Lawson, or one of the others who worked on the script, engaged in some form of plagiarism. Given the prominence of the film in 1943, it also seems unlikely that this fact went unnoticed to editors at *Harper's*, or to Lawrenson herself, especially since she was then married to Jack Lawrenson, an official of the Maritime Union. Of course, since both Lawson and the Lawrensons supported the left-leaning union, it might be possible that one or both of the Lawrensons suggested that he use the material in the script. It is not in Gilpatric's novel. [I am currently preparing an article on this issue because, as far as I know, it has yet to be noticed or explained.]

32. Lawson's message, as left-wing as it may be, is completely consistent with the arguments of the government-produced Capra series *Why We Fight*.

33. In *The Star-Spangled Screen*, Dick also discusses the effect of Lawson's politics. My conclusions again grow from viewing of both films and from my prior knowledge of Lawson's life and politics. The connections do seem rather obvious from the material itself. Dick's chapter "California Comrades," 211–229, is a useful study of the Hollywood left and the films of World War II.

Four "The Great Crusade"

1. Eisenhower's D-Day address, in Robert Torricelli and Andrew Carroll's edition *In Our Own Words: Extraordinary Speeches of the American Century* (New York: Kodansha, 1999), 139.
2. In the film *Gettysburg* (1993), based on Michael Shaara's novel *The Killer Angels* (1974), Union Colonel Joshua Lawrence Chamberlain makes a speech to his regiment that explores similar mixed motives but still demonstrates importance of the underlying cause for which the men are fighting.
3. Indeed, at least some idealistic soldiers entertained socialist political views that would be held against them after the war.
4. *Henry V* IV.iii.109–111. All citations from Shakespeare are from *The Riverside Shakespeare*, Second Edition (New York: Houghton Mifflin Company, 1997).
5. The initials "G.I." is usually said to stand for "General Issue" or "Government Issue," identifying standard equipment issued to individual combat troops and their units. See William L. Priest, *Swear Like a Trooper: A Dictionary of Military Terms & Phrases* (Charlottesville, VA: Rockbridge, 2000), 103.
6. Figures on total numbers in the U.S. military during the duration of the war vary, but I am using figures cited in James F. Dunnigan and Albert A. Nofi, *Victory at Sea* (New York: Quill/William Morrow, 1995), 321–322. Estimates of total numbers of eligible males are extrapolated from census figures from 1940—see *Statistical Abstract of the United States*, 71st ed., 1950, Bureau of the Census, U.S. Department of Commerce, Washington, DC, 1950, 8–9.
7. Some soldiers were not yet citizens while others were legally citizens but, because of minority status, did not really enjoy full citizenship rights, such as African Americans.
8. Such ideals were frequently violated in real practice. Women and minority groups suffered from chronic economic, social, and political discrimination. A glaring instance of racial and ethnic discrimination during the war was the internment of Japanese American citizens, many of whose sons were fighting in the American armed forces.
9. During World War II, more than a quarter-million women served in the military. Although their service was exemplary, they represented only a small fraction (roughly 2%) of the whole military, see Dunnigan and Nofi, 321–322. In discussing the war's cultural iconography, we are examining the imagery constructed at the time and afterward. This iconography represents G.I.s as male, as was predominantly the case. Thus, I refer to the G.I. as "G.I. Joe," a male figure.
10. Priest, 103.
11. Unfortunately, replacements were frequently left outside a unit's existing community, and they were often wounded or killed before they could assimilate.
12. In this passage, my detailed background information on Pyle comes from David Nichols' biographical essay at the beginning of his collection, *Ernie's War: The Best of Ernie Pyle's World War II Dispatches* (New York: Random House, 1986), 3–37. My analysis of Pyle's work and its significance is my own.
13. Nichols, 418–419.
14. Nichols, 419.
15. Reprinted in Nichols, 195–197; all quotations are from this edition.
16. Nichols, 195.
17. Nichols, 195–197.
18. For a detailed discussion of the enforcing and easing of censorship policies during the war see George H. Roeder, Jr., *The Censored War: American Visual Experience during World War II* (New Haven, CT: Yale University Press, 1993).
19. Nichols, 197–199.
20. Nichols, 197–199.

246   *Notes*

21. According to William Priest, "Dogface" originated from a Native American term for U.S. soldiers who were often unshaven. From World War I through the Korean War, it became a general term for the lowly, often-bedraggled infantryman, especially as described by others. It may make further reference to the sideshow stereotype of the "dog-faced boy," as an ugly, unwanted freak. Like many such derogatory terms, it is eventually embraced, ironically, as a badge of honor by those whom it describes. See Priest, 77.

22. See Bill Mauldin, *Up Front* (New York: Holt, 1945), 39.

23. My source for the cause of the blurriness of the D-Day photo is Robert Capa's *Slightly Out of Focus*, Paperback Edition (1947/1999. New York: Modern Library, 2001), 152.

24. Certainly, the Omaha Beach sequence of Steven Spielberg's *Saving Private Ryan* was influenced in part by Capa's photographs.

25. Geoffrey Perret identifies the mission as occurring in May 1943; see *Winged Victory: The Army Air Forces in World War II* (New York: Random House, 1993), 253.

26. According to film historian Lawrence Suid, Wyler used footage taken on the twenty-fourth mission, the one to Wilhelmshaven, whereas the actual twenty-fifth mission was an easier attack on the French coast. Wyler wanted the greater impact of a raid into Germany as the focus of the film. See *Guts and Glory* (Lexington: University Press of Kentucky, 2002), 96.

27. Randall Jarrell, "Losses," in *The Norton Book of Modern War*, ed. Paul Fussell (New York: W. W. Norton, 1991), 447.

28. Film scholar Thomas Doherty claims that Wyler follows Howard Hawks in his dramatic use of an actual aircraft taking off and landing. Although such an imitation is possible because *Air Force* had come out earlier that year, the inherent drama of a large aircraft moving from a standing start to full flight is so obvious that no one need borrow the idea. In England filming the real events, Wyler was probably far more inspired by direct experience than by Hawks' fiction. See *Projections of War: Hollywood, American Culture, and World War II*, Film and Culture Series (New York: Columbia University Press, 1993), 117.

29. *The Norton Book of Modern War*, 446.

30. The general release version had an added introduction by General Mark Clark, justifying why we had to destroy the village in order to save it—an army logic that, while associated with Vietnam, also has significance for World War II. See Mike Mayo's *Video Hound's War Movies* (Detroit, MI: Visible Ink, 1999), 358–359.

31. It should be noted that *The Battle of San Pietro* and other effective World War II documentaries may owe a great deal to the influence of the Spanish Civil War documentary *The Spanish Earth* (1937), made by Ernest Hemingway and Joris Ivens. Huston's understated and subtly ironic narration bears a tonal and structural similarity to Hemingway's in the earlier film (read by Hemingway himself in one version). Likewise, the integration of elements of daily life with the fighting, especially in a rural village, is also similar. Although *The Spanish Earth* never gained a wide public audience, Hemingway took it to Hollywood for private showings to movie industry luminaries, to raise money for the Loyalist cause. Certainly, many Hollywood writers, producers, and directors were familiar with its style and subject matter. See Carlos Baker, *Ernest Hemingway: A Life Story* (New York: Scribner, 1969), 307–312.

32. Also, it should be noted that Huston had far less access to the actual battle than might be assumed from viewing the film. Historian Rick Atkinson notes that Huston had to reconstruct battle scenes after the fact, not unlike Toland and Ford had done for *December 7th*. Huston, however, manages to make his reconstructions somewhat more convincing and effective. See Rick Atkinson, *The Day of Battle: The War in Sicily and Italy, 1943–1944*, Volume Two of *The Liberation Trilogy* (New York: Henry Holt, 2007), 290, 291–292.

33. It seems obvious from repeated viewings that several segments of film are used two or three times, a questionable technique though it does not mar the effect significantly.

34. Such grisly images, if seen by the American public when the first version of the film was available in 1944, would have doubtlessly had a shocking effect. The Army may have feared

the impact on civilian morale, reediting the film and delaying release until July 1945, after the war in Europe had been decided. See Jeanine Basinger, *The World War II Combat Film: Anatomy of a Genre* (New York: Columbia University Press, 1986), 293. Ironically, another film, *With the Marines at Tarawa*, made about the same time, was released to the public in 1944, and while shocking, stimulated an increased civilian commitment to the war effort (see Ken Burns' material on this in his own documentary *The War*, 2007, Episode 3).

35. In this paragraph, my factual information on the making of *The Story of G.I. Joe* comes from Suid, 92–97.
36. As the company prepares to spend the night in the captured town, the men learn that Private Murphy's fiancée, an army nurse, has arrived with her medical unit. What follows is an oddly sentimental and unrealistic marriage sequence that undermines the film's credibility.
37. Nichols, 419.
38. Rick Atkinson notes that approximately "one million U.S. soldiers…" were hospitalized for 'neuron-psychiatric symptoms'" throughout the war. See *The Day of Battle*, 508–509. He extrapolates from a number of sources; see Atkinson's notes on 710–711.
39. See *The Censored War* for more on the government's growing willingness to reveal some of the war's darker features.
40. Numerous critics have commented on the Flagg/Quirt feature in this and other films, including Hyams and Basinger. I myself noticed these features when viewing the film, prior to consulting any references. Any knowledgeable viewer will likely come to the same conclusion.
41. Harry Brown, *A Walk in the Sun* (1944/1971. New York: Carrol & Graff, 1985), 57.
42. The novel ends as they assault the farmhouse, at the point where Tyne stands up and leads the platoon forward. In the novel, it is Tyne, not Windy, who says that the assault "is" rather than "was" "so terribly easy." Brown, 187.
43. See Dick, 139–142.
44. Chuck Stevenson. "Bridge to Baghdad" (segment title). *48 Hours*. CBS Worldwide, March 29, 2003.

Five "Saddle Up! Let's Get Back to the War."

1. In this and the subsequent paragraph, my factual information about the flag-raising comes from James Bradley's *Flags of Our Fathers* (New York: Bantam Books, 2001), 201–212. Though controversies persist, I take Bradley's carefully researched work as my authoritative source.
2. Bradley, 235.
3. In this paragraph, my factual information about the poster comes from William L. Bird Jr. and Harry R. Rubenstein's *Design for Victory* (New York: Princeton Architectural Press, 1998), 9.
4. Information throughout this paragraph about the impact of Rosenthal's photograph comes from Bradley, 220–222.
5. Lawrence Suid, in *Guts and Glory*, Second Edition (1978. Lexington: University Press of Kentucky, 2002), argues that these four films were important in redeveloping the World War II genre. Jeanine Basinger has examined the close relationship of such films to those about the Korean War. Jay Hyams and Mike Mayo have each commented on the importance of 1949 and 1950 as pivotal years, with Hyams specifically noting the Cold War message in *Battleground*. These commentaries are insightful, but basic analysis of the time's political atmosphere yields similar conclusions about these films' relationship to the emergent Cold War. I base my arguments on my own interpretations of the films. Along with

Suid, see the following sources: Jeanine Basinger, *The World War II Combat Film: Anatomy of a Genre* (New York: Columbia University Press, 1986); Jay Hyams, *War Movies* (New York: Gallery-W.H. Smith, 1984); and Mike Mayo, *Video Hound's War Movies* (Detroit: Visible Ink, 1999).

6. The George W. Bush administration resurrected this argument to justify invading Iraq, spreading the fearful statement that "the smoking gun could be a mushroom cloud."

7. Joseph McBride comments extensively on the austere paternalism with which Ford sometimes treated Wayne. See *Searching for John Ford: A Life* (New York: St. Martin's Press, 1991).

8. McBride describes Wayne's unwillingness to serve during the war despite Ford's urging. *Searching*, 342–347.

9. Factual information regarding the development and production of *Sands of Iwo Jima* comes from Suid, 118–123.

10. Basinger, 168–170.

11. Suid, 120–121.

12. See McBride, *Searching*, which deals with the relationship between actor and director throughout a number of sections of the book.

13. McBride discusses the development of the character of Nathan Brittles in *She Wore a Yellow Ribbon*, one of several incarnations of this father-figure character. *Searching*, 457–459.

14. Suid, 122–123.

15. Bradley, 322.

16. Bradley, 322.

17. Because *Task Force* gains authenticity from genuine battle footage, we tend to respect the reality of all its documentary quotations. However, for the Pearl Harbor sequence, Daves also splices in staged shots, from the Toland/Ford *December 7th*, falsely authenticating those earlier fabrications (see chapter two). *Task Force* combines both actual and staged documentary footage with its own fictional material, thus conflating the fabricated with the recorded, significantly blurring fiction and history into a seamless and deceptive narrative. Of course, it is merely a very salient example of this tendency because so much wartime documentary combat footage was actually restaged.

18. Randall Jarrell, "Losses," in *The Norton Book of Modern War*, ed. Paul Fussell (New York: Norton, 1990), 447.

19. The prized toby mug from the film's opening was always left on the officers' club mantelpiece. A staff officer would signal an upcoming mission by turning the face of the mug toward the wall. These clubs might have civilian workers or guests, so this "secret" method was used to inform men of an upcoming mission and their need to get back on duty.

20. The British film, *The Way to the Stars* (1945), also begins at an abandoned airfield with overgrown runways. Hyams, 98, 110.

21. Savage is based loosely on Brig. Gen. Frank Armstrong, who in 1942 took over the poor-performing 97th Bomber Group and turned it into one of the best in the 8th Air Force. See Geoffrey Perret, *Winged Victory: The Army Air Forces in World War II* (New York: Random House, 1993), 245.

22. This is consistent with James Jones' conception of the "evolution of the soldier." See *WW II* (New York: Grosset & Dunlap, 1975), 54.

23. Jarrell, "Losses," 447.

24. Williamson Murray and Allan R. Millett, *A War to Be Won: Fighting the Second World War* (Cambridge, MA: Belknap Press of Harvard University Press, 2000), 554.

25. This paragraph's factual information on the project's development comes from Suid, 104–109.

26. Historical details in this paragraph on the Battle of the Bulge and the 101st Airborne's role in Bastogne come from Charles MacDonald's *A Time for Trumpets* (New York: Quill-William Morrow, 1985).

27. Division commander Maj. Gen. Maxwell D. Taylor was attending meetings in Washington—a fact noted in numerous histories of the battle.
28. Jones, *WWII*, 54.
29. Kinnie wakes the men by saying, "Off your cots and grab your socks." Here Pirosh alludes to the army commonplace, "Drop your cocks and grab your socks," unacceptable to a 1949 censor. Throughout, Pirosh alludes to aspects of army life not allowed on screen; he subtly communicates a special sense of authenticity to veterans in the audience while not risking offense to censors or the general public.
30. The woman character in the town becomes a commonplace in films about Bastogne, and many civilians, including women, were trapped in Bastogne with the troops; however, the Hollywood starlet image projected by Darcel does strain credibility as Suid notes, (104–109).
31. This is reminiscent of war as depicted by Stephen Crane in *The Red Badge of Courage*.
32. Wellman makes liberal use of combat footage to lend authenticity throughout the film. The grainy, gray tone of the combat film is complemented well by Wellman's somber, sound-stage set.
33. Hyams, 114, has accurately read this film, and this speech in particular, as a statement of Cold War policy in a World War II story.

Six   Longest Days in the "Good War"

1. Cornelius Ryan, *The Longest Day: June 6, 1944* (New York: Simon & Schuster, 1959). Ryan calls D-Day "the day the battle began that ended Hitler's insane gamble to dominate the world" (Foreword, n.p.).
2. Lawrence Suid comments extensively on the rehabilitation of our former enemies in *Guts and Glory*, Second Edition (Lexington: University Press of Kentucky, 2002), esp. 98–102.
3. The actual history also implicates our own politics during the Nazi rise to power, when more than a few Americans not only accepted but also admired Hitler.
4. In this paragraph, my source for information about the production and development of *The Longest Day* is Suid, 161–187.
5. As Philip Beidler notes in *The Good War's Greatest Hits: World War II and American Remembering* (Athens: University of Georgia Press, 1998), all these major novels were subsequently made into films, often with significant alteration and/or Bowdlerization.
6. One of the more important "epic" efforts was Samuel Eliot Morison's multi-volume, official history of Navy operations (1959–1962). Beidler discusses in great detail how the early television documentary *Victory at Sea* (1952–53) developed in relationship to Morison's efforts, 76–85. Morison also subsequently condensed his history into a single-volume trade book, *The Two-Ocean War: A Short History of the United States Navy in the Second World War* (Boston: Atlantic-Little, Brown, 1963).
7. In this paragraph, my information about the publication history of Ryan's book comes from Beidler, 152–162.
8. Beidler, 154.
9. Beidler, 154–155.
10. As Beidler explains in detail, the launching of Ryan's book also benefited from the full publicity apparatus of *Reader's Digest*, 155.
11. The "Angelus" is an old Roman Catholic prayer recited at 6:00 a.m., noon, and 6:00 p.m. Church bells have traditionally been rung at these hours to call people to the prayer.
12. Ryan, Foreword, n.p.
13. In his *Rhetoric*, Aristotle identifies "pathos" (emotion), "ethos" (personality or character), and "logos" (reasoning) as the three major "appeals" available to those who wish to persuade an audience.

14. Many film critics and historians have discussed Zanuck's project, including Basinger, Beidler, Dick, and Suid. The interpretation offered here represents my own historical and rhetorical analysis of the film.

15. Suid, 176.

16. Both Wayne and Ryan, then in their fifties, play airborne officers, Lieutenant Colonel Benjamin Vandervoort and Brigadier General James Gavin, who were in their thirties on D-Day.

17. Beidler, 161.

18. *The Longest Day* can symbolize the whole American war effort because it represents an amphibious assault. The Western Allies in World War II mastered amphibious warfare as no one has before, so "hitting the beach" symbolized the Western Allied offensive against the Axis. Despite important British contributions, amphibious warfare best symbolized the American way of war. It required massive resources and logistical support that could come only from a culture so devoted to integrating capital-intensive, technology-intensive, and labor-intensive modes of production. It also demanded the comprehensive organizational management at which America excelled. Therefore, amphibious assault was the most important application of American factory culture to fighting the war, and as the war's most strategically significant amphibious operation, the Normandy landings could stand for all the others.

19. In *Guts and Glory*, Suid provides thorough analysis of the making of *The Longest Day* and its influence on subsequent film projects. See esp. 168–189.

20. Some current military historians criticize Bradley while tending to idolize Patton—a shift from the more balanced perspective found in Ladislas Farago's *Patton: Ordeal and Triumph*, Wesholme Paperback Edition (1964. Yardley, PA: Westholme, 2005). The film does too readily accept Bradley's image, in part self-fashioned, as unambitious and duty-bound. After all, he was a professional soldier, and though more temperate than Patton, he also had an ego. Yet Bradley was no incompetent—in many ways he was a more balanced and capable leader than Patton.

21. Farago, 145–146.

22. Despite his military brilliance, Patton was politically naïve and insensitive, unable to comprehend fully the horror with which so many Americans and their Allies viewed the Nazi regime. Patton's rather casual dismissal of the importance of de-Nazification, along with his open hostility toward the Soviets, put him once again in the doghouse. He was relieved of command largely for these reasons, not simply for unpopular opinions.

23. See Carl Sandburg, *The People, Yes* (San Diego, CA: Harcourt Brace Jovanovich, 1990).

24. That is not to say that there were not imperial trends in American politics, domestic or international, before this; rather, there was a certain quality of openly imperial imagery and attitude that seemed to gain greater acceptance, first during the Nixon years, suspended somewhat in the wake of Watergate, and returning with the Reagan administration.

25. Clayton R. Koppes and Gregory D. Black, *Hollywood Goes to War: How Politics, Profits, and Propaganda Shaped World War II Movies* (Berkeley, CA: University of California Press, 1990), 66.

26. For example, we had condemned such tactics as mass bombing of civilian targets and unrestricted submarine warfare when used by the Germans, but we eventually employed these very same tactics even more massively.

Seven   Conscientious Objection

1. Working from William Bradford Huie's 1959 novel, Chayefsky turns a relatively conservative, pro-Navy book into a film highly critical of the military.

2. President Lyndon Johnson played upon Americans' fears of nuclear war in his campaign against Senator Barry Goldwater in 1964. Johnson attacked Goldwater's more aggressive stance on nuclear policy with the now-famous advertisement of the young girl picking flower petals, followed by the sound of an ominous countdown to a nuclear explosion.

3. Between 1945 and 1964, only a few American films had challenged the prevailing narrative, most notably Robert Aldrich's *Attack* (1956), which was not a major production. Antimilitary elements are evident in the films *From Here to Eternity* (1953), *The Caine Mutiny* (1954) and *Mister Roberts* (1955), and yet even these still generally support the overall mainstream narrative of World War II.

4. The film shows Charlie as more than a self-centered hypocrite. After Pearl Harbor, he had volunteered for the Marine Corps, but after a brief, terrifying experience on Guadalcanal, he sought help from his prewar contacts to land him his current job. His brother has died at Anzio, and his grief stricken mother overglorifies that death while still fearing her youngest son will run away to join the service.

5. Earlier, we had seen Charlie coming down the gangplank of a hospital ship, a scene similar to Tyrone Power's return from Dunkirk in *A Yank in the RAF*.

6. Another limitation of this film, consistent with a number of works that attack the war's mainstream narrative (e.g., *Catch-22*), is that, despite its more "radical" stance on war, it perpetuates obviously sexist stereotypes of women. In the midst of "rebelling" against military culture, many male writers and filmmakers seem incapable of overcoming their own embarrassingly adolescent attitudes toward women.

7. Mailer's was among the first major American novels about the war, and the first to offer the counternarrative. James Jones' work was the second novel in a planned trilogy, begun with *From Here to Eternity* (1951), also a successful film. The third book, *Whistle* (1978), came much later and was published posthumously.

8. Literary Naturalism, associated with the period from the late nineteenth and early twentieth centuries, continues to influence American fiction.

9. Stephen Crane's *The Red Badge of Courage* is somewhat of an exception in a canon of American naturalistic writing that deals mostly with social and economic issues, not with war.

10. Philip Beidler *The Good War's Greatest Hits: World War II and American Remembering* (Athens: University of Georgia Press, 1998), 100.

11. The f-word is also used as part of larger constructions. The absurdity of army life is captured in the acronyms SNAFU and FUBAR ("Situation Normal—All F——ed Up" and "F——ed Up Beyond All Recognition"). These expressions depend on the commonplace use of the f-word in military experience while also parodying the military obsession with acronyms.

12. What sexuality remains in combat is usually only in the realms of fantasy or forbidden homosexuality. In addition, for some characters, combat itself develops a perverse, eroticized quality, a sexual intensity associated with the adrenalin rush of extreme experience. Mailer and Jones explore all these issues in their novels.

13. See Carlos Baker, *Ernest Hemingway: A Life Story* (New York: Charles Scribner's Sons, 1969), 38–56.

14. My information in this passage about Mailer's military experience comes from Beidler, 98.

15. By this time, cavalry units in the U.S. Army no longer used horses (except in rare instances). Most often, they were mechanized units, equipped with armored cars, light tanks, half-tracks, and jeeps. They were used for reconnaissance and screening during mobile operations in Europe. In the Pacific, they often fought as infantry.

16. Beidler, 98.

17. In *Winesburg, Ohio*, Anderson offers his theory of "literary psychology" in the "Book of the Grotesque." He emphasizes how specific experiences tend to distort the lives of most characters, leaving them incapable of achieving psychological wholeness while still managing to continue with their lives in some fashion.

18. Baker, 495.

19. Ernest Hemingway, ed. *Men at War* (1942. New York: Bramhall House, 1955), xi–xii.

20. James Jones writes a partial memoir of his wartime experiences, interwoven with general commentary about war art, in an illustrated collection called simply *WWII* (New York: Grosset & Dunlap, 1975). In this recollection, he clearly identifies his assignments, and his wounds, to have been the same as Fife's. It is obvious by a comparison of the text of *WWII* and *The Thin Red Line* (1962. New York: Dell, 1998) that Fife is the character who most resembles Jones himself. Of course, Fife is still a fictional character, and he is not merely a thinly veiled portrait of the author.

21. The First Marine Division had landed on Guadalcanal early in August 1942, but after capturing the airfield and setting up a perimeter, its combat remained largely defensive until the end of November. New Marine Corps and Army units landed in December, and this enlarged American force continued the offensive campaign until its successful conclusion at the beginning of February 1943.

22. Jones, *WWII*, 54.

23. Jones, *The Thin Red Line*, "Dedication" n.p.

24. Scholar John Limon, although unfortunately dismissive of Jones, has made this argument in great detail in *Writing after War: American War Fiction from Realism to Postmodernism* (New York: Oxford University Press, 1994), 136–139.

25. Jones, *The Thin Red Line*, 41.

26. Jones, *The Thin Red Line*, 41.

27. Jones, *The Thin Red Line*, 442.

28. Jones, *The Thin Red Line*, 510.

29. See Heller's autobiography, *Now and Then: From Coney Island to Here* (New York: Alfred A. Knopf, 1998), 169–180.

30. Jones, *The Thin Red Line*, 41.

31. Joseph Heller, *Catch-22* (1961. New York: Simon & Schuster, 1994), 8.

32. The Snowden incident is narrated fully toward the end of the novel. Heller, *Catch-22*, 436–440.

33. Suid, 142–159.

34. Beidler, 94–108.

35. This support for American military preparedness to oppose global communism somewhat paralleled a structurally similar though ideologically distinct support for military preparedness to oppose global fascism from the late 1930s through the duration of the war. Certainly the military-industrial complex, and Hollywood's integration into it, first developed during World War II.

36. *Between Heaven and Hell* (1956) also deals with leadership problems in a former National Guard unit, but it focuses mostly on a rich young Southerner's learning, through combat, to respect the poor sharecroppers whom he had earlier regarded as "trash." The film also examines the abnormal psychology of an isolated unit to which the main character is transferred, and so it offers some interesting parallels to Francis Ford Coppola's *Apocalypse Now* (1979).

37. Stanley Kubrick released *Paths of Glory* one year later; however, he disguises his critique of the American military in a story about cowardly, autocratic French officers in World War I. It would be another six years before he would openly confront the American military-industrial complex in his brilliant satire *Dr. Strangelove* (1964).

38. *Beach Red* has probably influenced more recent World War II films. The traumatic amputation on the beach is echoed in Steven Spielberg's Omaha Beach sequence in *Saving Private Ryan* (1998). Clint Eastwood's *Letters from Iwo Jima* (2006) shows a more obvious influence of Wilde's sympathetic treatment of Japanese soldiers.

39. Lawrence Suid claims that *Beach Red* successfully "conveyed the message the director intended" (204), citing newspaper reviews and an interview with Wilde. Given the political tenor of 1967, a new antiwar film would likely excite newspaper critics. Moreover,

asking Wilde about the quality of his own film is hardly a means of getting an objective evaluation. The mere desire to believe an antiwar film to be good because one agrees with its ideas cannot change the facts of its quality.

Eight Now It Can Be Told: Reopening Old Wounds

1. James Jones, *WWII* (New York: Grosset & Dunlap, 1975), 255.
2. Rick Atkinson, *The Day of Battle: The War in Sicily and Italy, 1943–1944* (New York: Henry Holt, 2007), 508–509.
3. While much of the work on PTSD has come from the study of combat veterans, an increasing amount has also come from the study of civilians caught up in war, terrorism, or natural disaster, as well as victims of crime, sexual abuse, domestic abuse, or other trauma. For more on Posttraumatic Stress Disorder, see the *Diagnostic and Statistical Manual of Mental Disorders (DSM IV)*, Fourth Edition (Washington, DC: American Psychiatric Association, 1994), 424–425.
4. The film's protagonist is African American, whereas in the play, the protagonist is Jewish.
5. Not released until decades after the war, John Huston's *Let There Be Light* (1946) traces the treatment and recovery of psychological casualties. The U.S. Army, for which it was made, deemed it too depressing, despite its optimistic view of potential recovery.
6. Other specific poems include Randall Jarrell's "The Death of the Ball Turret Gunner" (446) and "Losses" (447), along with Louis Simpson's "On the Ledge" (519–520) and "The Battle" (520–521). Paul Fussell, ed., *The Norton Book of Modern War* (New York: W.W. Norton, 1991).
7. The word "essay" originates with the sixteenth-century French writer Michel de Montaigne, who conceived a literary form allowing for brief, open-ended reflections on any number of topics. These essays or "attempts" (from the French *essai*, to "attempt" or "try") reflect the writer's inner mental dialogues concerning experience, issues and ideas, and reactions to them. Unlike the "academic essay," a work of polished analytical and argumentative prose, the modern literary or reflective essay, in the tradition of Montaigne, reveals the mind at work in the process of constructing meaning.
8. Oral history originated as an ethnographic research method used to preserve the history of isolated, traditional, and/or indigenous cultures. It has developed broader applications as a general form of social history. When used in relation to war, it represents war more as social history than as military history. America's first real combat oral histories grew out of the Vietnam war.
9. The post-Vietnam narrative supporting that war depicts fighting men being betrayed by cynical politicians at home. The *Rambo* and *Missing in Action* films are salient examples.
10. Information in this paragraph regarding the development of this project comes from Jones, *WWII*, 11.
11. Some of these works had appeared in *Life* during the war, later in *Life*'s popular picture history of the war (1950), and in other illustrated volumes. See Philip Beidler, *The Good War's Greatest Hits: World War II and American Remembering* (Athens: University of Georgia Press, 1998), 65–76.
12. Jones, *WWII*, 13.
13. Like Fife, Corporal Jones also served as a forward company clerk and an assistant squad leader. Both character and writer were wounded by mortar fragments but were ultimately evacuated from combat because of aggravated ankle injuries.

14. *Whistle* parallels Jones' experiences once he returned to the United States after Guadalcanal. James Jones, *Whistle* (New York: Delacorte Press, 1978).
15. Jones, *WWII*, 16.
16. Jones, *WWII*, 16.
17. In one particularly graphic passage, Jones compares trying to teach young men to love killing with trying to teach their "dewy-eyed" sisters to be more open to sexual activity. See the specific passage in *WWII*, 30.
18. Jones, *WWII*, 69, 106–112, and 122–123.
19. Jones, *WWII*, 96.
20. Jones, *WWII*, 57–58.
21. Jones, *WWII*, 58.
22. Jones, *WWII*, 201.
23. Jones, *WWII*, 113–117.
24. Jones, *WWII*, 118.
25. Tom Lea, "War Is Fighting and Fighting Is Killing: Peleliu, September 1944," reprinted in *Reporting World War II: American Journalism 1938–1946*, 1-Volume Paperback Edition (New York: Library of America, 2001), 529–566. See 535 for quotation. Jones makes no reference to Lea's book, and indeed, he may have been unaware of it.
26. Jones, *WWII*, 13.
27. Jones, *WWII*, 54.
28. Jones, *WWII*, 256.
29. Jones, *WWII*, 256.
30. William Manchester, *Goodbye, Darkness* (Boston: Little, Brown, 1980), 134. All references are to this edition.
31. Marine Corps veterans Eugene Sledge and Robert Leckie also use the phrase "Raggedy Ass Marines," and it seems a commonplace of marine slang.
32. Earlier memoirs, such as Charles MacDonald's *Company Commander* (1947), Robert Leckie's *Helmet for My Pillow* (1957), and James Fahey's *Pacific War Diary: 1942–1945: The Secret Diary of an American Sailor* (1963), do not go much beyond traditional war narratives, either in style or content, though Leckie's personal revelations and Fahey's details sometimes vary from the expected.
33. Vonnegut's character Billy Pilgrim is transported back and forth through time—into the wartime past, a postwar present, and an extraterrestrial experience that seems timeless.
34. Owen's "Dulce Et Decorum Est" is found in Fussell, *Norton Book of Modern War*, 166.
35. See Ernest Hemingway, *By-Line Ernest Hemingway: Selected Articles and Dispatches of Four Decades,* ed. William White (New York: Scribner, 1967), 209–210.
36. Ernest Hemingway, *A Farewell to Arms* (1929. repr., New York: Scribner, 1969), 54.
37. Manchester, 384. The writer uses the fact that the men are pursuing daily life in the courtyard of a tomb to create a metonymic image of the combat experience itself—living daily life in the site of death and burial. Moreover, Manchester's staggering out of the tomb, seemingly dead but still alive, suggests both the raising of Lazarus and the Resurrection of Christ.
38. Manchester, 46.
39. See passage in Manchester, 70–72.
40. Manchester, 70–72.
41. Manchester, 72.
42. Manchester, 72.
43. James Jones, *The Thin Red Line* (1962. rpr., New York: Dell, 1998), 285.
44. Jones, *The Thin Red Line*, 286.
45. "Interview-based history" is the kind often produced by Stephen Ambrose and Gerald Astor. While not "oral histories," they make extensive use of interviews with veterans, resulting in much direct quotation or paraphrase.

46. Studs Terkel, *"The Good War": An Oral History of World War Two* (New York: Pantheon Books, 1984). All references are to this edition.
47. Terkel, 23. Historians generally agree that approximately 150,000 Okinawan civilians died during the campaign, most accidentally killed by both sides during three months of unusually violent fighting.
48. Terkel, 57.
49. Terkel, 38.
50. Terkel, 58.
51. Terkel, 39.
52. Terkel, 276.
53. Terkel, 282.
54. Russian literary critic Mikhail Bakhtin developed the terms "polyphonic" and "dialogic" to describe narratives that include many, multiform voices from the culture as a whole. Bakhtin contrasts such polyphony with the more "monologic" narratives that impose one view of experience, often from the top down. Polyphonic or dialogic narratives are often more complex and uneven because polyphony arises both because of and despite the writer's intentions. While the mainstream "Good-War" narrative tends to be monologic, oral histories like Terkel's have strong polyphonic qualities because they offer a textual space in which the culture may speak with its many voices. See Mikhail Bakhtin, *The Dialogic Imagination: Four Essays*, ed. Michael Holquist, translated by Caryl Emerson and Kenneth Brostrom, University of Texas Press Slavic Series 1 (Austin: University of Texas Press, 1981).
55. Terkel, 362.
56. Terkel, 364.
57. Terkel, 190.
58. Terkel, 193. It should be noted that Admiral Larocque remains a very controversial figure, whose opinions are viewed as extreme and whose factual statements are often disputed by the U.S. Navy and the Department of Defense.
59. Of particular note are two oral histories compiled and edited by Patrick O'Donnell: *Beyond Valor* (2001. New York: Touchstone/Simon & Schuster, 2002) and *Into the Rising Sun* (New York: Free Press/Simon & Schuster, 2002).
60. In general, it seems that literary representations of the war, whether in fiction or nonfiction, come from veterans with more extensive education. This fact highlights the importance of oral histories and interview-based histories because they can bring to light the experiences of a broader range of veterans.
61. Sledge's book is also the best known of these four because it caught the attention of scholar Paul Fussell, who republished a segment in a collection he edited, *The Norton Book of Modern War* (1990).
62. Introducing the Oxford edition of *With the Old Breed*, Fussell praises Sledge's unpretentious, direct style. Paul Fussell, "Introduction" to Eugene Sledge's *With the Old Breed: At Peleliu and Okinawa* (1981. New York: Oxford University Press, 1990), xi–xx, xi. All further references to Sledge are from this edition.
63. Sledge, 63.
64. Sledge, 60.
65. Raymond Gantter, "Foreword," *Roll Me Over: An Infantryman's World War II* (New York: Ivy Books, 1997), ix.
66. Gantter, "Author's Note," 398.
67. T. S. Eliot, "Gerontion," *The Complete Poems and Plays 1909–1950* (San Diego, CA: Harcourt Brace Jovanovich, Publishers, 1971), 21–23.
68. Roscoe C. Blunt, *Foot Soldier: A Combat Infantryman's War in Europe* (1994. Cambridge, MA: Da Capo Press, 2002), 80.
69. Blunt, vii.

70. Blunt, viii.
71. Blunt, viii.
72. General George C. Marshall conceived the Advanced Specialized Training Program (ASTP) to prepare talented soldiers for technical specialties, particularly engineering. Those selected entered U.S. Army programs at colleges and universities. By early 1944, however, rising casualty rates led the Army to eliminate most ASTP programs, transferring the men to the infantry, including Kurt Vonnegut and Robert Kotlowitz. Others went into combat engineer battalions, among them my father, T/5, Joseph Casaregola.
73. In *The Boys' Crusade: The American Infantry in Northwestern Europe, 1944–1945* (New York: Modern Library, 2003), Paul Fussell engages in a detailed discussion of the Kotlowitz memoir.

Nine   The Once and Future War

1. Jo Davidsmeyer, *Combat!: A Viewer's Companion to the WWII Series*, Revised Edition (Tallevast, FL: Strange New Worlds, 2002), 173.
2. Paul Fussell, *The Boy Scout Handbook and Other Observations* (New York: Oxford University Press, 1982), 260–261.
3. Stephen Ambrose, "Introduction," *Citizen Soldiers: The U.S. Army from the Normandy Beaches to the Bulge to the Surrender of Germany, June 7, 1944–May 7, 1945*, 13.
4. Ambrose's 2001 book *The Wild Blue* was found to contain some limited material from Thomas Childers' *Wings of Morning* (1995) without proper citation, leading to charges of plagiarism. Allegations of earlier instances also surfaced, but Ambrose dismissed them all as minor lapses in so much writing. These matters, however, are still in dispute. Most likely, his compiling methodology had betrayed him into treating quotations from books like passages from interviews. Without excusing this sloppiness, we can see how attempting so vast a production has its liabilities.
5. Cultural Studies grew from the work of British Marxist cultural and literary theorists in the 1970s, influenced as well by some aspects of poststructuralist and postmodernist theory. Maintaining the Marxist interest in socioeconomic issues and noncanonical texts, Cultural Studies has evolved into a number of distinctive ways of interpreting cultural practices. While contemporary Cultural Studies often reveals its material culture roots, it has largely abandoned the grand historical narratives of traditional Marxist theory, in favor of a more anti-foundational reading of history. Fussell's methods parallel those of Cultural Studies because he examines a wide range of social texts, many noncanonical, and because he seeks to critique established mainstream readings of history and literature. Yet he continues the pragmatic close reading associated with 1940s New Criticism, and Fussell rejects the theoretical and ideological reference points associated with more purely academic cultural analysis.
6. Fussell, *The Boy Scout Handbook*, 253.
7. Paul Fussell, *Wartime: Understanding and Behavior in World War II* (New York: Oxford University Press, 1989), 7.
8. Contrastively, Ambrose tends to skew his samples in favor of those who support his views because he works with veterans groups, commemorating specific units.
9. Fussell, *Wartime*, 5.
10. Fussell, *Boy Scout Handbook*, 254.
11. Fussell, *Wartime*, 296–97.
12. Phillip Beidler *The Good War's Greatest Hits: World War II and American Remembering* (Athens: University of Georgia Press, 1998), 170.
13. Beidler, 169.

14. The U.S. Army's Military History Institute in Carlisle, Pennsylvania, maintains a large storehouse of surveys of World War II veterans that reveal much about the veterans, leading us to a more complex understanding of their wartime experience. This Institute, served by a small but very helpful and efficient staff, is an excellent resource.
15. Describing the rising postwar birth rates, the term "baby boom" usually identifies those born from 1946 to 1964. Born between roughly 1935 and 1945, the Ambrose-Brokaw "pre-boomer" generation were too late to fight in World War II or Korea, and too early to be official boomers. Some "pre-boomers" fought in Vietnam, but most Vietnam veterans are baby-boomers born between 1946 and 1954. The "boomer" generation's large size marked it for labeling at the very time of its development, forever associating it with images of self-conscious, rebellious youth. Such superficial generational categories, however, often ignore class, race, gender, ethnicity, religion, and even region—factors that may have far more influence in a person's life than does the birth year alone.
16. James F. Dunnigan and Albert A. Nofi, *Victory at Sea: World War II in the Pacific* (New York: Quill/William and Morrow, 1995), 321. [This text is a brief encyclopedia or fact book about the American military in World War II, concentrating on the Pacific. Readers should not confuse it with the 1952 television documentary of the same name.]
17. Dunnigan and Nofi, 321–322.
18. This very problem of overgeneralization of generational categories is the subject of an interesting new book by Kenneth D. Rose, *Myth and the Greatest Generation: A Social History of Americans in World War II* (New York: Routledge, 2008).
19. William Manchester, *Goodbye, Darkness* (Boston: Little, Brown, 1980), 10.
20. The film is based, tangentially, on an incident reported in Ambrose's book *Band of Brothers*. One paratrooper, whose three brothers had been identified as dead or MIA, was recalled from duty and sent home. In the actual event, no great drama was involved as in the Spielberg film.
21. James Agee, "These Terrible Records of War" (1945) in *Reporting World War II: American Journalism 1938–1946*, 1-Volume Paperback Edition (New York: Library of America, 2001), 606–607.
22. The company's translator was killed, so Miller is given a replacement, Private Timothy Upham. Upham has no infantry or combat experience, having previously served only at a headquarters company. Ernest and naïve, his inexperience will prove fatal to his comrades during combat.
23. Miller may be based partially on Lieutenant Carl Anderson (Richard Widmark) in *Halls of Montezuma* (1950), who also suffered from a form of posttraumatic stress. Both Miller and Anderson had been high school teachers in civilian life, and both lead dangerous patrols resulting in high casualties.
24. Louis Menand criticized this film for lacking a sense of ambiguity, but Menand himself approaches the film rather narrowly. He fails to consider it in connection to the representation of combat in veterans' memoirs, and he ignores some of the complex elements of structure, character, and imagery. Louis Menand, "Jerry Don't Surf," *The New York Review of Books*, September 24, 1998, 7–8.
25. Based on the nonfiction book *The Ghost Soldiers* (2001), *The Great Raid* depicts the actual raid on Cabanatuan POW camp in the Philippines in 1945, when a task force of army rangers raided the camp to rescue the prisoners before the Japanese could kill them. Although accurate in portraying the intense cruelty of the Japanese camp garrisons, the film uses this material to construct a simple dichotomy between "heroic" Americans and "evil" Japanese. It thus resembles many films that were made during the war itself. As a POW-rescue film, it also connects with post-Vietnam POW films such as the Chuck Norris *Missing in Action* series.
26. E-Company (Easy Company) of the 506th Parachute Infantry Regiment. While the signifying call sign "Easy" (for E) is accurate, it is also ironic, since the men of Easy Company

did not have a very "easy" war. Of course, neither did the men in the hundreds of other Easy Companies in other regiments of the U.S. Army.

27. The film is based on the recovered writings of General Tadamichi Kurayashi, commander of the Japanese defenders of Iwo Jima.

28. Czelaw Milosz, *The Captive Mind,* translated by Jane Zielonko (New York: Vintage Books, 1955), 24.

BIBLIOGRAPHY

Ambrose, Stephen. *Band of Brothers: E Company, 506th Regiment, 101st Airborne from Normandy to Hitler's Eagle's Nest.* 1992. New York: Simon & Schuster, 2001.
———. *Citizen Soldiers: The U.S. Army from the Normandy Beaches to the Bulge to the Surrender of Germany, June 7, 1944–May 7, 1945.* New York: Simon & Schuster, 1997.
———. *D-Day, June 6, 1944: The Climactic Battle of World War II.* New York: Touchstone-Simon & Schuster, 1995.
———. *The Wild Blue: The Men and Boys Who Flew the B-24s over Germany.* New York: Simon & Schuster, 2001.
American Psychiatric Association. *Diagnostic and Statistical Manual of Mental Disorders: DSM-IV.* Washington, DC: American Psychiatric Association, 1994.
Anderson, Sherwood. *Winesburg, Ohio.* 1919. Reprint, New York: Viking Press, 1972.
Aristotle. *The Rhetoric of Aristotle.* Translated by Lane Cooper. 1932. Reprint, Englewood Cliffs, NJ: Prentice-Hall, 1960.
Astor, Gerald. *Crisis in the Pacific: The Battles for the Philippine Islands by the Men Who Fought Them.* New York: Dell, 1996.
Atkinson, Rick. *The Day of Battle: The War in Sicily and Italy, 1943–1944.* New York: Henry Holt, 2007.
Baker, Carlos. *Ernest Hemingway: A Life Story.* New York: Scribner, 1969.
Bakhtin, Mikhail. *The Dialogic Imagination: Four Essays.* Edited by Michael Holquist. Translated by Caryl Emerson and Kenneth Brostrom. University of Texas Press Slavic Series 1. Austin: University of Texas Press, 1981.
Basinger, Jeanine. *The World War II Combat Film: Anatomy of a Genre.* New York: Columbia University Press, 1986.
Beidler, Philip D. *The Good War's Greatest Hits: World War II and American Remembering.* Athens: University of Georgia Press, 1998.
Bernstein, Mark and Alex Lubertozzi. *World War II on the Air: Edward R. Murrow and the Broadcasts That Riveted the Nation.* Naperville, IL: Sourcebooks-MediaFusion, 2003.
Bird, William L., and Harry R. Rubenstein, *Design for Victory: World War II Posters on the American Home Front*, New York: Princeton Architectural Press, 1998.
Blunt, Roscoe C. *Foot Soldier: A Combat Infantryman's War in Europe.* 1994. Reprint, Cambridge, MA: Da Capo Press, 2002.
Bradley, James. *Flags of Our Fathers.* New York: Bantam Books, 2001.
Brokaw, Tom. *The Greatest Generation.* New York: Random House, 2004.
Brown, Harry. *A Walk in the Sun.* 1944. Reprint, New York: Carrol & Graff, 1985.
Capa, Robert. *Slightly Out of Focus.* 1947. Reprint, New York: Modern Library, 2001.

Capra, Frank. *Frank Capra: The Name Above the Title.* New York: Macmillan, 1971.

Chang, Iris. *The Rape of Nanking: The Forgotten Holocaust of World War II.* New York: Basic Books, 1997.

Crane, Stephen. *The Red Badge of Courage: An Episode of the American Civil War.* In *Red Badge of Courage, Maggie: A Girl of the Streets, and Other Selected Writings,* edited by Phyllis Frus and Stanley Corkin, 172–271. New Riverside Editions. Boston: Houghton Mifflin, 2000.

Cunningham, Chet. *Hell Wouldn't Stop: An Oral History of the Battle of Wake Island* New York: Carroll and Graf, 2002.

Davidsmeyer, Jo. *Combat!: A Viewer's Companion to the WWII TV Series.* 1997. Revised edition. Tallevast, FL: Strange New Worlds, 2002.

Dick, Bernard F. *The Star-Spangled Screen: The American World War II Film.* Lexington: University Press of Kentucky, 1985.

Didion, Joan. *The White Album.* New York: Simon & Schuster, 1979.

Doherty, Thomas Patrick. *Projections of War: Hollywood, American Culture, and World War II.* Film and Culture Series. New York: Columbia University Press, 1993.

Dower, John. *War without Mercy: Race and Power in the Pacific War.* New York: Pantheon, 1986.

Dunnigan, James F., and Albert A. Nofi. *Victory at Sea: World War II in the Pacific.* New York: William Morrow, 1995.

Eliot, T. S. "Gerontion." In *The Complete Poems and Plays 1909–1950,* 21–23. New York: Harcourt Brace Jovanovich, 1971.

Ellul, Jacques. *Propaganda: The Formation of Men's Attitudes.* Translated by Konrad Kellen and Jean Lerner. New York: Alfred A. Knopf, 1965.

Fahey, James J. *Pacific War Diary 1942–1945: The Secret Diary of an American Sailor.* Boston: Houghton Mifflin, 1963.

Farago, Ladislas. *Patton: Ordeal and Triumph.* 1964. Yardley, PA: Westholme, 2005.

Fussell, Paul. *The Boy Scout Handbook and Other Observations.* New York: Oxford University Press, 1982.

———. *The Boys' Crusade: The American Infantry in Northwestern Europe, 1944–1945.* New York: Modern Library, 2003.

———. *The Great War and Modern Memory.* New York: Oxford University Press, 1975.

———, ed. *The Norton Book of Modern War.* New York: Norton, 1990.

———. *Wartime: Understanding and Behavior in the Second World War.* New York: Oxford University Press, 1989.

Gantter, Raymond. *Roll Me Over: An Infantryman's World War II.* New York: Ivy Books, 1997.

Gilpatric, Guy. *Action in the North Atlantic.* New York: E. P. Dutton, 1943.

"Give Us the Tools." *Time,* March 3, 1941.

Hastings, Max. *Overlord: D-Day and the Battle for Normandy, 1944.* Reprint, New York: Simon & Schuster, 1984.

Heller, Joseph. *Catch-22.* 1961. Reprint, New York: Simon & Schuster, 1994.

———. *Now and Then: From Coney Island to Here.* New York: Knopf, 1988.

Hemingway, Ernest. *By-Line Ernest Hemingway: Selected Articles and Dispatches of Four Decades.* Edited by William White. New York: Scribner, 1967.

———. *A Farewell to Arms.* 1929. Reprint, New York: Simon & Schuster–Scribner's, 1995.

———, ed. *Men at War.* 1942. Reprint, New York: Bramhall House, 1955.

Hersey, John. *The War Lover.* New York: Knopf, 1959.

Holmes, Oliver Wendell. "Memorial Day." In *The Essential Holmes: Selections from the Letters, Speeches, Judicial Opinions, and Other Writings of Oliver Wendell Holmes Jr.,* edited by Richard A. Posner, 80–87. Chicago: University of Chicago Press, 1992.

Huie, William Bradford. *The Americanization of Emily: A Novel.* New York: Dutton, 1959.

Hyams, Jay. *War Movies*. New York: Gallery-W.H. Smith, 1984.

Jarrell, Randall. "The Death of the Ball Turret Gunner." In Fussell, *The Norton Book of Modern War*, 446. New York: Norton, 1990.

———. "Losses." In Fussell, *The Norton Book of Modern War*, 447. New York: Norton, 1990.

Jones, James. *The Thin Red Line*. 1962. Reprint, New York: Dell, 1998.

———. *Whistle*. New York: Delacorte Press, 1978.

———. *WW II*. New York: Grosset & Dunlap, 1975.

Koppes, Clayton R., and Gregory D. Black. *Hollywood Goes to War: How Politics, Profits, and Propaganda Shaped World War II Movies*. Berkeley: University of California Press, 1990.

Kotlowitz, Robert. *Before Their Time: A Memoir*. New York: Knopf, 1997.

Layton, Edwin T. *"And I Was There": Pearl Harbor and Midway—Breaking the Secrets* New York: William Morrow, 1985.

Lea, Tom. "War Is Fighting and Fighting Is Killing: Peleliu, September 1944." In *Reporting WWII*, 529–566. 1-Volume Paperback Edition. 1995. New York: Library of America, 2001.

Leckie, Robert. *Helmet for My Pillow*. 1957. Reprint, New York: ibooks, 2001.

Limon, John. *Writing after War: American War Fiction from Realism to Postmodernism*. New York: Oxford University Press, 1994.

Luce, Henry. "The American Century." *Life*, February 17, 1941.

MacDonald, Charles. *Company Commander*. 1945. Reprint, Short Hills, NJ: Burford Books, 1999.

———. *A Time for Trumpets*. New York: Quill-William Morrow, 1985.

Mailer, Norman. *The Naked and the Dead*. New York: Holt, Rinehart, and Winston, 1948.

Manchester, William. *Goodbye, Darkness*. Boston: Little, Brown, 1980.

Mannix, Patrick. *The Rhetoric of Antinuclear Fiction: Persuasive Strategies in Novels and Films*. Lewisburg, PA: Bucknell University Press, 1992.

Manvell, Roger. *Films and the Second World War*. New York: Delta/Dell, 1974.

Marchand, Roland. *Advertising the American Dream: Making Way for Modernity*. Berkeley: University of California Press, 1985.

Mauldin, Bill. *Up Front*. New York: Holt, 1945.

Mayo, Mike. *Video Hound's War Movies*. Detroit, MI: Visible Ink, 1999.

McBride, Joseph. *Frank Capra: The Catastrophe of Success*. New York: Simon & Schuster, 1992.

———. *Searching for John Ford: A Life*. New York: St. Martin's Press, 2001.

Melville, Herman. *Moby-Dick, or, The Whale* (1851). Illustrated by Rockwell Kent. 1930. Modern Library Edition. New York: Modern Library, 1982.

———. *Typee*. Illustrated by Mead Schaeffer. 1846. New York: Dodd, Mead, 1923.

———. *White-Jacket; or, The World in a Man-of-War*. 1850. New York: Grove Press, 1956.

Montaigne, Michel de. *The Complete Essays*. Translated and edited by M. A. Screech. London: Penguin Books, 1981.

Morella, Joe, Edward Z. Epstein, and John Griggs. *The Films of World War II*. Secaucus, NJ: Citadel Press, 1975.

Morison, Samuel Eliot. *The Two-Ocean War: A Short History of the United States Navy in the Second World War*. Boston: Atlantic-Little, Brown, 1963.

Murray, Williamson, and Allan R. Millett. *A War to Be Won: Fighting the Second World War*. Cambridge, MA: Belknap Press of Harvard University Press, 2000.

Murrow, Edward R. *This Is London*. New York: Schocken Books, 1989.

Nemerov, Howard. "Redeployment." In Fussell, *The Norton Book of Modern War*, 643. New York: Norton, 1990.

Nichols, David. *Ernie's War: The Best of Ernie Pyle's World War II Dispatches*. New York: Random House, 1986.

O'Donnell, Patrick K. *Beyond Valor: World War II's Rangers and Airborne Veterans Reveal the Heart of Combat* 2001. New York: Touchstone/Simon & Schuster, 2002.

O'Donnell, Patrick K. *Into the Rising Sun: In Their Own Words Pacific Veterans Reveal the Heart of Combat.* New York: Free Press/Simon & Schuster, 2002.

Owen, Wilfred. "Dulce et Decorum Est." In Fussell, *The Norton Book of Modern War,* 166. New York: Norton, 1990.

Perret, Geoffrey. *Winged Victory: The Army Air Forces in World War II.* New York: Random House, 1993.

Prange Gordon. *Miracle at Midway.* New York: Penguin, 1983.

Priest, William L. *Swear Like a Trooper: A Dictionary of Military Terms & Phrases.* Charlottesville, VA: Rockbridge, 2000.

Reporting World War II. 1-Volume Paperback Edition. New York: Library of America, 2001.

Roeder, George H. *The Censored War: American Visual Experience during World War II.* New Haven, CT: Yale University Press, 1993.

Roosevelt, Franklin Delano. "Fireside Chat, Dec. 29, 1940." In *Rendezvous with Destiny: Addresses and Opinions of Franklin Delano Roosevelt,* edited by J. B. S. Hardman, 164–73. Whitefish, MT: Kessinger Publishing Reprint, 2005.

Ryan, Cornelius. *The Longest Day.* New York: Simon & Schuster, 1959.

Sandburg, Carl. *The People, Yes.* San Diego, CA: Harcourt Brace Jovanovich, 1990.

Shakespeare, William. *The Life of Henry the Fifth.* In *The Riverside Shakespeare.* Second Edition, 974–1020. Boston: Houghton Mifflin, 1977.

———. *The Tragedy of Julius Caesar.* In *The Riverside Shakespeare.* Second edition, 1146–81. Boston: Houghton, 1977.

Sides, Hampton. *Ghost Soldiers: The Epic Account of World War II's Greatest Rescue Mission.* New York: Anchor-Random House, 2001.

Simpson, Louis. "The Battle." In Fussell, *The Norton Book of Modern War,* 520–521. New York: Norton, 1990.

———. "On the Ledge." In Fussell, *The Norton Book of Modern War,* 519–520. New York: Norton, 1990.

Sinclair, Andrew. *John Ford.* New York: Dial Press/J. Wade, 1979.

Sledge, Eugene. *With the Old Breed: At Peleliu and Okinawa.* 1981. Reprint, New York: Oxford University Press, 1990.

Spector, Ronald H. *Eagle against the Sun: The American War with Japan.* New York: Vintage Books, 1985.

Suid, Lawrence. *Guts and Glory.* Second Edition. Lexington: University Press of Kentucky, 2002.

Terkel, Studs. *"The Good War": An Oral History of World War Two.* New York: Pantheon Books, 1984.

Torricelli, Robert, and Andrew Carroll. *In Our Own Words: Extraordinary Speeches of the American Century.* New York: Kodansha, 1999.

Twain, Mark. *A Connecticut Yankee in King Arthur's Court.* 1889. New York: Heritage Press, 948.

Vonnegut, Kurt. *Slaughterhouse-Five, or, The Children's Crusade, a Duty-Dance with Death.* New York: Delacorte Press, 1969.

Wallace, Henry. "The Century of the Common Man," *Life,* February 12, 1941.

Wolfe, Charles. *Frank Capra: A Guide to References and Resources.* Boston: G. K. Hall, 1987.

Wukovits, John. *Pacific Alamo: The Battle for Wake Island.* New York: New American Library, Penguin Books, 2003.

Zedric, Lance Q. *Silent Warriors of World War II: The Alamo Scouts behind Japanese Lines.* Ventura, CA: Pathfinder Publishing of California, 1995.

Zicree, Marc Scott. *Twilight Zone Companion.* Los Angeles, CA: Silman-James Press, 1992.

FILMOGRAPHY (AND BROADCAST SOURCES)

48 Hours Investigates. "The Bridge to Baghdad." first broadcast March 29, 2003 by CBS.

The Americanization of Emily. Directed by Arthur Hiller. Hollywood, CA: MGM, 1964.

A Guy Named Joe. Directed by Victor Fleming. Hollywood, CA: Loew's-MGM, 1944.

A Midnight Clear. Directed by Keith Gordon. [United States]: A&M Films–Polygram, 1992.

A Yank in Libya. Directed by Albert Herman. [United States]: M&H Productions, 1942.

A Yank in the RAF. Directed by Henry King. Hollywood, CA: Twentieth Century-Fox, 1941.

A Yank on the Burma Road. Directed by George B. Seitz. Hollywood, CA: MGM, 1942.

All Through the Night. Directed by Vincent Sherman. Hollywood, CA: Warner Bros., 1941.

Apocalypse Now. Directed by Francis Ford Coppola. San Francisco, CA: Zoetrope Studios, 1979.

Attack. Directed by Robert Aldrich. Hollywood, CA: MGM, 1956.

Band of Brothers. Produced by Stephen Ambrose, Tom Hanks, and Steven Spielberg. [United States]: Dream Works Television and HBO, 2001.

Bataan. Directed by Tay Garnett. Hollywood, CA: Loew's-MGM, 1943.

The Battle of Midway. Directed by John Ford. Washington, DC: U.S. Navy, 1942.

The Battle of San Pietro. Directed by John Huston. U.S. Office of War Information, U.S. Army Pictorial Services, 1945.

Beach Red. Directed by Cornel Wilde. [United States]: Theodora Productions, 1967.

Beau Geste. Directed by William A. Wellman. Hollywood, CA: Paramount, 1939.

Between Heaven and Hell. Directed by Richard Fleischer. Hollywood, CA: Twentieth Century-Fox, 1956.

The Big Red One. Directed by Samuel Fuller. Los Angeles, CA: Lorac Productions, 1980.

Bombardier. Directed by Richard Wallace. Hollywood, CA: RKO Radio Pictures, 1943.

Buck Privates. Directed by Arthur Lubin. Hollywood, CA: Universal, 1941.

The Caine Mutiny. Directed by Edward Dmytryk. Hollywood, CA: Stanley Kramer Productions, 1954.

Casablanca. Directed by Michael Curtiz. Hollywood, CA: Warner Bros., 1942.

Catch-22. Directed by Mike Nichols. Hollywood, CA: Paramount, 1970.

Caught in the Draft. Directed by David Butler. Hollywood, CA: Paramount, 1941.

Crash Dive. Directed by Max Varnel. Elstree, Eng.: Danziger Productions, 1959.

Crossfire. Directed by Edward Dmytryk. Hollywood, CA: RKO Radio Pictures, 1947.

December 7th. Directed by John Ford and Gregg Toland. Hollywood, CA: Twentieth Century-Fox, 1943.

Destination Tokyo. Directed by Delmer Daves. Hollywood, CA: Warner Bros., 1943.

Destroyer. Directed by William A. Seiter. Hollywood, CA: Columbia, 1943.

The Dirty Dozen. Directed by Robert Aldrich. Hollywood, CA: Kenneth Hyman-MGM, 1967.

Dr. Strangelove: or: How I Learned to Stop Worrying and Love the Bomb. Directed by Stanley Kubrick. [United States]: Hawk Films, 1964.

The Fighting 69th. Directed by William Keighley. Hollywood, CA: Warner Bros., 1940.

Flags of Our Fathers. Directed by Clint Eastwood. Hollywood, CA: DreamWorks SKG, 2006.

From Here to Eternity. Directed by Fred Zinnemann. Hollywood, CA: Columbia, 1953.

Gentleman's Agreement. Directed by Elia Kazan. Hollywood, CA: Twentieth Century-Fox, 1947.

Gettysburg. Directed by Ronald F. Maxwell. [United States]: Esparza/Katz Productions, 1993.

The Great Raid. Directed by John Dahl. New York: Miramax, 2005.

Guadalcanal Diary. Directed by Lewis Seiler. Hollywood, CA: Twentieth Century-Fox, 1943.

Gunga Din. Directed by George Stevens. Hollywood, CA: RKO Radio Pictures, 1939.

I Wanted Wings. Directed by Mitchell Leisen. Hollywood, CA: Paramount, 1941.

Halls of Montezuma. Directed by Lewis Milestone. Hollywood, CA: Twentieth Century-Fox, 1950.

Hell Is for Heroes. Directed by Donald Siegel. Hollywood, CA: Paramount, 1962.

The Hunt for Red October. Directed by Joe McTiernan. Hollywood, CA: Paramount, 1990.

Joe Smith, American. Directed by Richard Thorpe. Hollywood, CA: MGM, 1942.

Let There Be Light. Directed by John Huston. Washington DC: U. S. War Department, 1946.

Letters from Iwo Jima. Directed by Clint Eastwood. New York: American Entertainment LP, 2006.

The Lost Patrol. Directed by John Ford. Hollywood, CA: RKO Radio Pictures, 1934.

Lucky Jordan. Directed by Frank Tuttle. Hollywood, CA: Paramount, 1942.

The Man Who Shot Liberty Valance. Directed by John Ford. Hollywood, CA: Paramount, 1962.

Marine Raiders. Directed by Harold D. Schuster. Hollywood, CA: RKO Radio Pictures, 1944.

The Memphis Belle. Directed by Michael Caton-Jones. London: Bountiful Company Limited, 1990.

The Memphis Belle: A Story of a Flying Fortress. Directed by William Wyler. Washington DC: First Motion Picture Unit, United States Army Air Forces, 1944.

Miracle at St. Anna. Directed by Spike Lee. New York: 40 Acres & A Mule Filmworks, 2008.

Missing in Action. Directed by Joseph Zito. Hollywood, CA: Cannon Group, 1984.

Mister Roberts. Directed by John Ford and Mervyn LeRoy. Hollywood, CA: Orange-Warner Bros., 1955.

Patton. Directed by Frank Schaffner. Hollywood, CA: Twentieth-Century Fox, 1970.

Paths of Glory. Directed by Stanley Kubrick. [United States]: Bryna Productions, 1957.

Pilot #5. Directed by George Sidney. Hollywood, CA: Loew's-MGM, 1944.

Platoon. Directed by Oliver Stone. London: Hemdale Film Corporation, 1986.

Prelude to War (aka Why We Fight, 1). Directed by Frank Capra. Washington, DC: U.S. Army Special Service Division, 1943.

"A Quality of Mercy." Directed by Buzz Kulik. Season 3, Episode 15 of *The Twilight Zone* television series. First aired December 29, 1961. Culver City, CA: Cayuga Productions, 1961.

Rambo: First Blood. Directed by Ted Kotcheff. [United States]: Anabasis N. V., 1982.

Sahara. Directed by Zoltan Korda. Hollywood, CA: Columbia, 1943.

Sands of Iwo Jima. Directed by Allan Dwan. Hollywood, CA: Republic, 1949.

Saving Private Ryan. Directed by Steven Spielberg. Hollywood, CA: DreamWorks and Paramount, 1998.

The Searchers. Directed by John Ford. Hollywood, CA: C. V. Whitney Pictures, 1956.

Sergeant York. Directed by Howard Hawks. Hollywood, CA: Warner Bros., 1941.

Since You Went Away. Directed by John Cromwell. Hollywood, CA: Vanguard Films, 1944.

The Spanish Earth. Directed by Joris Ivens. [United States]: Contemporary Historians, 1937.

Stand by for Action. Directed by Robert Z. Leonard. Hollywood, CA: Loew's-MGM, 1944.

The Story of G.I. Joe. Directed by William A. Wellman. Hollywood, CA: Lester Cowan Productions, 1945.

Task Force. Directed by Delmer Daves. Hollywood, CA: Warner Bros., 1949.

Tender Comrade. Directed by Edward Dmytryk. Hollywood, CA: RKO Radio Pictures, 1943.

The Thin Red Line. Directed by Terrence Malick. Hollywood, CA. Fox 2000 Pictures, 1998.

Triumph of the Will. Directed by Leni Riefenstahl. Berlin: Reichsparteitagsfilm from L. R. Studio-Film, 1934.io-Film.

Twelve O'Clock High. Directed by Henry King. Hollywood, CA: Twentieth-Century Fox, 1949.

A Walk in the Sun. Directed by Lewis Milestone. Hollywood, CA: Twentieth-Century Fox, 1945.

The War. Directed by Ken Burns and Lynn Novick. 14 episodes. Haydenville, MA: Florentine Films, 2007.

War Comes to America (aka Why We Fight, 7). Directed by Frank Capra and Anatole Litvak. Washington, DC: U.S. Army Special Service Division, 1945.

The War Lover. Directed by Philip Leacock. Hollywood, CA: Columbia, 1962.

War and Remembrance. Directed by Tommy Groszman. 12 episodes. Burbank, CA: ABC Circle Films, 1988.

The Way to the Stars. Directed by Anthony Asquith. London. Two Cities Films, 1945.

When Trumpets Fade. Directed by John Irvin. [United States]: Citadel Entertainment and HBO, 1998.

Winds of War. Directed by various. 12 episodes. Hollywood, CA: Jadran Film and Paramount, 1983.

Wing and a Prayer. Directed by Henry Hathaway. Hollywood, CA: Twentieth Century-Fox, 1944.

With the Marines at Tarawa. Directed by Louis Hayward. Washington DC: U. S. Office of War Information United States, Marine Corps Photographic Unit, 1944.

INDEX

Hitler, Adolf, 14, 15, 17, 34, 138, 142,
  144, 147, 203, 239n. 6,
  249n. 1
Hodiak, John, 129
*Hollywood Goes to War: How Politics,
  Profits, and Propaganda Shaped
  World War II Movies*, 39, 239n. 3,
  241n. 12, 250n. 25
  see also Black, Gregory D.
  Koppes, Clayton R.
  Office of War Information (U.S.)
Holmes, Oliver Wendell, Jr., 7, 11, 237,
  239n. 2
Holocaust/Shoah, 40, 80, 128, 191
Home of the Brave (play), 187
  see also Laurents, Arthur
Home of the Brave (film), 187
homosexuality, 59, 171, 251n. 12
Hope, Bob, 68
USS *Hornet*, 51
Huckleberry Finn, 178
  see also Twain, Mark
Huie, William Bradford, 250n. 1
The Hunt for Red October, 213
  see also Clancy, Tom
Huston, John, 89, 93–95, 97, 246n.
  31/32, 253n. 5
Huston, Walter, 52
Hyams, Jay, 243n. 10, 247n. 40, 247n. 5,
  248n. 20, 249n. 33

I Wanted Wings, 24, 68
If I Die in a Combat Zone, 189
  see also O'Brien, Tim
In Harm's Way, 149
*In Our Own Words: Extraordinary Speeches
  of the American Century*, 245n. 1
infamy, 32, 33, 34, 36
Into the Rising Sun, 255n. 59
  see also O'Donnell, Patrick
Ireland, John, 99
Ivens, Joris, 246n. 31
Iwo Jima, 2, 65, 107–109, 111,
  113–120, 227, 232, 233,
  258n. 27

Jaeckel, Richard, 70, 116
Jagger, Dean, 123, 125, 127
Jarrell, Randall, 91, 103, 122, 123, 128,
  174, 187, 246n. 27, 248n. 18/23,
  253n. 6
Joe Smith, American, 69
John Ford: A Life, 242n. 30
Johnson, Lyndon Baines (LBJ), 251n. 2
Johnson, Van, 4, 129
Jones, James, 99, 103, 129, 140, 149,
  163–165, 169–173, 174, 187,
  190–199, 201, 231, 248n. 22,
  249n. 28, 251n. 7/12, 252n.
  20/22/23–28/30, 253n.
  1/10/12/13, 254n. 14–29/43/44
Julius Caesar, 64, 244n. 21

Kamikaze, 56, 57, 65, 66, 67, 122
Keaton, Bern, 209
Keegan, John, 142, 143
Kelley's Heroes, 181
Kellogg, John, 125
Kelly, Capt. Colin, 66, 67, 72, 244n. 26
Kelly, Gene, 66
Kennedy, Arthur, 71
Kennedy, John F. (JFK), 32, 160
The Killer Angels, 245n. 2
  see also Shaara, Michael
King, Henry, 24, 123
Kissinger, Henry, 183
Koppes, Clayton R., 39, 239n. 3/5/9,
  241n. 12/17, 242n. 32, 250n. 25
  see also Black, Gregory D.
Kotlowitz, Robert, 204, 208–209, 256n.
  72/73
Kovic, Ron, 189
Kramer, Stanley, 187
Krueger, Lt. Gen. Walter, 58
  see also Alamo Force
Kubrick, Stanley, 160, 252n. 37
Kurayashi, General Tadamichi (Japanese
  Imperial Army), 258n. 27

Laurents, Arthur, 187
Lawrenson, Helen, 244n. 31